Previous Books

By Peter Dale Scott

The Politics of Escalation in Vietnam (1966, with Franz Schurmann and Reginald Zelnik)
The War Conspiracy (1972, 2008)
The Assassinations: Dallas and Beyond (1976, with Paul Hoch and Russell Stetler)
Crime and Cover-Up: The CIA, the Mafia, and the Dallas-Watergate Connection (1977)
The Iran-Contra Connection: Secret Teams and Covert Operations in the Reagan Era (1987, with Jonathan Marshall and Jane Hunter)
Coming to Jakarta: A Poem about Terror (1988, 1989, poetry)
Cocaine Politics: Drugs, Armies, and the CIA in Central America (1991, 1992, 1998, with Jonathan Marshall)
Listening to the Candle: A Poem on Impulse (1992, poetry)
Deep Politics and the Death of JFK (1993, 1996)
Crossing Borders (1994, poetry)
Minding the Darkness: A Poem for the Year 2000 (2000, poetry)
Drugs, Oil, and War: The United States in Afghanistan, Colombia, and Indochina (2003)
The Road to 9/11: Wealth, Empire, and the Future of America (2007)
The War Conspiracy: JFK, 9/11 and the Deep Politics of War (2008)
Mosaic Orpheus (2009, poetry)
American War Machine: Deep Politics, the CIA Global Drug Connection, and the Road to Afghanistan (2010)
Oswald, Mexico, and Deep Politics: Revelations from CIA Records on the Assassination of JFK (1994, 1995, 2013)
Tilting Point (2012, poetry)
The American Deep State: Big Money, Big Oil, and the Attack ion U.S. Democracy (2014, 2017)
Dallas '63: The First Deep State Revolt Against the White House (2015, 2018)
Walking on Darkness (2016, poetry)

By Freeman Ng

Joan: A Novel of Joan of Arc (2014)
Who Am I? A Personalizable Picture Book (2015)
Haiku Diem 1 (2017)

Poetry and Terror

ASIAWORLD

Series Editor: Mark Selden

This series charts the frontiers of Asia in global perspective. Central to its concerns are Asian interactions—political, economic, social, cultural, and historical—that are transnational and global, that cross and redefine borders and networks, including those of nation, region, ethnicity, gender, technology, and demography. It looks to multiple methodologies to chart the dynamics of a region that has been the home to major civilizations and is central to global processes of war, peace, and development in the new millennium.

Titles in the Series

Tommy's Sunset, by Hisako Tsurushima

Lake of Heaven: An Original Translation of the Japanese Novel by Ishimure Michiko, by Bruce Allen

Imperial Subjects as Global Citizens: Nationalism, Internationalism, and Education in Japan, by Mark Lincicome

Japan in the World: Shidehara Kijūrō, Pacifism, and the Abolition of War, Volumes I and II, by Klaus Schlichtmann

Filling the Hole in the Nuclear Future: Art and Popular Culture Respond to the Bomb, edited by Robert Jacobs

Radicalism, Revolution, and Reform in Modern China: Essays in Honor of Maurice Meisner, edited by Catherine Lynch, Robert B. Marks, and Paul G. Pickowicz

The "Other" Karen in Myanmar: Ethnic Minorities and the Struggle without Arms, by Ardeth Thawnghmung

A Localized Culture of Welfare: Entitlements, Stratification, and Identity in a Chinese Lineage Village, by Kwok-shing Chan

Malay Kingship in Kedah: Religion, Trade, and Society, by Maziar Mozaffari Falarti

Refining Nature in Modern Japanese Literature: The Life and Art of Shiga Naoya, by Nanyan Guo

Heritage Politics: Shuri Castle and Okinawa's Incorporation into Modern Japan, 1879–2000, by Tze May Loo

Visualizing Modern China: Image, History, and Memory, 1750–Present, edited by Matthew D. Johnson, Joshua Goldstein, James A. Cook, and Sigrid Schmalzer

Yokohama Street Life: The Precarious Career of a Japanese Day Laborer, by Tom Gill

The Bonin Islanders: Narrating Japanese Nationality, by David Chapman

Memory, Reconciliation, and Reunions in South Korea: Crossing the Divide, by Nan Kim

Neonationalist Mythology in Postwar Japan: Pal's Dissenting Judgment at the Tokyo War Crimes Tribunal, by Nariaki Nakazato

Ethnic Capital in a Japanese Brazilian Commune: Children of Nature, by Nobuko Adachi

Peace in the East: An Chunggŭn's Vision for Asia in the Age of Japanese Imperialism, edited by Yi Tae-Jin, Eugene Y. Park, and Kirk W. Larsen

Poetry and Terror: Politics and Poetics in Coming to Jakarta, by Peter Dale Scott with Freeman Ng

Poetry and Terror

Politics and Poetics in *Coming to Jakarta*

Peter Dale Scott with Freeman Ng

Foreword by
Robert Hass

LEXINGTON BOOKS
Lanham • Boulder • New York • London

Published by Lexington Books
An imprint of The Rowman & Littlefield Publishing Group, Inc.
4501 Forbes Boulevard, Suite 200, Lanham, Maryland 20706
www.rowman.com

Unit A, Whitacre Mews, 26-34 Stannary Street, London SE11 4AB

Copyright © 2018 The Rowman & Littlefield Publishing Group, Inc.

All rights reserved. No part of this book may be reproduced in any form or by any electronic or mechanical means, including information storage and retrieval systems, without written permission from the publisher, except by a reviewer who may quote passages in a review.

British Library Cataloguing in Publication Information Available

The hardback edition of this book was previously catalogued by the Library of Congress as follows:

Library of Congress Cataloging-in-Publication Data Available

ISBN 978-1-4985-7666-6 (cloth)
ISBN 978-1-4985-7668-0 (pbk)
ISBN 978-1-4985-7667-3 (electronic)

For Daniel Ellsberg

Contents

ACKNOWLEDGMENTS   xi

FOREWORD Poetry and Terror: Some Notes on *Coming to Jakarta*
  by Robert Hass   xiii

Introduction   xv

I. INTERVIEWS WITH FREEMAN NG   1

   Introduction: The Stream One Lives By   3

   I.i–I.iii Wind-driven ghost of snow   5

   II.i–II.iii As if in a small plane   11

   II.iv–II.v The blind man's prophecy   15

   Appendix to II.iv–v "shalt lose all companions"   23

   II.vi–II.vii We who desired to prepare the soil   25

   II.viii–II.ix The world like myself   31

   II.x–II.xi Cave of winds   35

   II.xii–II.xiii Indonesia   41

   II.xiv–II.xv This world that can only be dominated   47

   II.xvi–II.xvii The ruthlessness that made possible   53

   II.xviii–III.ii Part of the enemy   59

   III.iii–III.v An ovenbird's nest   65

	III.vi–III.vii The brooding toils of energy	71
	III.viii–III.ix Like the heroes of all good tales	79
	III.x The stream one lives by	85
	III.xi–III.xii The known and unknown roadways	87
	III.xiii–III.xv Like giant doomed stars	93
	III.xvi–III.xvii The cool hissing of the bullets	99
	IV.i Beyond the mists	105
	IV.ii–IV.iii The music changing	113
	IV.iv–IV.v Those baffled eyes	121
	IV.vi Truth and nonviolence	127
	IV.vii–IV.ix Its propensity to distance	133
	IV.x–IV.xii Portending deluge	139
	IV.xiii–IV.xiv If a sentence is left dangling	145
	IV.xv ¡Djakarta se acerca!	151
	IV.xvi–IV.xviii Whirr of low wings	157
	V.i–V.ii The shadow play	165
	V.iii Let there be the courage	171
II	Trauma, Poetry, Politics, and the Mystery of Hope	179
III	America's Culpability in Indonesia, and Why We Should Acknowledge It	189
IV	"Gaps" of Consciousness; or, How Writing *Coming to Jakarta* Led Me to Deep Politics	193
	Preface to Chapter 5	205
V	The CIA and the Overthrow of Sukarno, 1965–1967	207
	Epilogue to Chapter 5 (2015)	225
VI	Catastrophe and Hope: Art and Better Politics	227
PERMISSIONS		239
Notes		241
Index		277
About the Authors		285

Acknowledgments

That this book exists is due entirely to the inspiration and long-term efforts of Freeman Ng, who believed that my poem *Coming to Jakarta* deserved a larger audience but needed interpretation. It was his idea to conduct interviews over many months, and to post them online at www.ComingToJakarta.net. It was later his idea to convert the interviews into a prose book. I am deeply indebted to his painstaking efforts, which have led me to understand my poem better than I ever did before.

I also wish to thank the following people for their help:

My long-time editor Mark Selden, who published four essays later developed in this book, and encouraged me to write the core chapter 4 about how writing *Coming to Jakarta* helped develop my thinking about deep politics. I am greatly indebted to his years of patient and inspired editing.

My friend and colleague Robert Hass, for permission to reprint a portion of his generous and generative essay, "Poetry and Terror: Some Notes on Coming to Jakarta." This essay, like Freeman's interviews, contributed to my understanding of my own poem.

Doug Buckwald, for his helpful editing of this book when still in manuscript.

David Webster, author of *Fire and the Full Moon: Canada and Indonesia in a Decolonizing World.* David invited me to lecture at Bishop's University in March 2014 on Indonesia; and also arranged for me to read from *Coming to Jakarta* for the first time in North Hatley, Quebec, the locus for so much of the poem. That lecture led to parts of chapter 6.

Members of my two poetry groups, specifically Alan Williamson, David Shaddock, Dawn McGuire, and Anita Barrows, for their helpful comments. Also Bryan Sentes, Jim Reid, and Doug Buckwald, for similar help. And

Prof. Ronald Stroud and Emily Munns, whose expertise helped me clarify small but important facts.

I need also to acknowledge my debt and gratitude to three major influences in both my life and this book. The first is Czeslaw Milosz, who taught me so much about poetry in general, and how poetry can engage political matters as well. The second is James Laughlin, not just for publishing *Coming to Jakarta*, but for reinforcing and personally subsidizing a poetic tradition (that included William Carlos Williams, Ezra Pound, Denise Levertov, Robert Duncan, Thomas Merton, and Gary Snyder) with which I could identify.

The third great influence in my life, my friend Daniel Ellsberg, is directly involved in this book. Not only does he figure in the climax and open cloture of the poem itself, but also, years later, he read this manuscript and helped give it a greater depth, precision, and coherence.

As in my other books of the last quarter century, I must thank my wife, Ronna Kabatznick, most of all. My love for her, developing more and more through many years, has enhanced my ability and energy to love and care for this world. My life truly changed that day I met her, when my friend Daniel Ellsberg introduced me to her, at the first public reading in Berkeley of *Coming to Jakarta*.

Foreword

Poetry and Terror: Some Notes on Coming to Jakarta

Robert Hass

Coming To Jakarta is as its subtitle informs us, a poem about terror—the subliminal half-repressed terrors of private consciousness, terror as political violence, often tribal or ethnic, the savage kind we know mostly from newspapers because it occurs in countries where poverty or chronic instability has bred the rage to fuel it, and also terror as a reasoned instrument of political policy. What makes the poem so unexpected is not that it is about the first kind of terror, or even the second, but that it is also about the third, and that it tries to understand the relation among the three, for it has not been the case in the twentieth century that anyone who knew enough to write such a poem would write a poem at all. Our political and literary cultures are so separate that only very occasionally does a Washington reporter's or a foreign correspondent's novel attempt to bridge them. Our political poetry is a poetry of moral feeing or, more rarely, of witness, but even the poetry of witness has had for the most part something like a foreign correspondent's perspective. The poetry of homelessness can express anger at the sight of the sick and poor huddled in growing numbers over subway vents. It may even record what it is like in a refuge for homeless women, or portray the lives there, or enter them imaginatively, though this would more likely be the territory of literary prose. What it would not do is attempt to describe and analyze the whole network of causes from the deinstitutionalization of the mentally ill to the cuts in federal housing to the effect of the Reagan tax cut on real estate speculation in the inner cities and the boom in fraud this created for federal bureaucrats and the savings and loan business, even though this would begin to be a fit subject for Dante. In fact, the writing about this set of connections would leave literary prose behind as much as poetry. It would be relegated to investigative journalism.

So what Peter Dale Scott has undertaken in his long poem is both immensely ambitious and mostly unparalleled. A new reader, trying to take bearings, will see that the poem is an heir to Ezra Pound's *Cantos*, this time with footnotes. Or rather, side notes in the manner of Coleridge's *Rime of the Ancient Mariner*, to which it also seems, in the obsessive telling of a strange tale, to allude. It is a powerfully literary poem, and like *Cantos*, it does not so much assume as propose an education most of us do not have—not only in, say, how American foreign policy toward Chile was developed, but also in epic poetry. It wants to integrate these materials—and Pound's ideas about Martin Van Buren's ideas on the US banking system, and the gradations of class in Scott's childhood in Montreal, and the ideas of duty proposed by Krishna to Arjuna—not just in order to understand the nature of terror, but to produce an aesthetic effect that might be called the sensation of understanding, the formal feeling of understanding. That effect amounts to an assertion that the quieted anxieties and nightmare terrors of private lie and the political violence we glimpse in the newspapers, tortures, starvations, hysterias, mob frenzies, and the secret world through which arms, money, drugs, and agendas of political manipulation pass, that we also glimpse, though more fleetingly, when fragments of a pattern emerge in the investigation of some scandal or other, also the visible and semi-visible processes of government, and the common sense that our world is spinning out of control or sunk in a deathly inertia of habitual closed circuits of action—that all these can be integrated in a poem, despite the fact that our lives among these phenomena does not feel integrated, and the fact that these materials are, therefore, the ones that would seem to sink the very possibility of poetry.[1]

Introduction

I owe the existence of this book to the vision and persistence of my friend and co-author, Freeman Ng. It grew out of the twenty-eight hours of interviews Freeman conducted with me about my poem *Coming to Jakarta*, which was written after a night of panic, and which came slowly to focus on the US-backed massacre of Indonesian leftists in 1965.

Just as writing the poem had been an important learning and healing experience for me, so did the interviews prove to be, as well as the writing of this book and even the final editing of it. Without such a lengthy interactive process, I would never have dared to write a book so conceptually wide-ranging.[1]

Those interviews, edited, form chapter 1 of this book. For those not already familiar with the poem *Coming to Jakarta*, chapter 1's edited transcripts of Freeman's interviews with me may be the most important part of the book. Like the poem itself, these discussions view the massacre through the personal and poetic lens of the panic attack I experienced in November 1980, when I briefly, and not for the first time, feared I was going insane. The problem of how to stay sane in an insanely violent society emerges as a major theme of both the poem and this book, first for myself and then in general.

In chapter 2, I meditate on the experience of writing the poem, and on all serious poetry, as a disruption of the presentational self and the presentational world by disturbances from somewhere deeper within us, and how these disruptions of established order contribute to cultural evolution (ethogeny).

In chapter 3, as in my poem, I return to my obsession with the massacre, driven by a sense that it is important to air and deal with America's covert involvement in that crime. The extreme violence and terror of that episode can stand as an epitome of the intolerable resort to violence that both characterizes our current civilization and threatens its nuclear destruction.

I return at greater length to the themes of art, healing, and political consciousness in chapter 4, which serves as a bridge between my discussions about the poetry of *Coming to Jakarta*, and chapter 5, my 1985 political prose account of the massacre. (chapter 5, a prose summary of insights I had through writing the poem, is based on remarks I used in a debate with former CIA chief William Colby at a convention of Asian scholars. The chapter itself in this form was published repeatedly in Indonesia, even though officially banned by the Suharto government.)

In chapter 4, I write primarily about writing the poem as a cognitive process. But it was also, and more importantly, a healing one. The healing process is the more important: from being a rational but alienated anti-war activist at the poem's outset, I become more committed to nonviolence with all my being, intellectually, emotionally, and spiritually, at its end. But in the chapter I mostly try to explain how writing the poem was also an essential step in the evolution of my ideas about deep politics, deep events, and the deep state.

Finally, I conclude with chapter 6, an essay which looks at the slow emergence of Indonesia from the shadow of the massacre, and at cultural evolution from the perspective of literary responses to political catastrophes. In this way it reaffirms how poetry, seen in this light, has helped and still can help address our social psychoses, refine fundamental human truths, bring us closer to them, and thus help empower us to modify the violent structures by which we are now governed and misgoverned.

From this perspective, traumatic breakdowns can be seen as having a beneficial effect. To quote from the hymn "Patmos" of Hölderlin, whose traumas ultimately overcame him, "Wo aber Gefahr ist, wächst. Das Rettende auch" ("Yet where danger is, grows also what saves").

POSTSCRIPT

When most of this book was written, I had no reason to think that either Indonesia or America would, in my lifetime, become open to examining the truth about the United States and the Indonesian massacre. But as we shall see in chapter 6, in Indonesia at least there is a new spirit of reconsidering the government's half century of propaganda about the massacre. This change is due chiefly to two remarkable films by Josh Oppenheimer, "The Act of Killing" and "The Look of Silence," that managed (thanks to the Internet) to be seen by Indonesians, despite vigorous official efforts at first to prevent this. This new awareness has changed Indonesian history.

I cannot refrain from mentioning that in 2014 Oppenheimer, in an unsolicited email, wrote me that "your writing about Indonesia has been an important inspiration for this whole project, and I have revisited it again and again. Above all Coming to Jakarta, but also your survey of American involvement in the genocide."

I. Interviews with Freeman Ng

The following interviews were conducted in 2012 and were originally posted at www.ComingToJakarta.net. They have been edited for this book and slightly expanded to include occasional references to all three volumes or movements of my long poem *Seculum*. These are *Coming to Jakarta: A Poem about Terror* (1988), a poem dedicated to my father; *Listening to the Candle: A Poem on Impulse* (1992), a poem dedicated to my mother; and *Minding the Darkness: A Poem for the Year 2000* (2000), a poem dedicated to my wife Ronna Kabatznick.

[I use these square brackets to show the editorial additions.]

Unless otherwise noted, quotations and page references to *Coming to Jakarta* are from the American edition, published in 1989 by New Directions and now available as an e-book.

—Peter Dale Scott

Introduction

The Stream One Lives By

It was my great privilege to spend about thirty Saturday afternoons, in a fourteen-month period from November 2011 through January 2013, sitting with Peter Dale Scott in his Berkeley home, in the two big chairs in his living room, with the painting by his mother (Canadian abstract artist Marian Dale Scott) behind them and my low-end camcorders and a couple of thrift store table lamps for extra lighting in front of us, asking him questions about *Coming to Jakarta*, his book-length poem combining autobiography with an exposé of the 1965 Indonesian massacre.

Apart from our purpose—to bring more readers to the book and to record his own thoughts about it for posterity—I valued these sessions simply for the pleasure of Peter's company. I first met him when I was an English major at Berkeley, and though I pretty much sleepwalked through college, making almost no friends, engaging in no extracurricular activities, and doing just enough to pass, I saw that he was different from my other professors—more willing to engage with his students on equal terms, and more genuinely interested in our lives—and (with an assist from the one lifelong friend I did make in college, a fellow member of a poetry writing class I took from Peter) stayed in touch with him after I graduated, and began looking for his published poetry.

The first thing I discovered in my search was that he wrote prose books about politics as well—an aspect of his life we students had had no knowledge of—and then I discovered *Coming to Jakarta*.

What makes *Coming to Jakarta* so unique and so essential is not just its application of poetry to politics, but its merging of the political with the personal. The poet does not just catalogue the details of the world order that produced the massacre, but explores his own complicity in it. And he doesn't limit his investigations to that one instance of human cruelty, but pursues the theme across years and cultures and even into his own childhood, to his own terrors and acts of terrorism.

I don't know if the noble experiment of human civilization will ultimately succeed, but I suspect that more will be needed for survival than the many progressive voices that correctly decry the sins of our society, but from a self-righteous distance that ignores the "deluge of emotion / we all carry within us." We need not just a corrected politics, but reintegrated desires. Not just an exposé of the evil in this world, but a willingness to admit our part in it and its part in us. Not just the painstaking connecting of historical dots that Peter undertakes in all his political writing, but his plunge, in *Coming to Jakarta*, beneath the surface sheen of our outward acts, to examine the "green furtive shadows" of our selves.

—Freeman Ng

I.i–I.iii

Wind-driven ghost of snow

> There are three desks in my office
>   at one I read Virgil's
>   descent into the underworld
>
> at one I try to sort out
>   clippings of failed Swiss banks
>   or of slow killings on meat-hooks
>
> in a well-guarded Chicago garage
>   but the third desk this one
>   is where the typewriter
>
> stares at me with only
>   a sheet of white paper

Freeman: I first met you when I was a student at UC Berkeley, an English major attending some of your English department classes. For a long time, that was the only area of your life that I knew about.

You begin the poem referencing three areas of your life.

Peter: There really were three desks. The third one was just a typewriter table. It was true that I had one where I kept everything to do with my teaching English (including Virgil and Dante). Then at the second table were all my files and drafts on deep politics research, such as "killings on meat-hooks // in a well-guarded Chicago garage." That was in fact a very famous murder, of loan shark William Jackson by Jack Ruby's Chicago mob associate Dave Yaras.

The third desk was just a little typewriter table, back in the 1980s when we still used typewriters. This amphitheater of letters on keys was nested in an office typewriter. That nest contained "every poem / the mean vaults at the back of my head / would rather kill me than let go of."[2]

When I said that "the page blurs / to the size of a movie screen," that is pretty much what happened when I shifted my mind from an external to an inner attention. This first section, I.i, was not consciously written as the beginning of a long poem. Instead I was conducting a little experiment: Put in a piece of paper, don't think, just allow the fingers on the keys to help something come out.

As I did this, my mind started to change and became less focused. As my mind became less focused, what I saw became less focused. It became a movie screen and then all these images started bubbling up out of the back of my mind. This was a form of relaxed automatic writing.[3]

Right away, when this poem came out and surprised me, I liked it. I shared it with Robert Pinsky, who was later poet laureate, but at the time was on our faculty. He said, "Take the last two lines off. The rest of it is just what you need." In the last lines of the original version, I came back to the real world and heard the banging of the radiator pipes in the room. I don't remember the exact lines, but they were in the order of "I am returned to my senses / by the radiator clanging in my room."

But Pinsky said, "Don't come back to the real world; just end with the question, *'Have you something to tell me?'*" By dropping the two-line radiator ending, I went from a closure to an open closure. (You could say that the rest of *Jakarta*, begun many weeks later, was a belated answer to the question.)

[This was my answer in 2011 to Freeman. Since then I have come to believe that in October 1980, when I wrote this section, I was already on the verge of the mental crisis (described in I.ii) that I would experience some three weeks later. In other words, the conscious choice I made was perhaps governed by a deeper unconscious impulse for change, one I was still a bit slow to recognize when speaking to Freeman in 2011.]

What had happened in the course of this writing, as I went through all these crazy bits of language, was I ended up with "swift / alpine cloudburst hail." Here "alpine cloudburst" recalled hail actually falling on me in the Alps in the midst of a thunderstorm. There was lightning, too, which I don't mention here. Actually, the hair on the back of my head went up from the lightning. It was very close by, and I was more than a little scared for my life.

Then, "You / wind-driven ghost of snow // down the side of the dark / oak outside my childhood window." Here I had actually transitioned to this real memory of another scary experience, brought up out of my unconscious, of when I was eight. There was a frightening all-night snowstorm, which may have been suggested to me here by the alpine hailstorm. I was a very young boy. That night outside my window I thought I saw a ghost coming towards me. It was actually the snow on the side of a black tree trunk, but it looked like a ghost.

At the age of eight, I "knew" it was snow on the side of the tree. And I was also terrified because I "feared" it was a ghost coming straight into the room. I stayed up most of the night and ended up with the flu. I got sick from this episode. My mother was not pleased.

Long poems usually begin with an invocation, but I didn't begin to have the idea of a long poem until some weeks later, after I had this horrible night in Watertown, Massachusetts.

Once I started writing again, I realized that the first poem from weeks earlier was in fact an invocation. I do think that, in a way—you asked why I did it—I was opening up my mind to something different, even though I had no idea at the time that it was going to be more than this one poem. I didn't know that yet.

Freeman: The hail is kind of an invocation: "Hail, ghost!"

Peter: Yes, exactly. It's hail dropping, but it transitions into, "Hail, you." Yes, exactly so. The poem leaps from word to word to word. But underneath the leaps, I think you can trace these subconscious connections. (The ambiguous word "Mosaic," for example, can connote either a pattern of disparate bits, or the reception of unsecular truth on a mountaintop.)

It's difficult for the brain—as opposed to a computer—to jump from one word to another word that has no apparent rational association. Yet there are little neurons there that can do it on an unconscious level. In a poem, you want to get back to letting the neurons do their own far-out choosing rather than having the frontal lobes do the sensible choosing. That's what is happening here in this little sequence.

Freeman: Although Pinsky had a certain evaluation of that passage, "stand-alone poem," did part of you know that it was going to be longer?

Peter: Not consciously then, no, not at all. I thought I had a complete poem. In fact, I'm not sure now, but I think I only saw the poem as an opening quite some time after I started writing the part from Watertown, Massachusetts. For reasons we haven't got into yet, I started writing a whole lot of sections very quickly. At some point in writing all of those sections, I realized that the first poem that originally I thought was independent, really belonged with this sequence.

[What really intrigues me now is that I had to write four more sections over the space of some weeks, before I recognized that I was writing "a poem about terror." Yet in this section the "alpine cloudburst," and much more overtly the "wind-driven ghost of snow" brought up, almost immediately, memories of terror in my distant past. I remember now that after finishing this section, typed out in a half hour or less, I was shaking, the way one might shake after being almost hit by a car. So my conscious intention of experimenting in a different poetic style may have been less important than a latent need, of which I was not yet aware, to get to the level of a deep trouble in my mind.]

Freeman: Let's move on to I.ii. What was the situation there?

Peter: I was back east in 1980 right after the election of Ronald Reagan, and I had had too much to drink. That was the beginning of it. I was very frightened that I was going to throw up. I had a very vulnerable stomach in those days. It was quite frequent that I could be incapacitated for twenty-four hours by throwing up.

So the immediate fear was that I would miss my plane to Canada, and that might mean I would miss my next plane, the day after that, to fly back to Berkeley. It would be one huge mess. But that fear—which was what you might say a sensible fear—became something much more irrational. It was a fear that I was going insane. That was the next step.

My fear got even worse than that. It was that my life had always been insane and that everything that I had ever done had been a mistake. It was a terrible dark night of the soul in Watertown. I talk in this part of the poem about:

> giving one last broadcast too many
> > about the Letelier assassins
> > the heroin traffic
>
> a subject I no longer hope
> > to get a handle on
> > and want so much to vacate
>
> till I think of Noam
> > the East Timor massacres
> > he cannot publish.

That afternoon before I got drunk, I had seen Noam Chomsky. And I'd said to him, "Noam, I've just had a book suppressed by my publisher." And Noam said, "That's so odd. I just had a book suppressed by *my* publisher." (The difference was that his book eventually came out from a second publisher. My book that was suppressed never came out at all. The poem will talk about that later on.)

I had put a year of very hard work into that book, which was about the John F. Kennedy assassination, and its treatment by the House Select Committee on Assassinations. As I say in the poem later on (IV.i), it was in the Pocket Books Spring Catalog.[4] You could see a picture of it. The initial print run was to be 250,000 copies.

Then months of silence from the publishers, through which I slowly began to realize in horror there would be no book. I was numb. All that work for nothing! It made me think that really all the research I'd done for ten years that was in the background of that book, was really all for nothing! [What I was really lamenting, I belatedly realize, was not so much the work I had put into this book as the final blow to the hopes I had had for so long, of persuading America to return to the prospects of the Kennedy era, including what Kennedy had called for, in his American University speech of June 1963: "the pursuit of peace."]

"Giving one last broadcast too many": I had also given a broadcast that day about CIA involvement in the heroin traffic.[5] I did a lot of broadcasts of that kind. They made absolutely no difference to anything. So suddenly, I had enough sense to see that my life right then didn't make sense. That was very scary.

Then in this section, I think of other people. I was scared I might go insane, and then I think of two of my other friends, not wholly unlike me, who really had recently gone insane.[6]

Freeman: That could have been your fate had you only had the first two desks.

Peter: [laughs] Well, that's right. . . . I don't want to get too far ahead in this poem, but writing *Jakarta* became a healing process for me. And first of all, to get well, I had to realize I was sick. At this stage, it was the awareness that something was really wrong.

Freeman: I want to move on to I.iii. I wonder if you could talk a little bit about the two lakes.

Peter: The two are Lake Memphremagog, where (this all comes later) T.S. Eliot once spent a summer, and Lake Massawippi, where I had summered with Americans from the CIA and other elite institutions. They would come up from America to spend their summers at Lake Massawippi.

I had a little view into the higher levels of American society—or what I like to call a "roof experience"—because some of these elite people liked to come for their summer holidays to North Hatley. We'll talk about that when we get to it [II.iii, viii].

One last thing: I say, "I am piloted by the Greek immigrant taximan." The taxi-driver who took me from the airport to see my father and mother that day: he really was a Greek. And of course, it evokes the idea of people going into the underworld and being taken across the river by Charon, who takes people across the river Styx into the underworld and the realm of Persephone.

As I will explain later on (discussing IV.xv) *Coming to Jakarta* came to represent for me an entry to a kind of underworld, the world of contemporary terror.

Freeman: In the meantime, we end Part One in a literal state of suspension: airborne, or about to be airborne again. Could you talk about the sensation of "losing hold," both at that moment in your life and at this moment in the writing of the poem?

Peter: I'm so glad you asked that. On one level, I am letting go of sick obsessions: both the hyperrational obsession with a sick politics, and now more importantly my obsessive conviction that I was going insane.

[I think, after writing and editing this book, that I meant primarily "losing hold" of my self-control, that is, the very panic attack that was so scary in itself at the moment, yet was the gateway for opening up to a needed self-exploration and change.]

But on another level it also means that what I called "the mean vaults at the back of my head" are losing hold of their repressive control of my creative subconscious. By the time I write those last five lines, I must have recognized that what I was writing was going to lead to something larger and new: "The long voyage home // to where / we have never been."

II.i–II.iii

As if in a small plane

I am back on the lake
    the lake I will write about
    the complacent water

mindlessly sheening itself
    under our wharf
    where I stare down deep between the boards and see

beyond distorted caricatures of self
    green furtive shadows
    the slime of bottom weed

Freeman: You were talking about the technique you used to write some of the early sections of the book, the automatic writing.

Peter: In I.i I was using a technique that was a self-conscious attempt to see what would happen if I just let my mind wander. After I had this crisis in Watertown that we talked about, I was not thinking about experimenting or using techniques. To a large extent, I wasn't writing the poem; the poem was writing me. I spent years editing and enlarging the poem, correcting the poem, but the first draft of it just tumbled out of me.

For example, I say in II.i, "I see this is going to be . . . a poem about terror." When I wrote that, I still had no idea that it was going to be a poem about Indonesia. That comes two sections later; thus it hadn't happened when I wrote this.

Freeman: So the terror was provoked by just the remembrance of almost having drowned?

Peter: My panic attack in Watertown set me hunting for antecedents to my discomfort, to what I was "haunted" by. I began by recalling when "Harry and I were trapped // under the rowboat / we had tipped on purpose." We were both about ten with a big rowboat; and we said, "Let's tip it over and see what it's like to be underneath, and then we'll tip it back."

Once the boat was overturned, it was much harder to tip back than we had anticipated. Harry was trying to get out on one side, I was trying to get out on the other side, and we were neutralizing each other's efforts to right the boat. We couldn't talk because we were underwater. That was probably one of the first real death scares I had in my life. It was over very quickly but not the memory of it.

Freeman: I really love the stanza, "beyond distorted caricatures of self / green furtive shadows / the slime of bottom weed." It's a great image of what the whole poem will eventually do. There are surface appearances which almost by definition are caricatures, and when you look beyond them, you encounter terror.

Peter: At this point, I'm remembering Lake Massawippi and looking down through our wharf, which did have these curved boards hard to lie prone on without hurting your face. Yes, the self is in fact something where we have murky depth below the surface of our "person" or presentational self. What appears on the surface, which is what many people would think of as reality, is I think a caricature of deeper things that are closer to the truth. Indeed, you get into slime and ugly refuse, but that's what the human psyche includes.

Freeman: Can you talk a little bit about Lake Massawippi and the people you vacationed with there?

Peter: Well, I have to explain that on Lake Massawippi there was a "Canadian side" and an "American side." The more elegant houses and the nicer part of the northern end of the lake were on the "American side." It was really Americans who had built the resort up.

Lake Massawippi is just north of the border. Before the Civil War, you had families from Baltimore, Richmond, Philadelphia who would come up and summer in New England. After the Civil War, many of these families didn't want anything to do with New England, so they went further. After 1870 they could travel by rail to North Hatley at the north end of Lake Massawippi, and they developed the town as a resort.

I talk about the Summer Social Register. That's a register that for years gave the summer addresses of all American high society from the East Coast, St. Louis, even California.

I was shocked to see that these names I knew from childhood were printed in the Summer Social Register.

Our location on the American side of the lake was kind of odd because (like Raleigh Parkin, mentioned later on) we were Canadians. My father had just spent some time on a Guggenheim in Cambridge, and he knew from Cambridge some of the American people who summered in North Hatley. That's one reason, I think, why we first decided to summer in North Hatley, on our drive back from the year in Cambridge. But it meant that I didn't really belong.

I certainly didn't belong on the Canadian side which we weren't even near. We only knew the mostly American set, but we were not American. I felt both a fascination with these cultivated Americans and also a great sense of being different from them. This reinforced a mixed sense of alienation and admiration which I had felt through the previous wonderful year at Shady Hill School in Cambridge, Massachusetts.

Freeman: These rich Americans, whom you would later write about. . . .

Peter: They mostly weren't very rich. Many were intellectuals, Harvard professors. Hamilton Fish Armstrong was editor of *Foreign Affairs*, the journal of the Council on Foreign Relations. Two or three people were said to be in the CIA. This Joan, she had a husband who did something very covert. She wasn't sure and never could decide if it was the CIA, or perhaps something even more important and more secret than the CIA.

Freeman: These sections begin and end, once more, by invoking the imagery of planes. "It is at this moment / rising up as if in a small plane // I see what I have to do."

Peter: Earlier in this narrative I was literally in planes. There while rising above I experienced getting things under control. And now I use it as a simile, but it's being suggested in a sense by the movements of the poem in the earlier parts.[7]

Memory work is beginning to lift me out of my despond and liberate me.

II.iv–II.v

The blind man's prophecy

> I am writing this poem
> > about the 1965 massacre
> > of Indonesians by Indonesians
>
> which in an article ten years later
> > I could not publish
> > except in Nottingham England with
>
> a friend Malcolm Caldwell who has since
> > himself been murdered
> > no one will say by whom but I will guess
>
> seeing as this is
> > precisely poetry

Freeman: We have arrived at last at the subject of the poem.

Peter: Yes. At the end of the preceding section, it says, "It is at this moment I see what I have to do." Then for the first time it becomes really a poem about terror on a very large scale, because I start talking about a massacre in Indonesia.

It happened in 1965 and the killing was so massive that no one has even a general idea of its scale.[8] It was almost certainly more than half a million, possibly more than a million; and it is remembered, after the holocaust of the Jews, as perhaps the largest massacre of the twentieth century.

Freeman: Could you—for the benefit of those, like me, who didn't know anything about the history of this until this book came along—could you just briefly summarize the sequence of events, the major players involved, and the American connection?

Peter: Yes. Indonesia from the moment of its independence until 1965 had been ruled by a man called Sukarno, who in 1965 was threatening to nationalize all American oil investments there. (Some people would call him a dictator, but he was in fact elected at one point.) He was not a communist but a neutralist, trying to straddle both the communist and non-communist worlds. This was the time when the Third World, and India in particular, were trying to create a bloc of neutralist countries between the Soviet bloc on one hand and America and its allies on the other. After India, the largest country in the neutralist bloc was Sukarno's Indonesia.

In the '50s, John Foster Dulles attacked neutralism as being a kind of threshold for communism. The CIA supported a rebellion to overthrow Sukarno back in 1958; and they had to admit it because a CIA pilot was shot down and America had to negotiate for his release. So there was no secret about CIA involvement in 1958.

U.S. involvement in 1965, when Sukarno was replaced by the more right-wing General Suharto, is a much more controversial issue. There is little disagreement among historians now about U.S. support for Suharto and his colleagues after some generals were murdered in September, in the so-called Gestapu incident that was promptly blamed on the Indonesian Communist Party (PKI). And increasingly historians are beginning to recognize that America supported and facilitated the ensuing massacre.

But there is much less support for my contention in prose that the United States and Britain played a key role in arranging for the murders. One of my contributions in prose was to show that Congress didn't like neutralists either and voted to terminate any more aid to Sukarno. But, lo and behold, the Defense Department and the CIA went on giving aid anyway. However, it now wasn't going to Sukarno and the government, it was going to the Indonesian army, which was the obvious candidate to get rid of Sukarno and replace him. [See chapter 5.]

In essence, that's what happened in 1965. The result was that most of the communists were eliminated, most of Sukarno's top supporters were gone, and before you knew it, Sukarno himself was retired. One of these generals, Suharto, took over and ruled Indonesia for more than three decades, until 1998. The doors were open to investment and a lot of capital came in from America, the West generally, and Japan; and Indonesia became a capitalist nation.

My position is that the CIA, State Department, and Department of Defense desired and facilitated this terrorist violence in Indonesia in 1965, though probably not on the scale it reached.[9] And, just jumping ahead a bit, they used the same model in Chile, in looking to the army to get rid of another left-wing government in Chile in the years 1970 through 1973. (We'll come to that in section IV.xv.) They actually used what happened in Indonesia as a way of disseminating terror among all factions in Chile as well. This was what is called a strategy of tension, which led people to accept an army takeover.

The United States sanctioned massacre again in 1975 with East Timor, when Ford and Kissinger endorsed Suharto's invasion of a former Portuguese colony that had never been part of Indonesia. (It was contiguous to it: one end of the island, West Timor, was Indonesian, and the other end had been a Portuguese colony and was now seeking independence.) And it's very dramatic that in the *New York Times Index* in 1975, there were six columns on East Timor. It was an area of uncertainty and contention back then, so there were many entries in the *New York Times Index*. Then in 1976 there was another massacre that was comparable to Indonesia's a decade earlier. (It was in a much smaller country so the absolute numbers were smaller, but it was the biggest massacre at the time.) And for the year 1976, just one entry of five lines about East Timor in the *New York Times Index*. [See IV.xvii.]

In other words, if it's really big, like a massacre, it's too big to get into the US papers. Unless it's somebody else's massacre, like Cambodia. That got very full coverage. Rwanda got reasonable coverage, Darfur got reasonable coverage, but one of the best signs that Washington wanted the massacres in Indonesia and East Timor was the absence of coverage.

Freeman: You write at the end of this section about the psychological reasons why the public might turn away from news like this as well.

Peter: Yes.

Freeman: It's a really powerful passage. I really love the image of the faraway avalanche, the "first . . . mumurations / of the spreading / killer wind."

Peter: I'll never forget that. It is a beautiful winter day in the Engadine, very clear, and then suddenly you see this avalanche. You see it first, coming down, it was two or three miles away, and then you feel it on your face. I used that as a metaphor for seeing, not directly, but in newspapers and so on, that this massive event is happening in Indonesia, and in a sense feeling it in my heart, although the massacre was even farther off than the avalanche.

Freeman: It's a powerful image not just for an individual encountering numbers like . . . "many more than one million."

Peter: Which make no sense to us. We can't compute that.

Freeman: But still, emotionally. . .

Peter: Yes, way beyond emotional. In fact, what you're talking about here is almost more on the subject of the problem even than the massacre itself. It's the psyches that most Americans carry around that are conditioned to deal with the controlled world that we live in; and they're inept at dealing with these massive events that were happening in our lifetime and with which we were connected through living in America, which was partly responsible for them. You could read the *Time* magazine articles, read "500,000 dead," and it's not going to sink into the average psyche because the average psyche isn't equipped to deal with that.

[After writing the Appendix to this section, I realize I should say a little here about the murder in Cambodia of my friend Malcolm Caldwell. Malcolm was a maverick British Labour Party activist who was far more influential in the international anti-war movement than I was. His murder in December 1978 remains a mystery, except that it is clear that a team came to kill him in particular, and not other members of the party.

I ostensibly think of him in this section because he was the man who first persuaded me in 1975 to write about Indonesia, but in fact I was very shaken by his murder, and not just because I both liked and admired him as something of a role model (despite the fact that his Marxism and admiration of Pol Pot were wholly alien to me).[10] His death reinforced my own sense of increasing isolation and vulnerability as I devoted more and more of my energies to anti-war research. Although I was already used to getting rare occasional death threats, by phone, mail, or directly (e.g., IV.xiv, "we are going to get you"), these threats became much more ominous and disturbing after Malcolm was killed.

As I make clear in chapter 4, I have no evidence for my speculation that Malcolm was killed by the CIA's former Cambodian clients, the "Free Khmers" or Khmer Serai. This idea was wholly fanciful, "precisely poetry," though perhaps not much further from the truth than other unproven hypotheses.[11] It grew from something I had been told, I think by Malcolm himself, for which there is also no corroboration. This is that Malcolm, who had good friends both in Phnom Penh and in Hanoi, made his 1978 Asia trip in the hope that he could dissuade these two Marxist countries (the first a client of China, the second of Russia) from going to war. I could easily imagine, without any evidence, that some in the CIA would not wish this effort to succeed.

In other words, Malcolm was putting to the test a faith we shared, that individuals could by skilled action blunt the belligerent drives of history. In Malcolm's case the test failed: three days after he was killed, Vietnam invaded Cambodia. This conspicuous failure, by someone far better positioned than me, also contributed to my self-doubt about the futility of giving "one last [heroin] broadcast too many" (I.ii), and thus the panic of self-doubt and self-alienation that begins the narrative of the poem.

Malcolm's murder is, I now believe, a key link between the recognition in II.iv and the immediately preceding moment of clarity in II.iii, when "I see what I have to do". But I don't think I could have recognized this, until I had written the important Appendix to this section, "shalt lose all companions".]

Freeman: In the next section, you talk about EP, Ezra Pound.
Peter: Right.
Freeman: Can you elaborate a little bit on how he's connected with all this?

Peter: The most obvious way that Ezra Pound is connected to this poem is that Ezra Pound tried (in his words) to write "a poem including history." That's a very ambitious project for poetry, which very few poets take on. I hadn't really intended to do it myself, but this poem has been dealing since I.ii with the fact that I was terribly upset. Something was bugging me. I had to write about it. And then I had learned it was to be a poem about terror.

Now, finally I realized, I have been carrying around these horrible facts about Indonesia, and I can't share them with anybody in America. I have to get them out. That means that I'm writing a poem including history. So it was time for me to deal with the fact that I was doing what Ezra Pound did. But I was very ambivalent about Ezra Pound: because although I loved him as a poet; I thought he was kind of a village idiot when it came to politics.[12]

What I am particularly attacking in this section was Pound's great respect for the splendor of ancient civilizations created by strong warriors. He singles out this T'ang Chinese emperor T'ai Tsung (Taizong, 599–649 CE) as a model emperor, partly because he both wrote and sponsored poetry. But I said he was "felicitous in his assassins": he was also a killer. His time was not just a time of great peace, it was a time also of great violence.

[I believe in retrospect that I was misled by my nonviolent prejudices in this negative assessment of Taizong. Although his reign indeed saw much violence, the net effect was to consolidate the peace and prosperity of what is generally considered to be a golden age of Chinese history.]

Another emperor that Pound admired was Justinian, who was called a "fountainhead" by Pound. Then I list all these charges against Justinian. He was responsible for a massacre in northern Italy, Cisalpine Gaul, and his gratuitous destruction of the Gothic kingdom opened the Po to the Lombards, meaning that when he destroyed the kingdom that was there, there was a vacuum and a much more barbarous people poured in. [I based my account chiefly on the "Secret History" by Procopius, a contemporary account whose objectivity has since been severely challenged.]

Freeman: What happened to Pound later? Why did they put him "in the wind and rain"?

Peter: One of his most disastrous errors was to believe that Mussolini was like Jefferson. He actually wrote a book comparing the two. When the war came, he accepted an invitation to broadcast on Italian radio.

He started this in 1939, which was dubious, but not, from the American point of view, illegal. But when America declared war in 1941 on Germany and Italy and Japan, and Pound continued to broadcast on Italian radio, that made him eligible to be tried and convicted for treason.

The U.S. Army took Pound, who they deemed to be very dangerous; and in a detention center outside Pisa, they built a special little outdoor cage for him. They had plenty of cells and they could have detained him in a prison block; but no, they built a special stockade for him, and put him there until he really did, I think, briefly go insane. Then he was treated better, and he began to heal. As part of "his" healing process, they gave him a typewriter and paper, and, like me, he started putting pages into his typewriter, and he wrote the Pisan Cantos.

It's very clear to me that the Pisan Cantos are part of a healing process in which he says a lot of things which contradict the ideology of his earlier cantos. I say "it was hopeful" his epic "was botched in places," because we still haven't understood the reasons for what is so wrong in our century.

So "it is has not yet been from truth / we have gone into war." There's still the hope that if poetry can help find the truth, that that will heal the world, make it more peaceful, and rid us of the kind of terrible guilt, too deep, that we have to deal with: terror, a terror which is not just in us, but comes from a sense of past massacres in which we are vaguely implicated, and from which we profit. The massacred Indians of North America, for example.

Freeman: It's an enormous task that you come to see yourself taking on in this section. Despite the fact that you end by rejecting the prophecy of Tiresias, it's still rather ominous that you end on it, and the story of Ezra Pound is a rather harrowing example to find yourself.

Peter: That's right, and the example of Odysseus is a bit harrowing, because he was told by a prophet, Tiresias, "You will lose all of your companions" (Od. 11:114). "All of them"! And he does. He's shipwrecked and is washed up on the island of Calypso, and he is the sole survivor.

This is all hopeful, in a sense. "I was moved to reject / the blind man's prophecy // *Odysseus / shalt lose all companions*." Odysseus. Who is Ulysses in Dante's and Tennyson's poems, has become a symbol, an incarnation of the inquiring spirit in Western civilization—searching (in Tennyson's words) to "follow knowledge like a sinking star, Beyond the utmost bound of human thought." [As I note on sections II.xii—II.xiii, this symbolic Odysseus/ Ulysses appears in all three books of *Seculum*.]

"Kung and Eleusis:" You might say, the light and the dark, the yang and the yin, the rational and the irrational, Confucianism, the most rational religion in the world, and Eleusis, which was a Greek mystery religion.

[*Minding the Darkness*, the third part of the trilogy in which *Coming to Jakarta* is the first, seeks an equilibrium between yang elements associated with my father (to whom the first volume, *Coming to Jakarta*, is dedicated) and yin elements associated with my artistic mother (the dedicatee of the second, *Listening to the Candle*).][13]

So I end with a quote from Tiresias' prophecy (Od. 11:114, as quoted by Pound, Canto 1/5), that Odysseus (after a "dark voyage") "shalt lose all companions." This is still very early in the poem, and I recall identifying affectively with these words—feeling that my own researches deeper and deeper into unshared secrets had isolated me. In other words, Pound's use of the phrase "shalt lose all companions," which applied so prophetically to his detention in a cage at Pisa thirty years later, was still as I wrote it scarily applicable to myself, not yet properly recovered from my own little crisis and sense of loss in Watertown. (I may also have been thinking of my father's going beyond the usual limits of a professor's life, and suffering his own period of mental anguish and isolation.)

[After writing the Appendix to this section, I see a deeper and more existential coherence in the movement of the poem from II.iv, with the loss of my friend Malcolm Caldwell, to II.v, with Pound isolated "in the wind and rain," and the mythic prophecy that seekers like Odysseus/Ulysses, in their exploration of "Kung and Eleusis," shall "lose all companions." Coming into perspective is the long-term pattern of an otherworld or yin balance to the yang of external reality, a fitting segue to the pastoral memory of II.vi.]

Appendix to II.iv–v

"shalt lose all companions"

In the course of discussing this poem and interview with my friend Dan Ellsberg, who during the Vietnam War suffered a much more abrupt loss of friends than I did, I realized that this particular Homeric/Poundian quote was much more important in the poem, and in particular to my 1980 Watertown crisis, than I had ever acknowledged to Freeman. Dan encouraged me to think more about this.

It was not long after events in 1964–65 "changed me from a Latinist into an [anti-war] activist,"[14] that all invitations, public and private, ceased to arrive from my former colleagues in the San Francisco Canadian Consulate. In 1968, I visited a former close friend at his desk in the Canadian Embassy in Washington; and tried to give him a copy of my first book, *The Politics of Escalation in Vietnam*. He refused to accept it; and, when I asked why, he pointed to the cover and said, "Take the title, for example!"

Of course, as my politics changed, I acquired new friends, some of them among my best. But I felt far more distant from many of my new revolutionary lunch companions ("men with their Sunday morning / rifle range target practice," IV.ii), than I had with old friends I had lost. And of the new friends I respected, at least two were dramatically murdered: Malcolm Caldwell (section II.iv), and former Congressman Allard Lowenstein, who used to join me on two-man panels where he would talk about the RFK assassination and I the JFK assassination. Allard's murder on March 14, 1980, only a few weeks after I last had dinner with him in New York, had a particularly chilling effect on me, yet for reasons I explore in chapter 4 I did not consciously think of it when writing this poem a few months later.[15] Malcolm was a closer friend, but his murder in Phnom Penh was so exotic, so far outside my own lifestyle, that it was not as threatening to me as Allard's.

Another new friend from the Vietnam War who I lost in 1980, but in a different way, was Bob Silvers, the editor of *The New York Review of Books*. He had published my 1970 article on the Tonkin Gulf incidents after he had it OK'd by former ONI officer Bill Bader, then with the Ford Foundation (and, he whispered to me, "really with the CIA").[16] Then in 1970 I submitted what I considered a more important and original analysis of North Korea's capture of the U.S. Navy spy ship *Pueblo*. This was an event I considered to be a U.S. provocation analogous to Tonkin Gulf but even more flagrant, and in this case clearly intended to force a more belligerent war policy (including a call-up of army reserves) on a reluctant White House.[17] This time, Bob notified me, Bill Bader did not approve. The article was not published, and the pleasant lunches with Bob at Patsy's Restaurant gradually ceased to happen. My status as a *New York Review* contributor was essentially over, though for a few eventful hours in 1980 it seemed as if it might be revived (see below, IV.xiv).

The most tragic of my friendship losses in this period, by far, was that with the Polish poet Czeslaw Milosz, with whom I had translated a number of Polish poets, including himself and Zbigniew Herbert.[18] The loss began in 1967: Milosz observed me on an anti-war panel with Noam Chomsky, who Milosz described to me the next day as "one of those intellectuals of no sense / who destroyed Weimar"[19]. It is striking to me now that the loss of my friendship with Milosz, a major influence in my life (as noted above), is not mentioned at all in *Coming to Jakarta*. I came to write about this loss poetically in about 1983 (*Crossing Borders*, 133–38); and then later, less plaintively (after our partial reconciliation), in *Listening to the Candle* (128–33, ca. 1998); and *Walking on Darkness* (32, ca. 2014).[20]

In 1980, the year in which Czeslaw won the Nobel Prize in Literature, our separation may have been so acutely painful to me that I could not bring myself to acknowledge it in this poem.[21]

II.vi–II.vii

We who desired to prepare the soil

>   the trees so overladen
>   their limbs seemed
>   to tell us by their gestures

>   of relief at being picked

Freeman: One of the more difficult aspects of this poem for me is all the political references. They begin to come hot and heavy in today's session. I'm glad that, before we get to them, we can begin among the Winesaps.

Peter: Yes. This is a kind of a bucolic interlude in the poem, if you like. I wasn't planning this consciously, but the section supplies the kind of pastoral element that is so often present in an epic poem.

It's about the village of Compton, where I used to visit my rural cousins, and where once at about the age of ten (as I wrote in I.iii)

>   I rode by sleigh
>   to the Compton railway station
>   on the lap of the fur-coated gentleman

>   whose initials *L St L*
>   on the gold band of his walking-stick
>   next to my left eye

>   meant he was the local M.P....

>   going up to become Prime Minister

You couldn't drive to the railway station in winter. You had to go by sleigh, because the road was closed but the sleigh could slide over the snow.

I was sitting on the lap of Louis St. Laurent, who very shortly afterwards became the prime minister of Canada. His family origins were in the same village of Compton, where his brother still ran the general store.

During the war, most of the Compton men were away in the army. Even though I was then only from thirteen to sixteen years old, all those wartime summers I was needed in Compton to pick the apples. The apple trees were bowed down like this [gesture], you take the apples off, and the branches rise back up as if they were saying, thank you.

Then the evening, everything was so quiet in those days. There were few cars out. No civilian cars were manufactured for the length of the war. These were jalopies that were mostly made in the '30s, and more and more of them died. You have to have lived in a snowscape to know how quiet the world becomes when there's heavy snow, no traffic, and the snow somehow drinks all the sound and absorbs it.

I say, "Why shouldn't everyone be able to do this?" Although I haven't had terribly much agricultural experience, I really actually believe all of us city dwellers would be healthier if we had a shot of agricultural experience, as I did in Compton and recall here.

Sometimes it's not so easy. In this section I remember a much later week of absolutely exhausting stoop labor. I was hitchhiking. I had no money, on purpose. I had left home with only five dollars, to see what it would be like to survive with no money and no ID.

Before I knew it I was in Ontario picking tobacco, which I'd never done in my life. I was actually priming, the hardest work there is in a tobacco field, because it's stoop labor. The prime leaves are the ones at the very base of the plant. You have to pick those leaves and put the leaves into the boat, which is a very narrow cart being pulled by a horse between the rows.

You're done for if you can't keep up with the boat because you have to put the leaves in it. Out of the nine of us who started working in that field, almost half were gone after one or two days. It was very hard work. I only did it for one week. I have absolutely no ambition ever to do it again, but I'm very grateful that I did it.

I think everybody would understand the whole social structure of society if they understood what the *braceros*, the immigrant labor from Mexico, are doing here in California in the cotton fields and so on. It's very hard work.

Freeman: That part probably doesn't come into other epics of the past.

Peter: Maybe not.

Freeman: They evoke the bucolic, but they don't take the next step the way you do here.

Peter: That's a nice thought. Ezra Pound evokes the bucolic, but he never writes about stoop labor.

Freeman: Nor does he go on to talk about the refugee nephew of Freud.

Peter: Yes. By the way, I consider my mother to be a co-author of this poem, in a sense, because as I have said earlier, it took almost a decade to finish it. When I first wrote this section it probably ended with the girls in the shade, singing Hungarian songs, which was very nice. My mother said, "But you know there was a darker aspect, too."

I said, "What do you mean?" and she told me about Freud's nephew. My mother told me about it on the phone, and I went back to the typewriter and re-wrote the section, adding the information that he had settled just outside of bucolic, idyllic North Hatley.

He was a pacifist. He hurt no one. He was very popular in the village, even though his English wasn't very good. But he got into a problem with people who hunted on his land. After he objected, someone shot and killed him. The coroner in the village exonerated the shooter.

My mother was a very astute, wise woman, and she didn't allow any sort of cant in this poem. She made sure that I didn't overpraise primitive rusticity, because it has its down side.

Freeman: Well let's move on to the next section and your father.

Peter: My father was a poet, too. He was also a political figure. All my life, through my 20s, my great ambition was to be different from my father. I didn't want to teach university. I wrote poetry, but I didn't take it very seriously. And at one point I vowed to not have anything to do with politics.

I have to say that I flunked in all three ambitions! [laughs] I ended up being somewhat like my father, but I hope I'm also like my mother who was so much gentler than my father.

My father spent a lot of his time not at home, but away at conferences. I'm talking particularly about the conferences he went to with an American organization, the Institute of Pacific Relations, which was looking ahead to what a Pacific Rim was going to look like, and America's role in it.

China was in turmoil. In America, there were two schools of thought. The FDR government was solidly pro-Chiang Kai-shek. But even members of the government were reporting that it was a corrupt government, not likely to survive. My father was with the Institute of Pacific Relations, the IPR, and some of those people were looking critically at Chiang Kai-shek.

The famous examples were John Fairbank and Owen Lattimore, both named in this poem, but there were other in the State Department who were also critical—John Paton Davies, Jack Service. And these people came under terrible attack from the right after the war.

Although the Chiang Kai-shek government had less and less base in China, and was eventually driven out, they had millions and millions of dollars in gold that had been given to them by the U.S. government, which never reached the people, but stayed in the hands of people like T.V. Soong, Chiang

Kai-shek's brother-in-law. Soong at the time—this is in the poem—was rumored to be the richest man in the world.

He had been able to fly his gold out of China, and use it to corrupt American politics, and to back people like Joseph McCarthy who were attacking all the U.S. officials who had warned that the Chiang Kai-shek regime was corrupt.

So these quotes about John Fairbank and about Owen Lattimore are ridiculous from my point of view. They were what was said about them by the people who, in the Joe McCarthy era, were winning. They were successful in getting people like them driven out of the State Department, closing down the IPR.[22]

This was very hard on my father, who had once looked to America as a democratic corrective in Canada to the top-down influence of England. He had believed America would support a more democratic, polycentric, reasonable approach to the future. He took great heart in the creation of the United Nations. He thought that this could be, possibly, the end of wars. The war itself had been very hard on my father, forcing him to shed his former pacifism. Then the war ended and he was again hopeful.

In 1953, I think it's worth mentioning, the UN sent him to Burma. That was my father's sole exposure to Asia and his sole exposure to Buddhism. And he came back extremely impressed with U Nu, the leader of Burma, and the Buddhist culture he saw in Burma. Of course that ended, too, in 1962, when U Nu was overthrown in a military coup.

In the 1940s my father in effect had a bit of a nervous breakdown, very minor compared to Pound's, but that's when he "lay on the floor / and talked to the ceiling." Of course, that era was terribly hard on many people, like Freud and H.G. Wells, who in that era—the 1930s, 1940s, and early 1950s—had believed in rational [as opposed to cultural] progress.

Freeman: When I think about this passage, in the light of current events, I find it one of the more moving passages in the poem, despite the more explicit horrors that follow. There's something very noble about the character of you, the child, growing up in this world and discovering bit by bit these things that happen. Why would they tap our phone? Why would they. . . .

Peter: They first tapped my father's phone when in March 1932 there was a hunger march of the unemployed, and the police broke it up violently. My father was a lawyer. He wasn't a member of the bar at that time, but he wrote an article saying that the police behavior in this was reprehensible.

The police, not just the local police, but the RCMP, which was the federal police, then treated him as a subversive. There was no doubt about the tap: in those days when they tapped your phone, you heard tap, tap, tap. When I was writing this poem—it'll emerge later in the poem (IV.xiv)—I also had my phone tapped, in really spectacular ways.

Why? My father was a college professor. He was very anti-communist, by the way. But once he successfully defended a communist whose civil rights had been violated. (His victory voided the Quebec Padlock Act, which authorized the padlocking of premises where Marxist literature like *Das Kapital* had been discovered.) My father is remembered in Canada as a constitutional lawyer, who fought and won some civil rights cases. He joined the bar eventually and fought and won, on appeal, five or six of the more important constitutional civil rights cases in Canada.

That cheered him, but it happened after the period that I'm writing about, when he was "getting out of politics." He quit the political party he had helped found and lead.[23] [I'm very moved, in fact, re-reading the Brecht quote at the very end of this section. I see his sense of failure then as similar to my own sense of failure which provoked this poem.]

The party still exists [and in 2011, at the time of this interview, it was the opposition party in Canada with a new name, the New Democratic Party (NDP)]. It has gained ground very slowly, but after the 1940s my father had nothing to do with that.

And I later found, in his copy of Brecht, which I read, he found something he had underlined:

> we who desired to prepare
> the soil for kindness
>
> could not ourselves be kind.

So one of the steps of healing in the poem is this initial sense of reconciliation with my father, to whom the poem is dedicated. It is a step towards a larger reconciliation with the yang world he represents.

II.viii–II.ix

The world like myself

> At those wartime Hatley parties
> there was Lily Dulles
> *the Jersey Lily*
>
> so when I went to Oxford
> I picked out her cousin
> Allen by the family name
>
> years before a Korean bullet
> deDullicized his head

Freeman: We've come today to the section about adolescence. I thought maybe you could give some background information about your personal history here.

Peter: Yes. As I discussed earlier in the poem, quite fashionable Americans came up from the States to spend summers at North Hatley where we also summered. It's just 90 miles from Montreal, but it's much farther for them.

One of the people who came up was this woman Lily Dulles. Of course, the name "Dulles" is famous now in history, because of Allen Dulles and his brother John Foster Dulles, the head of the CIA and the Secretary of State who dominated U.S. foreign policy in the 1950s.

But this was earlier. I heard the name Dulles in 1940 about Lily. She was a very charming woman. She had class and she came out of high society. (Virginia, as I thought from her strong Southern accent, but actually suburban Philadelphia.)

Then I went to Oxford in 1950, and one of the people I met there was the son of Allen Dulles, also called Allen. He was later shot in Korea.

I identified with him, because we each had a quite dominating father who was well known. (I don't think we shared this between ourselves, but I read about it later in a biography of the Dulles brothers, *Dulles*, by Leonard Mosley.) My father was nothing like as famous as Allen or John Foster Dulles. But he was famous in the Canadian milieu, so for me he was comparable.

We each had to deal also with a father who philandered. Allen, by the time he had "a Korean bullet [in] his head," was really a terrible mess; and mostly defined himself, according to Mosley, by how much he disliked his father.

I myself loved my father, but I was ambivalent about him.

Freeman: When I first read, "deDullicized his head" I thought it killed him.

Peter: No, but it is said to have damaged him somewhat mentally. When he says to his father, "I'm never coming home to you, ever," that may have been after the bullet went through his head. I'm not sure. I knew him, of course, before—not long before. But he did survive.

Freeman: I always liked that little line. It works just as well now. I thought of being deDullicized as a way of describing the loss of a person's personhood, but it also works in this case. The bullet took away something about him that was . . .

Peter: Yeah, and it's also an introduction to what I'm talking about with this woman Marian, whom we mustn't confuse with my mother Marian. This Marian was born Marian Horwitz and became (when I knew her) Marian Wintersteen; but her mother (whose maiden name was Dulles) was Lily Dulles's sister. So I treat Marian as if she were a Dulles. And in a sense that whole society world was breaking up, in the 1960s and 1970s; and that's why I talk about these parties, where Marian, for example, was quite on the side of the student protests, and radicalism became chic.

The young in this particular set were moving away from their parents the way I was moving away from my parents. I give this image of how I was a radical by day, and would then go to a dinner party and wear black tie, and then late at night we would take off our black ties and take off almost everything, not quite everything, and jump into the swimming pool.

I take that as a kind of the image of American society in a way, losing its black-tie formality and breaking up—deDullicizing. Then I describe the scene with Lily. [Years later Lily told me that the reason she was childless was because of her husband who came from a very prominent, posh, main line, social-rank family in Philadelphia. He had contracted a venereal disease and given it to his wife, and that's why she couldn't have children.] She was quite bitter about the man, and that's what interested me. Just as I am developing a politics that resented the role played in American foreign policy by John Foster Dulles and Allen Dulles, so I'm finding that within the family even, there was resentment of these unprincipled patricians.

Particularly moving and poignant for me, was the younger Allen Dulles, resentful of his father's very notorious philandering. It was very common in the CIA: the husbands traveled for long periods and the wives stayed at home; and so the husbands slept with somebody else, usually inside the agency station.

I had these glimpses into the structure of high society. The first time I saw high society it was from outside and I was awed by it, but here I begin to see that it's flawed, and precarious, and capable of breaking down.

I'd just like to say a word about this final scene about the squirrel.

Freeman: Wonderful, wonderful scene.

Peter: It's not about the Dulleses at all, but about an equally famous family in Canada. There were four big country houses in a row, all on Lake Simcoe, and all owned by branches of the same family, so there were no fences or anything between them. And this man had married into the family, but he's preserving what I learned later is the quite common practice of "blooding" among anyone who "rides to hounds," as they say, who's engaged in the old practice of fox-hunting. They wanted their children to get used to the sight of blood.

More than the sight: "He blooded the face / of his three-week-old son." This was incredible to me. The transitive verb "blood" in the English language means to smear blood on the face of a foxhound, or on the face of somebody who's going to join the restricted elite of those who go fox-hunting. You know, it's no accident that these traditions go back to the Middle Ages and even further, because the ruling class was in origin the warrior class. And it's still preserving itself by blooding an infant child. [And then I learned later—it's not in the poem—that the mother had been very angry that the father had done this; and she was the one from the traditional family and he was the one who had married into it and wanted to affect its customs.]

Freeman: It's yet another example of how in the book I think, you're so good at constantly tying the personal to the political and the political to the personal, and revealing, on either side, the depth of complexity.

Peter: Right. All of this of course is on a personal level; but yes, I do see deep political implications in this talk about the Dulleses and their like. The tale of the squirrel is a little synecdoche for the irrational violence that survives in society under the fragile veneer of polite behavior. This theme of civilized irrationality, or perhaps I might say, "residues of civilized irrationality," is developed in the next section, and is important to the poem.

Freeman: Well, we can move right on to the next section, which also unites the personal and the political.

Peter: It certainly did for me. Here I had been given this scientific approach to sex and, you know, "frogs, the birds and the bees"—the cliché. And then I found a whole shelf of books on sex in my father's study, from Bertrand Russell to Malinowski on sexual promiscuity in Melanesia. From these

I had an introduction to sex that was completely different, depicting a permissiveness that was for me at that time terrifying. I still got some kind of jolting charge from writing about this, much later, in my poem about Indonesia. [There may be a link here to my father's womanizing, something that impacted heavily on my adolescence.]

And when I went into the Berkeley library doing research about Bali (this was not in the book I was looking for, but in another book about Bali) there was a series of photographs of all these bare-breasted women. (Until recently it was normal for the women of Bali to go around bare-breasted. That's how they got married.)

And here was this extraordinary civilized reaction to the book in Berkeley: somebody had cut out all the pictures of the breasts. I gave three alternative explanations: "lecher puritan aesthete or all three." But having thought about it since—Krause's book is still there in the UC Berkeley library if anyone wants to go check it out—I suspect it may have been an art student who was preparing a collage and just pillaged the book for little pictures of breasts that they could put in a collage. But I don't know.

Freeman: It's typical of *your* book that you suggest all three possibilities.

Peter: I'm moving here into the realm of unknowing. You know that the whole idea since the enlightenment is that the world is knowable and that science is gradually sort of revealing all mysteries. But here, even in this curious little anecdotal detail where the book has been irrationally violated—we don't know why. And in the context of sex, there's so much in sex that is irrational and we don't know.

Freeman: Perhaps the person that cut the breasts out did not fully know himself, why.

Peter: Yes. That would be the "all three." I think of those Puritans who are notorious for their pornographic obsessions. One was a Canadian member of parliament who was always trying to ban smut, cut down on pornography. He had, as it turned out, a huge collection of pornography in his office. So, yes, I do link it to politics.

But, while on the topic: this may be the first section where I talk about drugs. This was how the Western world forced its way into Bali. Bali was the last of the Indonesian islands to be subdued, I think in 1906. But in the nineteenth-century British traders came and started trading opium. At first I think the island didn't want to trade, but eventually they became addicted to opium.

That was what opened up the island to trade generally. But the biggest commodity by far in 1859, 87 percent of the total, was opium. And in the end they were all addicted. In the royal palace there was so much smoke that the lizards — this is from Clifford Geertz, the famous anthropologist — the lizards were also addicted and falling off the wall. It was the weird way that the West came to the East and corrupted it.

II.x–II.xi

Cave of winds

>   EP however nuts
>   you may have been
>   in your Wagnerian way
>
>   you were right to talk about banks
>   the problem of stored desire
>   which becomes no one's

Freeman: Today's section involves a wealth of political and historical references.

Peter: It's dense.

Freeman: It's dense.

[laughter]

Freeman: Before we jump into it though, I want to say one thing about the poetry. This section [II.x] begins with one of my favorite lines in the poem, "The problem of stored desire which becomes no one's."

I don't know the extent to which that's your line or Ezra Pound's—

Peter: I don't know myself whether it's me or I'm just copying.[24] [laughter] It might be me. "The problem of stored desire which becomes no one's." It's really true, here in the whole society, right now, of course, because we're in crisis. But even when we're not in crisis and people are dutifully saving up for their retirement and depositing all of that postponed pleasure fulfillment, putting it in the bank.

It creates a power in the bank which in theory, ought to work toward for the benefit of society; but in practice, in the 1930s, which is when I'm talking about, it produced wars. Not in the interests of society.

Freeman: We've talked a little bit about the poetry, and now let's jump into the footnotes.

Peter: Let me try to give an overall view of what's happening in II.x. Right after World War I, two young men, Adolf Berle and Lincoln Steffens, were attached to the U.S. peace mission to Versailles; and they went off on a jaunt to Moscow to talk to Lenin.

Then they met Lenin and they both liked him, but later Berle became an ultra-imperialist in his old age. He was the uncle on her mother's side of this Marian whom I knew, who was also a Dulles on her mother's side. So he's connected in a way to the Dulleses.

At the time he said, "Why can't we just have peace?" It was such an obvious idea that only a very low-level diplomat would have thought of it.

[laughter]

Peter: That's why I think of myself and my naïve way when I was at the UN, and the Americans were saying we had to go on having nuclear tests. In 1957 I wrote a memo for my boss in the Canadian Delegation, saying, "Our allies are saying we have to have these atomic tests that are creating all this fallout," which was becoming a big health threat in the 1950s.

"So: Why don't we limit tests to underground tests?" A perfectly obvious thing to suggest, but it had absolutely no purchase whatsoever inside the diplomatic machine. Six years later when Kennedy was willing to talk to Khrushchev, the same obvious idea was presented then, and we got the 1963 Test Ban Treaty.

I had my own direct experience of how bureaucracies get into a kind of bureau-think that is not capable of dealing with simple and obvious ideas. And that was the experience of Berle, in 1920, whenever it was. (He ended up being, essentially, an advocate of war in his old age.)

Freeman: I also see these sections as illustrative of the final line of the previous section, "The world like myself / in its unintegrated desires." I see both sections, II.x and II.xi, as being about the world's unintegrated desires.

Peter: For me in particular, because I had four years' experience of bureaucracies that bureaucracies are paralyzed by this lack of common interest. You have people there representing labor, people representing corporations, and the result is a kind of paralysis.

I don't think anyone is ever going to make much sense of this section on a first reading. If they bother to use the sidenotes, then maybe these will help them see how the Morgan Bank induced America to join World War I, in order to ensure that the loans it had made to Britain got repaid.

You can't flash on that instantly. If I could draw an analogy—in II.xi I'm showing there are two sides to Adolf Berle: the young man who wanted peace, and the old man who's been thoroughly conditioned by bureaucracy, to think in terms of power and war.

John Foster Dulles is another complex man. In the 1950s I was not capable of thinking good things about him. He just epitomized for me—he and his brother Allen Dulles, who was then head of the CIA—they epitomized the concentration of American power that was running the whole world, and incidentally dominating the Canadian Foreign Service. When I was in the Third Committee at the UN, I was always having my arm twisted, not literally but metaphorically, by American diplomats, to make sure that Canada voted with America on everything.

But there were two sides to John Foster Dulles too. A lot of the rhetoric in II.xi about peace is quoting from Dulles, who in his own way had a dream of "a continuing United Nations."

The United Nations as first created soon became an instrument of American power over the Third World. It's not that anymore, but it certainly had become that in the 1950s when I was there.

But there were two sides to John Foster Dulles.

I think one of the general thrusts of *Coming to Jakarta* was, as part of a healing process, to try and see the two sides to just about everything, even something as apparently purely evil as a massacre of a million people. I have already suggested that II.vii about my father was a step in that process.

Freeman: The world like John Foster Dulles in its unintegrated desires.

Peter: [laughs] Yeah. But again, we talk about the world and its unintegrated desires. That's exactly the picture which I am relaying here. The language is not mine about the Versailles conference as a "cave of winds," where there were all these special interests pulling and tugging.[25]

Then Pound. I'm talking about Pound's ambivalent relation to this. But I say "EP when counterintelligence / threw you in a cage," he was arrested by the American military police in Italy, and literally put in an outdoor cage at a concentration camp for prisoners, because he had broadcast for Mussolini.

He didn't see himself as broadcasting for Mussolini. He just thought himself sharing his ideas about Social Credit, etcetera, on Italian radio. But from the point of view of the law, he was broadcasting on the radio service of a country with which we were at war. So he was very lucky, in fact, that he was not tried and convicted for treason.

Then I talk about how he never objected to the wealth of Barney and Cunard. These were two powerful women in Paris with inherited fortunes. Natalie Barney was a banker's daughter, and Nancy Cunard was the daughter of the head of Cunard Steamships. Their wealth helped sustain the Left Bank counterculture of that era. [I make other references in the poem to the interaction between high culture and wealthy patronage, not yet aware that my poem would eventually be published thanks to Pound's wealthy patron, James Laughlin of New Directions.]

Then when he was in Italy fulminating against banks, Pound was partly crazy. It almost gave him extra insight because he didn't think normally; and he saw, accurately but distortedly, that banking maneuvers were leading the world to war.

At first the Dulleses were trying to hold the whole prewar world together. They had quite close connections to Germany, which grew out of the fact that they had been personally involved in negotiating and then administering a resolution of the German debt problem from World War I, the so-called Dawes Plan.

At a certain point in the 1930s, despite the connections with Germany, Allen Dulles felt that Hitler had to go, because he was threatening the Anglo-American world system. Foster, poor man, liked peace, like I like peace. He didn't want to go to war with Germany, and that was one of the few times that Allen and his brother disagreed.

Allen steered a very tough line. Roosevelt agreed with Stalin and Churchill that their policy would be unconditional surrender. And Allen Dulles would have none of it. He was only the head of OSS in Bern, Switzerland; but he went ahead and negotiated his own conditional surrender with the Nazis in Italy, with all kinds of terrible consequences, like collaboration with Nazis in the CIA after the war, and so on, and so on.[26]

Allen Dulles represented a kind of deep power that was not conferred upon him by the Constitution in any way whatsoever, but a power backed by other bankers which ignored the official policy of Roosevelt, the Head of State, of an unconditional surrender of the Nazis. Dulles just went ahead and made his own deal. He suffered no consequences for his insubordination because a number of bankers supported it in New York.

Freeman: That's quite a tale of woe painted in these two sections, but you end on, I guess, an optimistic note about "a continuing United Nations."

Peter: Or is it irony?

Freeman: Because these are the words of John Foster Dulles.

Peter: I just want to make clear the context is that I'm taking, from a favorable biography of John Foster Dulles which I don't agree with, quotations of words by John Foster Dulles which I do agree with, even though I felt that the man in his complete life experience did more to betray than to live up to the spirit of the words. But the rhetoric is fine.

Freeman: You sort of affirmed, I feel, your belief in these words by tagging on the biblical quotation at the end: "let us run with endurance" [Hebrews 12:1].

Peter: Yes.

Freeman: Which I assumed Dulles did not say.

Peter: John Foster Dulles did say them. Dulles, whatever you say about him, was a very religious person and he played a big role in the Presbyterian

Church and World Council of Churches. That was what he really wanted to see, was a world united by everyone under their own fig tree [Micah 4:4], with their own religion, and so on.

Anyway, so the words are great rhetoric but there's a certain irony to them in context:

> Van Dusen honors
>
> that spiritual quest
>   for *some great creative purpose*
>   *a continuing United Nations*
>
> *autonomy for subject peoples*
>   *control of military establishments*
>   *religious and intellectual liberty*
>
> *let us run with endurance*
> *the race that is set before us*

II.xii–II.xiii

Indonesia

        but when Foster and Allen agreed
        on the magic formula

   to help eliminate Communism
       in Iran Guatemala
       Standard Oil and United Fruit

        were not unhappy

Peter: I see that this is a very difficult section to listen to, because there are so many references that are brought up. It's sort of like rapid camera, you know: flipping through a whole lot of background scenes at once.

Can I explain one thing about the first one, when I say "I could think only of / an eleven-year-old / and four adults," the reference is to John Fairbank, who by the time of this section was beginning to be the number one China scholar in America and a little later was flying to Washington all the time to advise on how Washington should deal with the emerging communist People's Republic of China.

When I was eleven, as I have shown earlier in the poem, I had spent a year with my parents down in Cambridge, Massachusetts; and perhaps my father's best friend down there was John Fairbank.

When I say an eleven-year-old and four adults, that refers to me, my father and mother, and John and Wilma Fairbank. We would go canoeing together, and then sit by the river bank and have a picnic.

I was eleven and I was allowed to taste the wine. And it was tragic to me much later that when I saw John Fairbank again we had very different views about Vietnam. I myself was often accused during the Vietnam War that

I was not active enough on one side or the other, but like a former diplomat I was always trying to reconcile things, naively hoping that Americans could be persuaded to pull back from its Vietnam misadventure. But I was nothing like John Fairbank, who was working with the government and was here in effect telling the anti-war Concerned Asian Scholars not to be "concerned" about the war but just do their research.

So I was no longer on his side and the moral situation here was painful to me. It was even more upsetting when Wilma came to my house for tea and

> talked of Franz Schurmann's
> *abandonment of a promising*
>
> *scholarly career*
> *for simple journalism*
> *one of John's best students*

[I believe Franz later commented to me that he had never been Fairbank's student at all.]

Freeman: I think it is very typical of the poem, too, that you mix these different views of people. "The dark gods" of the twentieth century were also ordinary people. It was ordinary people who created this world we live in.

Peter: And Allen Dulles: he had a mistress, Mary Bancroft, who really did say to him that he made "Germany safe again / for the Junkers and Prussians / and of course Sullivan and Cromwell," which was the law firm of Allen and his brother, John Foster Dulles.

That is what they were doing, the two of them again, when they sent the CIA into Guatemala—where Allen's bank, Schroder Bank, had investments and it was interlocking with United Fruit—and particularly Indonesia where the big American oil companies, what are now Exxon and Chevron, had big investments there and were very concerned because Sukarno, the head of Indonesia who was overthrown in this massacre I talk about, had threatened to nationalize them. So they were indeed trying to make the world safe for Sullivan and Cromwell and their clients.

Freeman: It's a significant section in the poem as a whole, because I think it's the first—it's one of the first times in the poem when you come to Jakarta, the outskirts of Jakarta.

Peter: Yes. I think maybe that when I say Indonesia at the end of section I.xiii, as a sort of end point, with all this banking and intelligence intrigue through the two sections, that is, the first use of the word since II.iv, where I talked about the massacre for the first time.

Freeman: In the next section, you'll digress again. It's a poem full of circlings around as you try to come to this topic that neither you nor your reader really want to talk about.

Peter: Yeah. When I wrote these sections, I had not yet come up with the concept of deep politics, but I'm very definitely talking about deep politics in here.

I'd like just to look at Operation Sunrise, which is remembered in some history books as a noble peace effort—you know—Allen Dulles at his best because he was able to take the German armies in Italy and much of Austria out of the war.

But at the same time, of course, he was disobeying Roosevelt, because Roosevelt had promised the Russians unconditional surrender, and here was Allen Dulles negotiating a conditional surrender, and he was ordered by Washington not to do it and nevertheless he did it.

Why? Because one of the things they did was save Italian Superpower. The Resistance movement was on the point of blowing up the dams in northern Italy to make it difficult for the Germans to withdraw. Negotiating the surrender quickly meant that the dams weren't blown up. And the head of OSS in Europe, J. Russell Forgan, was a director of Italian Superpower. His own investment was saved by Allen's doing this.[27]

[Neither Freeman nor I thought to discuss the small personal anecdote at this point about my dealings with the former CIA officer turned author, Richard Harris Smith.

> and after I told Dick Smith
> the ex-CIA historian
>
> that Allen's OSS boss
> Forgan was another director
> of Italian Superpower
>
> his typescript came back
> with this small detail altered
> into a lie indicating
>
> someone found it significant

This small discovery—about the CIA's diligence in lying—was in fact an important factor in my political education, following my earlier discovery that *The New York Times* would not correct an obvious falsehood in their pages concerning the North Vietnamese condition for peace talks to end the Vietnam War (see below on IV.ii).

I knew that Dick was ex-CIA, and was still in touch with the Agency. Yet, despite the fact that the Vietnam War was still raging, we were close enough to share our manuscripts with each other. When I read in his MS a fact I had given him—that one director of Italian Superpower, "a banker, James Russell

Forgan," was Deputy Commanding Officer, European Theater of Operations, OSS—I was eager to see if that fact would survive CIA scrutiny. It did not. The book, as finally published, stated that one director of Italian Superpower "was a Chicago banker whose son, New York banker James Russell Forgan, [was] commander of OSS in the European Theater."[28]

What was important to me in this episode was not just that the CIA would lie (something I knew by then) but that someone in it took the time to conceal a fact which I had myself discovered.

I shall say more about this in chapter 4.]

Freeman: So we move on to Foster and Allen.

Peter: Yes. Foster and Allen. Let me explain why Allen was "anxious to avoid / a family quarrel with Foster."

I became aware in writing the poem that the two brothers dominated Sullivan and Cromwell and had a lot to do with the foreign politics of America both before and after World War II, and particularly with CIA involvements in Iran (1953) and Guatemala (1954)—the first big CIA covert operations, which saved clients of Sullivan and Cromwell: the oil companies, United Fruit, and the International Railways of Central America, which was owned by the Schroder Bank, where Allen Dulles was a director before he became head of the CIA.

That doesn't mean that the two brothers were part of a well-oiled machine. They disagreed about World War II.

John Foster Dulles—we talked about this before—was a churchman. He was quite religious, and he was anti-war, and like Allen had very good friends in Germany.

John Foster Dulles spent a lot of time trying to stop World War II from happening, while his brother Allen was quietly machinating to get Roosevelt to come in on the side of the British and defeat the Nazis; because he saw the Nazis as a kind of a threat to the kind of banking capitalism that he profoundly represented. Allen was not a churchman.

I'm not taking sides here because I too am anti-war, but I'm also anti-Nazi.

Freeman: It's a characteristic of the poem and of your writing on deep politics that . . .

Peter: They dramatize these two conflicting . . .

Freeman: These are not monolithic conspiracies. These are human forces in the world, with all kinds of conflicting interests and beliefs.

Peter: Exactly. That, in a way, is one of the ways I was inspired by Ezra Pound. There was a lot that's not admirable in Ezra Pound, which we will pass over in this interview. But he saw the war coming and he went to his one friend in the Senate, Senator George Tinkham. (Pound always called him "Unkle George" with a "K.")

He tried to get "Unkle George" to stop the banking finaglings that were going on. Tinkham actually went to Morgenthau, the Secretary of the Treasury, and tried to stop Roosevelt's intrigues to come in on the side of the British.

Of course it was quixotic. It went nowhere. But maybe that's the sort of thing that poets should do, even though it is quixotic.

II.xiv–II.xv

This world that can only be dominated

I have since tried to imagine

describing on that veranda
    the sugary scent on a hot day
    from the corpses in Hamburg's rubble

how we who had been spared
    unlike young Harfie
    now smiling from his wheelchair

must think as survivors
    but I do not think our meeting
    could have come out otherwise

Freeman: For our viewers so far, I just want to reassure them that this sequence of very heavy, dense political sections, is coming to an end soon.
[laughter]
Peter: Yes, we are building to a climax where the political for the first time becomes personal. After the personal crisis in Part One of the poem, there are three more big parts: Two (political), Three (personal), and Four where I try to integrate U.S. politics and my personal life into a more coherent whole.

In the next session, we will see the political become personal after I realize two things: (1) that by teaching at the University of California I have become involved in the machinery of murderous repression; (2) much more seriously, that I had been in denial about this in 1975, when I downplayed the university's responsibility for the 1965 massacre. I should not have done this.

This sets me up in Part Three to "see myself," as I write, "as part of the problem" [III.ii]. Then I try to go beyond being "part of the problem" in Parts Four and Five.

Freeman: You have a very cosmic voice sometimes. In the meantime, "We must consider the five sons / of Meyer Rothschild." You began II.xiv with a quote from Franz Schurmann that refers to the replacement of gold bullion by a worldwide system of accounts. You quote him saying that it was "the most important force / for peace in the nineteenth century."

Later in this section, you'll talk about the creation of a world that can only be dominated and not governed. Can you talk about both those sides of it? In what sense was this system an important force for peace?

Peter: Earlier I quoted from Ezra Pound in this poem who had this crazy idea that the Rothschilds were responsible for war. I just had to insert that people who've actually studied the Rothschilds closely relate nineteenth-century peace to their creation of a global financial system. (Yes, you can virtually say global, but of course it was based in England and the countries of Europe.) Their banking system vastly freed up international trade.

Before you had to settle accounts by actually shipping gold, which is heavy and needs to be insured and so on. Now it could all be done by banking.

You don't have to look very long at the nineteenth-century history to see that it was (especially compared with the previous centuries in Europe) a century of unprecedented peace. And Frank Schurmann is saying this was because they had a banking system which connected countries easily for the first time. I just had to work that in. It's not by itself a very poetic section, I grant you.

Freeman: But it is typical. It does contribute to the peculiar poetry of the book, that you never simplify. You never oversimplify the characterization of any one entity, any one power, any one force. It's more complicated than that. The contribution of the Rothschilds to the world was not simple.

Peter: I gave two examples here, whereas generally they prevented wars from happening and used their own private communications networks to ease crises when they were getting too large. I don't want to overidealize the Rothschilds.[29] They were bankers.

But on the other hand, in the year 2012, the word "banker" has a terrible set of connotations after the downturn of 2008. Many people have attacked them, and earlier Ezra Pound also claimed that they were really responsible for everything that went wrong.

Systems evolve. Initially the Rothschilds were a force for peace. They changed with the Crimean War, because the Rothschilds were very sensitive to the persecution of Jews in Russia. They thought of the Crimean War as a war for liberation and emancipation to get the Russians out of the Balkans and so on.

They were partly responsible for that war. Then, as I say, they backed the financial ventures of Cecil Rhodes in South Africa, which led to the Boer War, which is the point where I would say that the British imperial system was becoming pathological.[30]

The Rothschild system contributed both to the build-up of the Pax Britannica and then to the breakdown of it; but fundamentally it was a system which worked for peace for about a century, and then also to the climax of an unprecedentedly violent war, World War I.

Freeman: Well, let's move on to the next section when you come back to your father. Why were you surprised to find that he had published in *Foreign Affairs*?

Peter: Well, because, as I say here, I thought of him as a radical. He helped found a socialist party in Canada, the Co-operative Commonwealth Federation (CCF), now the New Democratic Party (NDP). There's a big gap between this socialist party on the one hand and the Council on Foreign Relations (CFR) on the other, which has been called "Wall Street's think tank" and an engine for promoting capitalism and free trade and free movements of capital. But both were opposed to British imperialism.

My father in the 1930s was part of at least one big event of the Institute of Pacific Relations, which was then closely allied with the Council on Foreign Relations. My father saw it as a venue for devising a rational international polity to forestall war, but it could also be seen as a way of exploring an expansion of the U.S. banking system, if you like, into the Pacific.

Well, it didn't forestall war. But it was a try.

In this section, I remember, as a college student, having drinks in North Hatley with Gregor Armstrong. And I must add, developing an instant crush on this beautiful woman, her face still flushed from playing tennis at the Club in North Hatley.

She was the daughter of Hamilton Fish Armstrong, who was the editor of the CFR's journal *Foreign Affairs* when my father published there. And as I say, the brains behind the postwar War and Peace Studies Project, which projected the CFR's importance into postwar American foreign policy, especially after two of its members—the Dulles brothers—became Secretary of State and Director of the CIA.

Behind them was Hamilton Fish Armstrong who helped set up this Project. It was going on during the war, and I suspect it helped prepare secretly for a CIA.

Among other things I, as a young twenty-year-old, was pretty caught up by the mystique of actually talking to the daughter of one of these architects. I was just beginning to get involved in these things. I'm a little older in this section and have already been to Europe.

I've already seen Hamburg flattened by the war; and smelled the corpses in 1948, three years after the war, when they were still clearing square miles of rubble flattened by the U.S. Air Force.

Freeman: I didn't realize when you referenced that later in this section that this was something you witnessed personally.

Peter: This was a personal memory, and actually underlay my argument with her. I thought I was sent by NFCUS, the National Federation of Canadian University Students, but NFCUS teamed up with a project from WAY, the World Assembly of Youth [cf. IV.i].

I'm now pretty sure that the CIA, or shall we say the people who created the CIA, created the WAY as a way of countering Soviet influence around the world after the war.

I was sent to a seminar in Germany where fifty Canadians met up with fifty Germans and fifty students from the rest of Europe.

The fifty Germans were recruited from people who were anti-Nazi when it was very hard to find those people in Germany. Most of them were Social Democrats so I had a special feeling of kinship—I was a social democrat myself in Canada.

The SPD, Sozialdemokratische Partei Deutschlands, was attacked in a newspaper column by Gregor's stepfather Walter Lippmann, whom her mother had remarried. Lippmann in that era was the press guru on foreign relations. There's nobody as influential as him in American journalism today.

In his columns, he laid down the law on what American foreign policy should be, until he warned against fighting a war in Vietnam; and that meant that Lyndon Johnson cut him dead. And that meant that he no longer had standing in the White House, so it was the end of the Walter Lippmann era.

I remember my argument to her quite vividly: Lippmann had warned in an article that the SPD was dangerous, because it could sell out in a moment to the East. The future of Germany in 1949, which was when we were having this conversation, was still far from clear. You had a divided Germany. Everybody, including the powers that be, was concerned whether Germany as a whole would align with the East or the West.

Walter Lippmann was worried that the socialists would be elected to power in West Germany. He worried that this would lead the country into alliance with East, and Germany would be lost to the West and NATO and so on. But I had known and liked all these SPD students, and was quite sure this wasn't going to happen.

In addition, the CIA was already making sure that Christian Democrats would win in Germany, just as they were making sure that the Christian Democrats would win in Italy and that the parties of the center right would win in France.

It was far more determined than we knew then, but we know it now with the wisdom of hindsight.

What I'm really saying in this poem was I had a crush on Gregor, and how nice it would have been if she and I could have just talked about something more positive. [In retrospect I see Gregor as epitomizing my ambivalence about America—drawn to it, unsure about it, and not knowing how to engage fruitfully in dialogue with it.]

This was right after World War II, and it was time to think, "How are we going to make this a peaceful world?" I would've liked to have engaged with her on that level. But, as I say, I talked, mostly out of shyness, about the one thing I thought I knew something about. I'm a brash twenty-year-old in this section. I thought I knew all about the SPD because I had met some of them. It was a discussion that went nowhere.

Freeman: But what was the exact disagreement? What was the argument?

Peter: Well, she didn't really argue very much at all. I was saying dogmatically, "your stepfather's wrong to think the SPD will sell out to Moscow."

She didn't know or care anything about the SPD, so the argument was all coming from me. In a way, I was right not to worry myself about the SPD; but I think it was an asinine thing to have brought this up with a beautiful woman on a nice spring day, looking down at the sailboats on the lake below us. I am confessing here to an early example of my not being in a right relationship with those around me [one overcompensated later by my entering the Foreign Service].

Freeman: It's an image of world that wanted to just be able to talk about how to create a peaceful order, a peaceful world, a peaceful existence, and couldn't.

Peter: I think only people my age or thereabouts can remember what it was like after World War II, the horrors of the war itself, the relief that it was over, and the sense of an open future, that now we've supposedly learned from the errors of the past.

Everybody agreed the war was horrible, and so we were going to have a new world. That was our hope for the UN and the other things which started then.

The whole of my life has been seeing those hopes eroded and the institutions that created those hopes being converted into much more corrupt institutions.

II.xvi–II.xvii

The ruthlessness that made possible

> ...confused
> by a sudden surge
>
> of my old combativeness
> saying *you*
> *political scientists*
>
> *are part of the problem*
> and the students all
> starting to applaud I
>
> hushed them and turned
> to apologize *of course*
> *not you personally*

Freeman: We're almost at the end of this long dense Part Two of the book.
Peter: Yeah.
Freeman: But we do begin to make a kind of turn here, I think.
Peter: Yes.
Freeman: Back toward the personal.
Peter: Yes. Here I first turn up as a minor character in this political survey. Because I did debate this RAND professor, Guy Pauker, at Pomona College, and did apologize to him: "I didn't mean you, personally." But (although I did not yet know it) if there was any one man in America who was responsible for encouraging the Indonesian army command to carry out a massacre, it was Guy Pauker.

First, he encouraged them to do it, and then he published an essay in which he said he was losing faith in the army because he didn't think they were ruthless enough to do it. Then, finally, though it's not in this poem, he wrote a third essay, in which he was glad to see that in the end they were ruthless [for details, see chapter 5].

The ruthlessness was still going on when he said this, because the massacre took about six or seven months; and, in the middle of it, out came his essay saying they're doing a good job.

This is very important for the structure of the poem that I'm, as a figure, beginning to think that there was something wrong with my own polite persona that refused to think there was anything wrong with my academic environment.

The irony of my deference here is personal, almost comic. But it becomes a more serious issue in the next section. There I really come to grips with the role played by the University of California—which I begin to mention in this section—and above all the fact that I had "defended" the University of California against a radical critique. And that I had been morally wrong to do so.

That's going to change the whole nature of the poem, because I'm talking about a major social problem; and I begin to see, as I say in part III, that I myself, with my powers of denial, am part of that problem. My whole attitude of politeness and acceptance is part of the problem.

Freeman: Before we move on with that material, I want to go back to the beginning of II.xvi, and talk about Pound a bit more. Is that a similar story, a similar situation that you paint here? With Pound?

Peter: Later on I'm critical, but I think, here, I'm just asking a very simple question. OK Pound, you talked about banks, you talked about this episode when President Van Buren, your great hero, refused to renew the charter of the National Bank of the United States, which was in Philadelphia. And you didn't see the result, that the banks in New York came to replace it.

Pound just saw it as a heroic exploit of Van Buren, a New Yorker, to have opposed the bank. He did not see, as historians now see, that as one banking connection was being attacked it was being replaced by another (which was actually more connected to the Rothschilds Pound was so paranoid about).

I'm throwing in a kind of commentary: if Pound knows all of these things about banks and so on, "how come you never once mentioned the Council on Foreign Relations?" That is not a critique of him as a poet. But I think it is a way of acknowledging that he was so busy fulminating in Italy that he didn't have much time to do research as to what was really going on in America, because the Council of Foreign Relations helped guide America into World War II. Then—this reference to the communist Oumansky is in a relevant CFR memo—the CFR helped lead the CIA into saving Sullivan and Cromwell's client United Fruit in Guatemala, where the government had nationalized some of United Fruit's land. ["It is has not yet been from truth / we have gone into war," II.v.]

It is an example of when the Council on Foreign Relations, as part of what I'm nowadays calling the deep state, was able to tell the state what to do. Pound should have been a natural to talk about that, because the CFR represented banks and he did believe that banks were the root of all evil. But he missed the CFR. I'm making the point that Pound, way off in Rapallo, was not as knowledgeable a guide as he thought he was.

Freeman: I want to ask you about Penn Nouth, about this whole section in which you turn back to yourself, when you talk about yourself during this period of . . .

Peter: In the 1950s, I was not yet thirty and I was very proud of myself. I met Dean Rusk—what an important thing!—because my then father-in-law worked for the Rockefeller Foundation, and took me up to the top floor of the building where Dean Rusk had an office.

Then I was a diplomat at the UN. Oh, how important! I sat, as I say, "in the Cs of the United Nations," meaning where Cambodia, Canada, and Ceylon as it was then, and Chile, all sat together.

Penn Nouth, the prime minister of Cambodia, was sitting right beside me in effect. And we all had our translation microphones on, trying to understand each other or perhaps turning to the number six channel, which was pure silence—very convenient after lunch when you wanted to have a nap.

Freeman: This is a portrait of kind of a . . . callow youth?

Peter: Yes, I would say a callow youth: a callow youth who thinks that he is very bright and important because he has a PhD, and now he has at last a job and a secretary. Then for a while my life was a bit rocky, as we'll get into later; but now I have a job, I have a marriage, and I have a title.

One thing I don't have is any ideas in my head about anything. I'm just like everybody else: doing my job.

I thought you were going to ask me about the black on the page for the people who can see it.

such was the academic
language of Professor Fifield

Freeman: This is one of two places in the book where there are words blacked out.

Peter: That is correct.

Freeman: Can you explain what that was about?

Peter: First of all, I'll repeat what the language was. . . . By the way, if anyone has the Canadian edition which came out first, it's not blacked out in the Canadian edition.

Just before it, I have been quoting Professor Fifield's words about those members of the Indonesian officer corps who rebelled against Sukarno in 1958, which sound as if he was encouraging them to rebel again. It's very polite academic language. But when he was saying that these people cannot "be overlooked / in Indonesia's future," the only way they could get into Indonesia's future would be to throw out Sukarno. So here's an American academic sanctioning rebellion in Indonesia, in a book written for the Council of Foreign Relations.

Then I say, "such was the academic / language of Professor Fifield / not *in any indictable sense / a war criminal*" (the seven words blacked out in the U.S. edition). Then I go on to Guy Pauker.

Before I discuss what happened with the American edition, let me say that it was a great honor to have had this book published by New Directions. And, in a more personal way, to have been selected for publication by James Laughlin, who created a press which promoted so many great names of American modernist poetry. But the New Directions lawyer, when he saw this poem, sent me quite a long memo raising questions about twenty places in the poem, and I had to defend them all. This section was one of the two sticking points he wanted me to rewrite, but I said, "I'll do better than that, we'll just black it out;" and so we did.

Freeman: We've talked in the parallel series of podcasts on deep politics about this phenomenon of people not remembering.

Peter: Right. How we all repress things that are awkward, that don't fit. Events that don't fit in with the ordinary events of our life. We'll come to an important one at the end of the poem (V.ii), and we'll talk about it then. [Cf. also chapter 4].

Freeman: Here I guess we're about to see you not considering the possibilities that maybe were unthinkable at the time.

Peter: Also, thinking back to . . . this is in II.xvii, where I'm not quite as callow as I was in II.xvi. I'm now part of the anti-war movement. Actually, because of my diplomatic experience, I was quite early on in the anti-war movement. But when I met this man Guy Pauker [in 1965, the year of the massacre], I had not studied Indonesia at all.

I knew nothing about his connection to Indonesia. But I met him and I said, "You political scientists / are part of the problem." I was thinking of men like Professor Fifield who were writing about Vietnam and saying we should get more involved there.

Just like William Henderson from Mobil, who wasn't an academic, but an employee of Mobil, one of the U.S. oil companies that wanted, urgently, to get to the offshore oil in the South China Sea. Especially Mobil. Unlike most of the big oil companies, Mobil was chronically short on oil reserves, so they were actively pushing America to get involved in Vietnam, and then make the South China Sea safe for development, which it became.[31]

I'm still pretty wet behind the ears, so I say to Pauker, "Not you personally." But in fact Pauker really did have a lot to answer for personally. Maybe he was "not in an indictable sense a war criminal," but the blood of thousands of Indonesians was on his hands. By the way, I got to know him quite well, because I interviewed him about this section, and about things I also wrote about him in prose [chapter 5].

Then he got involved in something called the Nugan Hand Bank, which we will talk about in the next interview. This was essentially an Australian bank started by Special Forces and CIA veterans, which was directly involved in drug trafficking, drug financing, and drug imports into Australia.

I talked to him about all these things, and he was always doing two things at once: Defending himself against any specific charge, and also revealing that he had had a lot of time in his life to reflect on what he had done.

It was clear, whatever he said to me, that he was not entirely happy about what he had done. I would say that from a Gandhian perspective he had not been living in truth, and it was getting to him in subtle ways that are hard to put your finger on.

Freeman: Can you go a little bit into detail about what exactly he did? About this Indonesian army command school and so forth.

Peter: First of all, he trained future Indonesian leaders to be capitalist economists. Then in 1959 and 1962 he encouraged the military to take power in Indonesia. Then in 1964, which is the year before the massacre, he rebuked them publicly in an essay, saying: You lack the courage to carry out "a control function." You lack "the ruthlessness."

Imagine saying that. They lacked (in his words)

> *the ruthlessness*
> *that made it possible*
>
> *for the Nazis to suppress*
> *the Communist Party*
> *a few weeks after the elections*
>
> *in which the Communist Party*
> *won five million votes*[32]

He's encouraging them in effect to behave like the Nazis.

Then after the massacre he wrote another essay, saying in effect, "Ah, I see now that they did have . . ." and he used the word again, *ruthlessness*—the ruthlessness that was necessary to carry out "a control function" and take over the country.[33]

Freeman: That sounds like it was more than just his writings. You talk about him developing this program?

Peter: Oh, at Berkeley. Yes. At what point does something become criminal? What he did at Berkeley was to create a program, right on our campus here in Berkeley, where Indonesians (both civilians and military) came and were trained in capitalist economics. That is, economics that could only be implemented after a change of government.

They went back to SESKOAD, the army command school in Indonesia. Many of the principal figures in the coup in 1965, which was followed by this terrible massacre, had been trained in SESKOAD, by people who had been trained by Guy Pauker, here in Berkeley. This is setting up the stage for my personal sense of guilt, which becomes much more acute in II.xviii, which we haven't read yet. Because in that section I see the university's involved; and I have involved myself by my defense of the university, on this matter where I should not have defended them.

II.xviii–III.ii

Part of the enemy

> I was always going along
> at first with whatever
> sounded most reasonable

Freeman: We're nearly out of the woods of the dense political references. We just have a few more to explain in the middle here, and then we won't be encountering them again for a little while.

Peter: It'll be much more personal. Yes, the poem goes from external politics into self-examination and the personal. This is a kind of crucial turn in the poem, and II.xviii explains why.

Freeman: Let's begin with these two things that sounded reasonable, "this dispute among friends."

Peter: Yes. After the war, the Ford Foundation (working with the CIA) set up a lot of money to study China.

And John Fairbank (who we recall from II.xii was a personal friend of our family, and a very gentle man) believed in the importance of this, because he thought, as it says here, it was the best way to bring "the cold war to an end"—that is, in this way we would all understand each other better.

But a dispute arose when in the course of the Vietnam War we got a younger generation of Concerned Asian Scholars (CCAS) looking at all this, and seeing that the CIA had been involved with the Ford Foundation and that what the Ford Foundation was subsidizing served the purposes of the U.S. Army.

There was a dispute over this function, and I was a little bit on both sides, because I was a friend of John Fairbank and believed in greater knowledge and communication, but I was also against the CIA's enlisting the academy in the Cold War against Communism. I was a teacher so I felt personally involved.

But then I say whatever that dispute was, it seemed "less important than" another thing that the CIA and Ford did, which was to fund the "UC Indonesia project." This was a project involving the University of California at Berkeley where I taught.

They first taught the so-called "Berkeley Mafia" of economists at Berkeley; and in 1961–62 they sent a team over to Jakarta in Indonesia, to continue training people who joined the anti-Suharto conspirators in SESKOAD.[34] There were two consequences. They were training some of the people who became involved in the coup that led to the massacre. And they were also consolidating the team of economists who after the coup would run the newly capitalist country.

It was a quasi-socialist economy under Sukarno. The plan was to end that and have a free market capitalist economy, and the University of California was also training, first in Berkeley and then in Jakarta, the people who would achieve that. When I say this was a much more serious charge, it is because what UC was doing presupposed a change of government that would necessarily be violent. And my university was involved.

At the very end, I bring in Michael Harris, the former Embassy Labor Rep in Paris, who "felt himself superior / to the Ambassador" (in Indonesia), because he was preparing for a new government. And was working "with the CIA / the Asia Foundation [which actually was a CIA creation] // and those whom at first / I declined to mention."

This is where my guilt comes in, because in 1975 I wrote an account of the massacre in Indonesia, basing my work partly on the work of somebody else, a man called David Ransom.[35] I learned a great deal from the Ransom essay, in particular that the conservative U.C. business professor put nominally in charge in Jakarta, Leonard Doyle, was sent back to Berkeley after suggesting "that the University should not be involved in what essentially was becoming a rebellion against the government."[36]

[I consulted the UC Archives on this mission, and verified that Doyle was sent back home after—as I recall it, my own files having since been destroyed—showing "bad judgment" and for not being "a team player." Doyle when I interviewed him was reluctant to talk about his treatment.]

But I took issue with what the Ransom article said about the guilt of U.S. academics in general, and the University of California in particular. I called the term "Berkeley Mafia" "memorable but perhaps unfortunate;" and I added,

> Without wishing to absolve Berkeley of its responsibility for what happened, I would still distinguish between the Berkeley-trained civilians who instigated

and benefitted from the 1965 seizure, and the military who seized power and ordered the subsequent purge.[37]

When I came back to look at Indonesia some years later, I realized that in 1975 I had been in denial. That actually the University of California, my university, had played a larger role in this overthrow of Sukarno than I personally had been able to at that time recognize.

It hit me very hard. Remember this whole poem is about my being depressed. This is a point where the depression comes home. Up to now I have been discussing the political system as an objective "it"—out there, like the Council on Foreign Relations, or the Ford Foundation. Now after reflection I begin for the first time to see myself as part of the system, not outside it. And for the first time I have to recognize the forces of mental repression and denial about my involvement—one of my most important recognitions from the process of mental exploration and reflection in writing this poem.

Taken by itself, this failure of mine may not seem very important. But I saw it and still see it as one small personal example of the way nearly all of us adjust to and defend the system we are part of, and in so doing suppress from our consciousness the intolerable aspects of our system that need to be changed.

At the very end, I'm blending two different quotations. One is Nadezhda Mandelstam the Russian writer talking about what it was like living under Stalin. I interrupt the quotation from her in the poem but I'll give it without interruption here: "In our sort of life people of sound mind had to shut their eyes, with devastating consequences." Nadezhda is acknowledging the psychic cost of this repression, a cost that underlies my crisis in this poem. I'm now seeing that I too have shut my eyes, so I interpolate that quotation with another quotation from Guy Pauker, the UC professor.

Guy Pauker (the man to whom I said, "not you personally") is talking at a meeting of the Nugan Hand Bank—the bank set up by ex-CIA and ex-Special Forces people in Australia that in the 1970s became central to the importation of heroin into Australia. By that time Guy Pauker was on the board.

I've talked to him about it. He said he never knew what was going on at Nugan Hand. I think that's quite possibly true, but he "was" on the board. To the board he said, "the so-called Berkeley Mafia"—these were the people who were running the country after they had all been trained at UC Berkeley or by Berkeley in Jakarta.

Here I quote what he said: "I [Guy Pauker] talked them in to coming / to the University (of California) / running the country (Indonesia) today / fun to have around," Pauker said. And then I add, quoting again from Nadezhda Mandelstam "With devastating consequences."

This has meaning in the poem on a double level: (1) above all, of course, devastating consequences for Indonesia, for the hundreds of thousands who were massacred; but also (2) devastating consequences for me personally, when I have to face the fact that I have been in denial about my life working for an institution implicated in a massacre. [And devastating also, I would add, for the world and especially for America, whose leaders, by welcoming a massacre, had hardened their hearts. This paved the way to subsequent gratuitous U.S. wars in Afghanistan and Iraq, unprovoked wars that would I believe have been unthinkable in the 1950s.]

Freeman: The subtitle of this poem is, *A Poem about Terror*. You told me once it could have been equally subtitled, *A Poem about Denial*.

Peter: Yes, yes. Absolutely. It is a poem about denial, and it's a poem about recovery of repressed memories. That will be dealt with at the very end of the poem, we'll talk more about that, but they go together. We try to survive by just not thinking about certain things. This keeps us sane but also exposes us to a return of the repressed.

That's why there's really quite an important link with the beginning of III. ii, where I say, "To have learned from terror / to see oneself / as part of the enemy // can be a reassurance."

Buddhists say that there is *dukkha*, there is suffering. But there is a cause to suffering, and there is a way out of suffering: by seeing the cause. This is the point where I am beginning to see the way out of suffering. Because understanding the cause of my suffering, what it is in myself that could be part of the enemy, will help me cease to be part of the enemy, and to reach a better level of self, if that makes sense.

Freeman: Then in III.ii you begin to go into some of your past history, as it relates to seeing yourself "as part of the enemy." Feeling terrorized ...

Peter: Yes, but also remembering my own violence, and how they went together. How I was picked on by the kids, we lived at one time in a quite rough part of Montreal. As I say, I'd take out my sled, and young boys would take the sled away. (You have to keep in mind that it was the depression, and a lot of families were deprived then.)

I was in this bad relationship with other children, which produced badness in me. One sign was the fact that I hit Babs, who wasn't one of the rough children at all. But being a resentful young boy, I hit her (I think with a stone) so badly that she actually bled.

I have to tell you this was something that I probably hadn't thought about for a long time. But when I started writing this poem, I remembered, not only that I'd done it, that I was a violent little kid, but that it hurt me, as well as hurting her.

There was another event from this period that I also felt very badly about. I was chased by kids into our backyard, which was protected by a wooden fence. The boys outside were teasing me, "Nyah, nyah, nyah." And I say in the poem, though I don't remember it now, that they were throwing gravel.

I do remember that my response was to take a rock. I wanted to kill them, I suppose, but I threw it so hard it went right over the lane they were in and into the apartment of my future calculus professor, when I was later an undergraduate, and it landed in the nest of his typewriter.

We're beginning part III the same way we began part I, with looking at the nest of a typewriter—and in this case a broken window.

Freeman: Not just the typewriter, I was about to mention the broken window, which is, I think, a wonderful line of poetry. This broken window is black as the lake's bottom. Suddenly, the lake is back. Suddenly, the lake was never gone. There it is.

Peter: In these intense moments everything impinges at once. That was, again, for me, quite traumatic, to have broken that window, and to have my parents telling me that I have to go over and apologize to Professor Sullivan.

What kind of a little kid was I, who would do this? Part of the enemy!

Freeman: Part of the human race.

Peter: Part of the enemy, yes.

We mustn't forget to talk about III.i. I said that in Part I there was what turned out to be an epic invocation of the muse. Here I'm actually bringing in an epic poem in Javanese about how Sultan Agung of Mataram besieged Batavia.

Now, in fact, the siege failed and the Sultan lost. Agung, one of the last important kings, was trying to take over the whole of the island of Java. But the Dutch had already arrived. At first they were just trying to fit in, and had not taken over everything; they just had Batavia, which is now Jakarta, at the west end of the island, and a bit of land around it, not very much. Then this Sultan Agung got the idea: "Well, we'll throw them out."

He sent his whole army, and his whole army was massacred. And the Dutch in the end paid him 60,000 guilders. In return he delivered so much in commodities for export that in forty-one years the Dutch made a profit of 25 million guilders, of which almost 10 percent was sent back to Amsterdam.

This is imperialism in motion. But according to the Javanese epic, the winner was Sultan Agung. He got 60,000 guilders! Good heavens! In fact, he's lost his army. He failed to take the city. But it was a great victory, from the point of view of the court poets!

Freeman: Court poets are spinning what happened, essentially.

Peter: Yes. In a sense, it's like the intelligentsia of this country spinning America. Saying, what we're doing is for the good of Iraq, or the good of Afghanistan, or whatever. I'm beginning to think in two minds about even the role of poetry.

"There have always been poets." This is a lead-in to being part of the enemy. Poet, you better watch what you say very carefully, and refine it of false consciousness!

[In II.xviii I had a similar recognition of denial at work in myself. By the time I write the female or yin segment of *Minding the Darkness*, the third volume of this trilogy *Seculum*, I talk (p. 137) about "the great conspiracy // of organized denial / we call civilization."]

Here in III.i is perhaps my first glimpse that culture, even poetry, can be part of the false consciousness impeding our return to a healthy awareness.

III.iii–III.v

An ovenbird's nest

> ...and after a few hours
>   the first rainstorm of that summer
>   extinguished our hissing fire
>
> my hopes of belonging
>   to the pre-Cambrian north
>   No! If I am to use language
>
> then Lake Massawippi
>   the one lake
>   I could come back to
>
> is the one we must deal with

Freeman: I'd like to begin by reminding the viewer exactly where we left off last time, which was a rather momentous transition of the poem in which you come to realize, if not your complicity, at least your implicit relationship to the violence that you'd begun to research.

Peter: I think the word is *complicity*. To try and sum up very briefly, I think that I had been appalled just by discovering the facts of this huge massacre in Indonesia. This supplies the title, *Coming to Jakarta*.

First: That there had been this massacre. Then second, that America had been involved. And then third—Oh, hey, wait a minute—the University of California had been involved. The Berkeley campus had trained people who went back and helped prepare to take over the country.

Then fourth, after that, I remember that the first time I wrote about this massacre, I tried to excuse the University of California. I wrote an article in a book published in England that took issue with the critic who had said that the "Berkeley Mafia" (a term used in Jakarta about Suharto's economic team) were at the heart of it.

So what in me had tried to say, "Oh, no! not the *Berkeley* Mafia"? It *was* the Berkeley Mafia! So that's where we come now to part III, which is about myself, what is it in me? And in III.ii I acknowledge that I am part of the enemy. And in an odd way, that's "a reassurance."

Another thing happening all the way through the poem is that I'm gradually healing from a really genuine crisis, which I perceived at the time as close to a nervous breakdown, back in Watertown, Massachusetts. To see myself as part of the enemy can be a relief, because the problem is not some form of *kismet* or fate. It is something I can and must begin to deal with.

That's the situating where we are now. I'm looking at my childhood.

Freeman: Is this still being written with this sort of unconscious automatic writing?

Peter: I wouldn't say "automatic" any more. I'm beginning to know what I'm doing by part III. At the beginning of part II, I didn't even know why I was writing so furiously, or where it would go.

Then I realized it's going to be a poem about terror. Then I realize that I have to do this thing about Indonesia.

Here I'm beginning to put things together. For example, in III.iii I talk about the "first lake." That is the lake that I will talk about more in the sequel volume dedicated to my mother, *Listening to the Candle*, which was a really primitive lake. No signs of anything civilized or human, except that nearby there had once been a French-Canadian farmer and his family, and my mother's father had built or taken over a log cabin for our family.

Twenty years later, the survivors from the farmer's family were living in Montreal. My grandfather had gone back to live in England, where he died. I went back another twenty years after that, and couldn't even find where the farmhouse had been. And the road had all grown in.

So we didn't belong there.

Freeman: You literally couldn't go back.

Peter: Well, no. I could go back on foot, but the last time I went, which is not in the poem, I couldn't even find the lake. The lake is obviously still there. If I had gone with a compass and a topo map, I certainly would have found it. But there used to be a road up to the cabin, and now there was no cabin and no road.

We didn't belong there. "Not even the white horse." Horses are not native, of course, to Canada.

I didn't belong there. And I have to deal with the paradox that Lake Massawippi, full of Americans I'm different from, is where I belong: more than this other primitive lake, which still haunts me. That's why I come back to it in the second yin poem about nature, dedicated to my mother.

But in "this" long poem, dedicated to my father, there is this whole elaborate culture that I felt simultaneously part of, attracted to, and alien to. That's why, at the end of this section, I wasn't at the sherry parties. I went up on the hill to get away from them.

In a sense, it's a kind of coming back to something very important when I discover the ovenbird's nest. That was like a moment of truth for me at the age of twelve, even though what does it signify? Nothing, really.

But on another level, it does signify something: that basically I'm drawn back to nature and away from this culture which is partly Canadian and partly American.

The paradox is that I was certainly happier in America. The happiest year of my childhood was the year when I was not in Canada, where, even in this supposedly progressive Montreal school, I was quite ruthlessly teased by the other children.

That's why I was glad to be in Cambridge, Massachusetts, with people who didn't drag each other fully clothed into the gym, which just appalled me the next year back in Montreal.

I really hated that sort of violence. But it didn't happen at all at Shady Hill School with Miss Thorp, so that's why I was happy there.

So all of this is an exploration of my identity. Am I Canadian? Am I American? I'm certainly more Canadian than American, but there was a problem about that.

Freeman: At the end of this section [III.iv], the ghost comes back. The ghost that we first see at the very beginning of the poem.

Peter: I could only see the ghost in the darkness of night. In the dawn, I saw by daylight that it was just snow on the tree. But the world of daylight is not enough; "If we are to escape // we must go another way."[38]

Freeman: In III.v, then, we come to the "bright island of non-being." What was this place?

Peter: Cambridge, Massachusetts. The year my father got a Guggenheim and we moved down with our maid Georgette to a house in Cambridge, for him to write a book.

Maybe I could have spelled out this episode a bit more. I don't know if it's clear. The poet George Barker was coming downstairs; and Georgette was coming upstairs with a tray, because my father was sick in bed.

George Barker, being who he was (I didn't like him, although he's quite well-known as a British poet) just reached over, took the glass of orange juice off Georgette's tray, drank it, and put it back on the tray.

And this was too much for poor Georgette. There was nobody down there for her to speak French to. She barely spoke English. My mother searched very hard for a Roman Catholic church where she could speak to the priest, and she never really found a good one.

Thanks to George Barker, Georgette, within an hour, had totally flipped. And was standing with arms extended in a doorway. "*Je suis la croix blanche, et vous êtes la croix rouge.*" My mother had to take her back to Montreal.

Freeman: So you're . . .

Peter: Here is the theme of madness. It was the first time in my life I watched somebody go mad.

Freeman: I see.

Peter: Madness is what is frightening me in this poem, *Coming to Jakarta*. But in Buddhist terms, I'm beginning to see there is a cause and remedy to this suffering.[39]

Freeman: Your maid goes through a similar experience to the larger experience that you're having with the world, the incongruity of it, the unfittingness of it to our minds.

Peter: Yes! And in a sense, she and I are in the same condition, because we're both in a city that we don't know and don't belong to. But for her, it's too much; she has a breakdown and has to leave.

For me, in some odd way, I'm more happily adjusted than I've ever been in the city that I come from.

Freeman: You're in this new school.

Peter: Yes, a very good school, Shady Hill. It is true that my teacher there, Miss Thorp, was a granddaughter of Longfellow.

Freeman: What was the reference about "bad King George"?

Peter: Well, when I say "during the war," in that year 1940–41, Canada was at war. But America was not at war.

That's what I was debating about with the other children. There was quite a lot of pumping up of American patriotism. And there was going to be a big school assembly.

We, in grade seven, were going to all come out on stage, the whole class, and sing, "In seventy-six the sky was red, thunder rumbling overhead, Bad King George couldn't sleep in his bed. And on that sultry morn, ol' Uncle Sam was born."[40]

But Miss Thorp came to me and said, "Of course, if you don't want to sing those words, 'bad King George,' you don't have to sing them." It hadn't occurred to me not to sing them. Whatever my identity was, it had nothing to do with "bad King George." I too was anti-king.

Freeman: That's certainly a sign of the different place you were now in that they would consider that.

Peter: But they thought it was important. I didn't think it was important.

Freeman: Later on, you talk about Donald.

Peter: Oh, yes. I'm back now in Canada, Westmount (a suburb of Montreal). We're in Westmount again, but no longer up at the top of the mountain. The school was particularly difficult for me in those war years, because one way you could stay out of the army was to go to school. So in the back of my eighth grade classroom there were "boys" who were eighteen, nineteen, twenty. (I think at twenty-one you could no longer get away with this.) And they were extremely tough and boisterous and difficult. (I talk about that in *Listening to the Candle*, too [II.iv, pp. 22–28].)

They were always looking for someone to tease. Here I have to admit, guiltily, that rather than have them tease me, I was one of the people who, as I confess in this poem, once redirected their attention, by saying, "It's Donald's birthday."

This would happen, perhaps not quite once a week, but regularly: "It's Donald's birthday." Donald was an orphan. He lived in the Weirdale Orphanage, just a few blocks away from the school.

I'm really upset now to be confessing this: Donald would be stuffed into the waste basket: so deeply in, he couldn't get out. He had to wait for the teacher to come and help him to get out.

Perhaps as a result of that treatment, he left the school. He joined the Navy. German submarines were active in the St. Lawrence River, and Donald's ship was sunk. He died. (As did my cousin, Dick, by the way—that's in the poem later [III.xi, p. 85]. Quite a few boats were blown up in the St. Lawrence River.)

This is my early involvement in thoughtless, shameful, in a sense even ruthless, self-serving action which may have contributed indirectly to somebody else getting killed.

I'm already a kind of casualty here: My feeling about it was that I was a casualty.

Freeman: It's not the first example in the poem of your complicity in the very violence that you're trying to deal with in the book.

Peter: Exactly. We are "part of the enemy."

Freeman: At the very end of this section, as you said earlier, you narrate this habitual escape you make from that world. So perhaps that would be a good note to end on.

Peter: Could I just stick in a little bit more? Once again: the complexity of it is that I really found, with this kind of school experience at Westmount Junior High, I felt better off in the summers with Americans at Lake Massawippi.

But Lake Massawippi is far from ideal, because it's all organized about these races and games at the Club, in which I was always last or among the last.

This experience, I'm thinking to myself, of swimming in a 100-yard race, freestyle; of the winners, the splashing from their feet in my face. As I'm thinking, "Surely there must be some other way to grow up."

Freeman: This is the culture of the young father earlier in the poem who bloodied his child's face.

Peter: Well, that was perhaps a bit more upper class, but there was a very competitive culture at the Club.

The question which I ask as a teenager, "surely there must be some other way to grow up," is from one point of view the most important question in the whole poem. That things don't "have" to be.... Surely, they don't "have" to be as they are.

I just wanted to get that in, because I loved Lake Massawippi in a way, although I always had profound nostalgia for the other lake, where we didn't belong.

I also did not belong in those races. I was always having trouble with other children and that continued until I got to college. And then college was full of people like me, so this sense of being a freak ended to some extent then.

Freeman: To some extent. Although . . .

Peter: Although I had a sort of nervous breakdown there. Yes, I did. [laughs]

III.vi–III.vii

The brooding toils of energy

    I arrived in no mood
        for the obligatory pluralism
    of post-war Oxford

    where in our seminar
        on *Recent European*
    Political Thought

    we were persuaded to read three dons
        from the south side of Broad Street
    and three from the north

    my suggestion of Sartre
        meeting with a look which convinced
    even me I had just been joking

Freeman: In last week's installment, there was a line about the life around this lake and "surely there must be some other way to grow up." In the section before that there was a line about we humans not being fit for this world we live in.

In this week's installment, you sail away across the Atlantic, but you find yourself still in a world you're not fit for.

Peter: Looking back in 2012, I would say that Oxford now seems to have been yet another "roof" experience—like Shady Hill School, North Hatley, or Harvard in section III.ix—by which I was simultaneously inspired and alienated. (It was at Oxford that, by writing one short paper a week, I luckily overcame an acute writer's block—but this is not in the poem.)

When I was writing *Jakarta*, I recalled only the alienation. That's why I make the allusion to Wordsworth at Cambridge, after coming down from his idyllic childhood in the pastoral setting of the Lake District. He came to Cambridge; I went to Oxford. At Cambridge he saw these dons (teachers) doing their donnish theatrics and it made him aware of his own difference and also of his own innerness.

I was not yet a reader of Wordsworth when I went to Oxford, but I was aware of that same difference from not belonging. However, it didn't help me to discover something authoritative within. Actually, these two sections are about almost the opposite, about how I felt myself coming apart inside. I really did think I was going to go mad at that time, after my first crises at McGill and in Paris. I did for about three or four years.

It was in the end a relief to fail at Oxford, have a very minor crisis, and then say, "Oh, this is just a minor crisis I can deal with." And so: "Maybe I'm not going to go insane after all."

And considering all of that was sixty years ago, if I am insane it's not as visible as I was frightened it was going to be.

Freeman: There's the bit about you yourself deciding that you must have been joking about Sartre.

Peter: [laughs] That don! The challenge to the seminar was to choose authors to study from all the political thinkers in Europe, and I suggested, "Sartre." [Imitating the don:] "Sartre?" It truly "convinced even me I'd just been joking." And we ended up with six authors, all of them dons from Oxford. They say the British are insular but I don't think anyone was more insular than Oxford dons were in those days.

Freeman: In that section about the reading list, there's something I was puzzled about. This scene alone on Snowdon, straddling the hog's back, the dense fog: What's that a reference to?

Peter: Well I guess it's another allusion to Wordsworth, who climbed Snowdon and had a mystical experience. He saw the moon shining on the clouds and it opened up a whole universe for him.

I went up Snowdon in the morning and got caught in totally dense fog. I could see only about as far as from me to you. And I was trying to find the top and my only method was to keep climbing up.

I didn't make a very good choice. It was actually quite dangerous though I didn't know it until later. I ended up at the top of a jagged hog's back, and the only way I could proceed was with one foot on one side and one foot on the other side.

I inched forward into the fog. The analogy was like a rodeo rider. In fact, the mountain wasn't bucking like a bronco would buck; but not having any dimensions to check myself on anything, I did get quite giddy in that experience. However, I did not get the kind of insight that Wordsworth got.

Freeman: He found enlightenment; you encountered a kind of "endarkenment."

Peter: "Enfoggiment," yes. And as alone as at Oxford. But then in the end—this part is true and was very dramatic for me—the sun burst through and I saw a little hut and a cog railway; and the train—symbolizing civilization—was ready to take me down to the bottom. [Chuckles] It was not what Wordsworth saw.

Freeman: No, it was much more in tune with the kind of explorations you're engaged in this poem.

Peter: Right. I was very lucky. People die on Snowdon all the time when they get caught in the fog.

Freeman: Well the next figure after Sartre that you had a disagreement about was Hegel. I guess we can get into this more in the next section, but for now, what was the nature of the limitations you were running up against here?

Peter: Let me say, first of all, that Hegel became very important for me for about three or four years and I was reading him in German. I got very involved. It developed partly because of my alienation from Oxford. My dons were very down to earth, practical; they were language philosophers in the sense that they thought philosophy should just be about things that "people" say and mean, people in the streets of Oxford.

Hegel was brought up in discussion as something for them to attack—as being one of these German metaphysicians with grandiose metaphysical visions. We were required to read an attack on him by Karl Popper, *The Open Society and Its Enemies*, that I (and later not just I) found very crude in its polemics against Plato and Hegel.[41] Hegel interested me on many levels: (1) his suggestion that everyday reason or Understanding (*Verstand*) was inadequate and needed to be transcended, (2) that this *Verstand* had been the limiting characteristic of the eighteenth-century Enlightenment, leading to the irrational violence of the French Revolution, (3) that history was marked by the process of dialectic, wherein things were superseded by their opposites: medieval faith became post-Newtonian reason (*Verstand*), and now we were ripe to combine them in something else.

Hegel's dialectical process of thesis, antithesis, and synthesis can be seen as underlying my trilogy *Seculum*. The yang volume of *Coming to Jakarta*, dedicated to my rationalist father, is followed by a yin volume dedicated to my intuitive artist mother, and then a third volume structured around the search to reconcile, if not transcend, the tension between yang and yin.[42] This process unfolded very slowly in Hegelian fashion: I completed a draft of the first volume before realizing the need for a second, and likewise the second before the third.

Hegel was, by the way, a major influence for Sartre, as we see in this business about "the *world* was *an sich* / and I was *für sich*." Sartre picked up on

Hegel's idea in the Preface to his *Phenomenology of Spirit* that the objects in the world have essences, they are *an sich*, *en soi*, what they are, and humans, on the contrary, are pure existence without essence, *für sich*, *pour soi*, searching to create an essence.

According to existentialism as I understood it, humans are freedom—as opposed to that lamp over there which is a lamp without a chance to be anything else. I was drawn to this partly, I think, because of my incipient sense of our double existence between two worlds; and also, perhaps chiefly, because my dons were so opposed to this largeness of vision beyond common sense. I felt it really did correspond in some not very explicable way to intuitions I had. It made a kind of sense to me, just as Sartre made a kind of sense to me.

Today I am not interested very much in Sartre anymore. I still am interested in Hegel. His influence on Marx alone would make him important, I don't want to go into it too much, but as a philosopher, I think Hegel was the greatest philosopher until Alfred North Whitehead. And Whitehead in a way was developing from Hegel but, referring to recent quantum mechanics, came up with the idea that even the universe is a little bit fuzzy, and we humans are not as opposed to the universe as Hegel or Sartre thought we were—because some degree of freedom is inherent in the whole universe, not just in us.

[I hope it is clear that when I wrote "now I knew / the *world* was *an sich* / and I was *für sich*" I was satirizing my youthful self-certainty at the same time as my dons' pluralism. I "knew" things at twenty-two that one cannot know in maturity.]

I don't want to give a whole philosophy lecture here; but Hegel will, in the next section, be important to me and will lead to my being failed at Oxford because they didn't agree with my interpretation of Hegel.

Freeman: What's the literal translation of *an sich* and *fur sich*?

Peter: It's hard to translate. *An sich* means "in itself" (an object already defined) and *für sich* means "for itself" (a subject defining itself). Then for Hegel, the absolute was "*An und für sich*, "in and for itself." (already defined, yet in the process of realizing itself). That was a kind of totality, which neither objects could achieve, nor humans, because we humans would never have the degree of essence necessary to be absolute.

Freeman: So the Sartre suggestion was a joke, and now the Hegel was the same?

Peter: Well, Hegel got me into trouble with this famous don. I can give his name now: Isaiah Berlin, he was and is deservedly quite famous. And he gave us a lecture about Hegel saying that for Hegel, every moment was part of a grand orchestrated movement toward a fulfillment of history.

I called him on the words *every moment*, because, I said, Hegel recognized that there is accident in history.[43] And Isaiah Berlin didn't want to hear that, because it wasn't compatible with the lecture he'd just given.

As I recall, he said, "If Hegel wrote that he shouldn't have." [laughs] Hegel was messing up Berlin's interpretation of Hegel. So I kept writing my own version of things, and another don who was also my friend [John Plamenatz], said of one of my papers, "You write that, and they'll say that you're insane."

Freeman: Let me come to this next section here where you do come to believe that . . .

Peter: I'm going to go mad, yes. And madness was going to get me out of this mess I was in.

Freeman: Explain about the mess again.

Peter: I didn't fit in. I really didn't fit in at Oxford. This is a one-sided account of my life there because on another level I fit in very well, too well. I was poetry editor of the magazine *Isis*. I was going to be the editor-in-chief of the magazine. I went to lots of parties. I had a girlfriend. There was even a gossip column written about me and my girlfriend Caroline. And then I met this incredibly beautiful young woman, Sally Philipps, who was very briefly the great love of my life.

But I wasn't equipped to deal with all of that experience; and I felt always, inside, that somehow the cogs were missing. I was spinning wheels inside my brain and it was going to lead to a climax. I was in a situation which I was convinced was going to end badly; and the only way to get out of it was for everyone to see I was insane, and didn't belong there. And I didn't know what would happen after that.

It was really unsettling for me. Twice in my life I've been screaming on the floor with my hands and fingers stretched out. The first time, at McGill, my voice was not my voice. I was screaming things and from far off I was also listening to myself screaming. It was very scary the first time, and I was also convinced that it was a prelude to another bigger collapse.

And then at Oxford when I failed, I expected the collapse. Then it did happen again, but in a much more diminished way. My housemates were there (I was alone the first time). They calmed me down. It was all over in about three minutes and I never again thought I was going to go insane the way I had for about four years.

Well, actually that's not true, absolutely not true at all. (Just think of Watertown in part I.ii.) But those four years, of steady certainty that I was coming to a precipice, were over.

Freeman: Can you talk about the time you saw:

> beyond the humming phone wire
> and glistening black asphalt
> a face in the heavy clouds

> or was it
> > in the strange light
> > an intimation
>
> of those shapes in the brooding
> > toils of energy
> > and deluge of emotion
>
> we all carry within us

Peter: I think the poem is not really very accurate here: I don't think I saw a face in the heavy clouds, but I do think I had an ineffable experience. And I didn't have words to speak the ineffable, the unspeakable, so I spoke instead of that "face."[44]

I don't think I saw a face but I do think I had an experience. And it came from being blocked from getting to the beautiful church, Orcival, that I was planning to reach the next day, that I had seen many times in photographs but never in real life.

Freeman: What's the significance at the end of this section of the "toils of energy / and deluge of emotion / we all carry within us?" What do you think the connection is between that and these other subjects that you're writing about?

Peter: First of all, on the personal level, I don't imagine that I'm very alone in this. I think other young people becoming adult, coping with a future opening out which they don't know anything about, have to deal with the inner storms and confusions and violent surges of energy which are inside us but not really ours because we don't control them.

That, I think is on the personal level, of what I've been talking about here. But I want to relate that (and I think the poem does relate it) to the end of III. vi, when we plan a little rally and the plan is all set; then we cancel the plan, and something happens anyway.

It was really quite imposing that five of us very secretly planned a rally on the steps of the Student Union and then we secretly cancelled it; and I arrived there and people were standing around saying, "Why are there police on the other side of the street?" And the more of us who gathered on the steps, the more police there were on the other side of the street. Then, very dramatically, the Mounties [RCMP] came on horseback and trotted into the midst of the crowd. Pretty soon it was almost impossible for the traffic to move on Sherbrooke, one of the biggest streets in Montreal, because there were so many people milling about.

[I thought naively at the time that one of the five of us must have been a police informant. Now it seems much more likely that the police were just continuing to tap my family phone (cf. II.vii).]

Why am I talking about this in this context when I say "there being more than meets the eye / to the politics of reason"? This is perhaps the first time I ever became aware of there being politics under the surface, of all these other forces accumulating and asserting themselves and not part of the world as we think about it rationally.

It's a model both of the psyche which I'm giving at the end of III.vii, and also a kind of model for politics which I'm giving at the end of II.ix. [They illustrate the internal and external doubleness of the human condition.]

Freeman: "The world like myself . . ."

Peter: Right! Finish it.

Freeman: "in its unintegrated desires."

III.viii–III.ix

Like the heroes of all good tales

       I would go out in the moonlight
         boots squeaking on snow

    to empty the steadily filling
       buckets of maple sap
       into the boys' vats

    and stoke their banked fires
       the woods' shadows numinous
      with sugary smoke

    Freeman: Well, as predicted, you were ploughed.
    Peter: Right, this is what they said—"ploughed" (i.e., "failed," in their Oxford English). We are coming to the mid-point of the poem. And it is really a turning point, because I had been very worried about having a nervous breakdown and going insane. And then I was failed and I didn't go insane; and on the contrary, escaped into the woods—like these two mythical heroes Yvain and Erlangga who, as we can talk about, found strength by going back to nature.
    That moves me forward, so I become a bit more assertive now. Instead of being just a victim of everything that is happening to me.
    The way we see that, is when I go back to Oxford, instead of blaming myself for not being part of Oxford, I see Oxford as inflicting pain on my former tutor Michael Foster, whom I really revered very much.
     Berlin told me *"your Hegel questions // sounded almost like Michael Foster."* But I felt then, and still do, that this was no shame but more like a badge of honor.

Freeman: This is Michael Foster?

Peter: This is Michael Foster. Yes. As opposed to the "famous don," Isaiah Berlin, a much more famous man and a wonderful man in his way. But I was convinced then, and still am, that he didn't know (and didn't want to know) as much about Hegel as Michael Foster did.

Freeman: I think this next section ("it was back to Canada // and a small school / for the over-privileged / in the woods of the Seigniory Club") you going into the woods to empty the maple vats is one of the better stretches of poetry in the book. I often think about those high trees and your thoughts about them.

Peter: The boys were allowed to make their own maple syrup. So that's why they had these fires, to boil down the sap. And they had to go to bed at a certain hour; but I could go out and make sure that the fires would last through the night. So I was stoking fires and smelling the sap; and it was very, very nourishing for the soul, I do have to say.

If you live in cities, you think that cities dominate nature. If you live in the country, then cities seem like small, little islands of something not altogether desirable, called civilization, in a matrix that is larger and older. That's what I believed and later wrote down.

Freeman: You certainly get that sense of civilization as an island in a larger world of nature when you read these old legends like Yvain and the Arthurian matter and things like that. That's a European hero, but the other Indonesian hero that you mentioned . . .

Peter: . . . Erlangga . . .

Freeman: . . . and he's important to this poem.

Peter: Yes, this is perhaps the first moment in the poem where we actually do start "coming to Jakarta," in a narrow sense of describing Indonesia. Both Yvain and Erlangga are mythical figures based on real historical figures. Both of them, in the mythic accounts of them, suffered a setback, retreated to the forest, and came out of the forest stronger.

This is said of the historic king Erlangga, who was a king in Java. Yvain is based on a Welsh king, Owen. It's probably just a myth, but in its way it speaks truth. In the myth, Yvain was torn between his love for his beloved and his love of chivalry and his career. So he was not very well integrated, and he went off on many escapades chasing after evil knights; and totally forgot that in a year he was supposed to be back to see his beloved.

As a result, she threw him out and he went mad.

It's very relevant to the background of this poem. Being mad he went into the forest, encountered a lion, and became the Knight of the Lion. And the lion represents all the strength of nature while he, in the company of the lion, emerged a more complete hero and was able to have a happy reconciliation with his beloved.

Erlangga—I think I won't say more about Erlangga now because we will in III.xii.

Freeman: The significance of Erlangga for now is that he's a figure from *Indonesian* mythology.

Peter: Right! And he does almost the same thing.

It is interesting to me that two cultures converge. Chrétien de Troyes wrote about Yvain in France in the twelfth century, and there is no way he could have been aware of the Indonesian culture; but the two different traditions make a similar point in roughly the same time period about the relationship between civilized life and nature. I do believe that there are certain archetypes in literature that slowly emerge in synchrony, as part of cultural evolution all around the world.

Freeman: It's an aspect of "that which is within us."

Peter: Yes! And very much of course what was happening in my life, in that I was, in effect, meditating during that year 1952–53 in the forest. That was a year when I was teaching children, and had certain chores to do; but I did quite a lot of reading. I learned Greek, I read all of Gibbon and some other major books. One of the most important was Kierkegaard's *Concluding Unscientific Postscript*, which helped persuade me of the limits to Hegel's over-defined presentation of reality, and indeed to all social science.

Another very important book in this vein, which I read after seeing a review, was Erich Heller's *The Disinherited Mind*. I read it as a history of the loss of faith in Absolute Truth after Hegel, and the increasing importance of art as a substitute.

But all in all, it was a quiet year, and very much what I needed after all the hustle in Oxford. At the beginning of it, I thought I was turning my back on university life forever. But at the end I was energized enough for a fresh try, from a fresh perspective.

Freeman: I was surprised that the students were freaked out by the lynching story.

Peter: I was surprised, because the most hateful thing about that school was its culture of violence. I believe that the U.S. military still subsidizes, as it did then, the making of Hollywood movies which celebrate the massacring of enemies—in those days they were the Japanese. And these movies make people revel in the thought of our power and how we can kill people. And the students, from the age of eight to seventeen, literally did cheer when the Japanese were being burnt to death by napalm before our eyes. So we had this little bit of "civilization" in the midst of nature there.

That's why it was such a relief to get out of that, and go into the forest. Later I had the courage to test the student reaction to an account of an actual lynching, and it was astonishing to me how they wouldn't let me finish reading the extract. It was a memoir by W.H. Davies who was an English poet, or rather Welsh poet, who visited America.[45] And he saw a lynching, which he described in a matter-of-fact way. And these two things were true: (a) they wouldn't let me finish reading it, it was too much for them; and (b) they wanted me to promise that it wasn't true.

Freeman: Some moral there.

Peter: Yes, I think so.

Freeman: I would not have guessed that any group of kids. . . . I would have thought that they would have found it fascinating or entertaining, for the violence.

Peter: Or maybe they were in a sense being strengthened in their inner core by going out and doing the maple syrup in the forest as well. Maybe a city group would not have that same degree of sensitivity.

Freeman: Maybe the planners of the future will have to be careful not to locate their schools in places like that.

Could you say a little more about Michael Foster, what his unhappiness was, what his story was?

Peter: I want to. I never knew him very well. He looked like a monk; even his hair was more or less tonsured. He was single, he lived at Christ Church, which was the richest and most elegant of the colleges. I have to repeat a bit what I said about Hegel in an earlier session: that the dominant feeling at Oxford was that continental thought, which had just been defeated in World War II, was the source of dangerous, large metaphysical ideas; and it was the job of Oxford professors to shoot these ideas down, as Isaiah Berlin was doing.

Michael Foster was perhaps the last in the tradition of nineteenth century English metaphysical thinkers who took Hegel very seriously. So he knew his Hegel very well. Above all there was just something unworldly about the man. He was very quiet. He had a little bit of a lisp and a tremor, which suggested to me that perhaps there was some lack of ease within. But he exhibited great composure.

I don't know why Isaiah Berlin said I "sounded almost like Michael Foster." (As if that would make me see that I'd been an idiot.) But Michael Foster had been my tutor.

Freeman: If anything, that was affirming.

Peter: I said to Berlin, a little brashly, "I take that as a compliment."

Freeman: You mentioned earlier that you were aware of Foster's unhappiness.

Peter: I think it was that he showed a kind of remoteness from the world. You couldn't imagine going out and drinking a beer in a pub somewhere or watching a cricket game. He had a great serenity that was based on a certain amount of abnegation, giving up.

[After I left Oxford he published a short book, *Philosophy and Mystery*, in which he asserted that spiritual realities exist that are inherently mysterious and not accessible through science. Though I have never seen the book, I suspect my exposure to Foster's earlier thinking helped prepare me to write *Listening to the Candle* and *Minding the Darkness*.[46]]

It's funny because it wasn't just me who had this admiration for him. I had a much more secular Canadian friend, Cranford Pratt, who I didn't expect to respect Foster so much. My friend didn't write an exam on Hegel. He passed, after writing about something else. But he shared my respect for Michael Foster.

Freeman: Foster's another one of the many figures in the poem so far that were not at ease in the world and didn't make it.

Peter: Exactly, and I guess I felt that identification with him precisely because he validated a way of not being at ease with the world, or at least not being at ease with Oxford. [laughs] But I was different when I went back. Oxford had me cowed at the beginning. They persuaded even me "I had just been joking." But now at the same way that I had the courage to read students the story about the lynching, I had the courage to ask him, "in effect . . . *How can you stand it here?*"

He didn't indicate to me that there was any problem, but that was the way he was. He certainly wasn't wearing his heart on his sleeve or anything like that.

I wanted to say something about III.ix. We have said almost nothing about meeting with the Harvard Junior Fellows and above all this climactic moment at the end of III.ix. This was a house in New York a year or two after I had been writing my McGill PhD dissertation in Cambridge. It was the apartment of a man who actually did become America's Ambassador to Italy. He wrote a big and quite a good book about economics. I had become so aware of the stringencies of the Cold War—that I said this shocking thing. (*"That's why / some people in Europe / are not so upset // to see Russia get the bomb"*)

What I meant was that, as a Canadian, I could see a case for having two nuclear powers in the world and not just one. But it was literally so shocking that, as I recall it, everybody—there were maybe fifteen or twenty people in the room—stopped talking. The man who had brought me, who was very close to me and later the best man at my wedding, took me aside and said, "Peter, you really mustn't say things like that, even if you're joking," which I don't think I really was.

I began to see civilization, if that's what we should call it, as much more constrained and limiting to our freedom and our real aspirations, compared to just being out in the maple trees and putting wood on those fires.

III.x

The stream one lives by

> she may seem no more than a
> rest within space
>
> no more than a
>   pivot
> for the restless movements of the stars

[In our original videos, Freeman and I agreed not to discuss this section, a love lyric to my first wife Maylie, but I now think it is important to talk now about when and why I added it to the poem.

As I recall, it was added, for two reasons, shortly after the furious weeks of writing a first draft of the poem, which I first envisaged as being about everything of relevance in my life. On the one hand, I realized that I had written overwhelmingly—as in the patrilineal genealogy of the next section—about males; and that in particular my love for Maylie (or indeed for any woman) was flagrantly absent. I reflected about this conspicuous absence and this inspired the image that opens the section ("The stream one lives by / one hardly hears"). At that time I had not yet imagined there would be the sequel (*Listening to the Candle*) that would be dedicated to my mother and would remember Maylie and my children, along with two earlier loves. However, just as Maylie was a pivot about whom my life rotated, so I placed this section as a "pivot" at the exact mid-point of the poem symbolizing Maylie's place at the center of my adult life, heart, and mind.[47] (And also a counterbalance to the hyperactive male activities that had sickened me.)

At the same time, as I began to focus on the shape and development of the poem as a whole, I realized that this section, at both the chronological and narrative middle of the poem, would supply an organizing "pivot" for its movement and return. It is at the point where I am beginning to fulfill in the poem my mother's words, "Think for yourself . . ." (II.ii) and to escape what in III.xiii I call the legacy of "excessive inheritance." I believe it is true that Maylie contributed, more than anything else at the time, to this gradual shift.

But I was not thinking of epic strategies when I first drafted this section; I was still immersed in emotion from the anxiety that precipitated the poem. Years later I can perceive a certain irony in the words "to think of escape / is meaningless / and one feels free // even to scream rather than escape." The words that follow

>   indeed could one ever scream
>   this way at God I wonder
>
>   how exonerate her
>   for the criminal defects
>   of the whole establishment
>
>   including life itself
>   she first delivered me from –

are stronger clues to an ambivalence I was not yet ready to admit or confront openly, even to myself. The fact is that 1980–81, the year in which the poem began to be written, was also the first year that we both screamed "this way" at each other—a way I could not have imagined even a year or two earlier. The section both summarizes an overwhelming sense of gratitude to her I felt then (still feel, years after her death in 2001) and also raises, if only to dismiss it then out of hand, the thought of "escape."

In between these two poles was an unspoken gap, an emptiness of heart, that I can now easily see (as then I could not) was a major factor in the emotional sickness and self-alienation that we encounter at the beginning of the poem, and gave rise to them.

The poem can be read less as a description than as a prayer, or as a "tribute" in the sense of gift or peace offering, to the woman I still loved so much. But only three or four years after writing this section, while still revising *Jakarta*, I essentially moved out of our house. And in 1992, by mutual friendly consent, but on her initiative, we agreed to divorce.

Writing now, a third of a century after composing this pivot poem, I see for the first time that the whole poem (and not just this section) also expressed my grief at losing the bliss of our first married years, a loss due in large part, like my loss of other friends, to my obsessive research into the Indonesian massacre and other crimes: my loss in short of Maylie, of my happy marriage, of my youthful hopes, of the sixties optimism I shared with so many.

>   Odysseus
>   shalt lose all companions (II.v)]

III.xi–III.xii

The known and unknown roadways

>it is all coming out
>>the funeral I must have forgotten
>
>Dick Scott
>
>torpedoed in the St. Lawrence
>>I have not escaped death's nudge
>
>they are emerging now
>
>from the house of my dream
>>*the dead*
>>*and the survivors*
>
>*the fallen apples of the dead*
>>*beyond ourselves*
>>*the yet untasted*
>
>*tree of life*

Freeman: We have two really interesting sections today. They're very different in a lot of ways. They're very unique.

Peter: They're both about ancestors, though.

Freeman: But they're both about ancestors, and they're both a kind of an invocation of the mythological.

Peter: And seeing the tragedy of the past in the present.

Freeman: Now, the first section is your past.

Peter: Yes, my family.

It is more specifically the male lineage of my father, to whom this volume is dedicated. [By the time I wrote this late section I had probably begun the next volume of the trilogy, *Listening to the Candle,* which is dedicated to my mother; and there (e.g., IV.vii) I make references to her ancestors, mostly in the female line.] Robert Hass notes "this male lineage of the Scott family" in III.xi, and rightly adds that it "is meant, I think, to remind us of the procession of warrior kings in book six of the *Aeneid.*"[48] It became slowly clearer to me as I wrote and rewrote *Coming to Jakarta,* that it and all three epics chiefly evoked in it (*Aeneid, Iliad,* and *Mahabharata*) are, as Hass writes, about "maleness." And this section, like the genealogical sequence in *Aeneid* 6 links maleness (through my warrior uncles) to conflict and death.

Freeman: We had a hint already earlier in the book of your childhood experiences with terror, with complicity in terror, with death, but now, in this section, it floods in in a much more overwhelming way.

Peter: I felt that in myself, particularly because I was just barely too young—by one year—to be drafted into the Canadian army for World War II. The class ahead of me ended up in the army. Actually, the class immediately ahead of me ended up occupying Germany after it was defeated, but the class before that was "in" the war. Two of my favorite teachers were killed in the war.

I came to feel I had always been protected from death. I lived in Canada; and death, during the war, was over there in Europe. But in this section, I'm realizing there had been an enormous amount of death in my family in every generation. My father was one of the five surviving boys in a family of seven; my grandfather was one of the three surviving children of nine. All three of my father's older brothers signed up for the army in World War I. Two of them were wounded, along with my grandfather; and the third one was killed. The story of Uncle Harry's death is in this section.

My grandfather was the Padre of the First Division. He wrote a memoir afterwards, *The Great War as I Saw It,* which has just been reissued. In it there's this very moving scene, how his son was also in the First Division; and in a terrible battle—the Battle of the Somme[49]—his son was killed and hastily buried.

With a small party, my grandfather went out between the lines at night to look for his grave. It's literally true that he saw in the mud a hand with this little ring on it.[50] It's the family ring with what I call a "fake crest," because my grandfather had acquired it himself from the English kings of arms. (A century ago, they would sell you a coat of arms, so now males in my family can wear a ring with a little stag's head.) The ring is mostly famous in our family memories because my grandfather found it there on the buried hand of Uncle Harry, who's now buried in one of the Canadian army cemeteries in France.

But that experience of death was also in the generation before. My grandfather was one of the nine children, of whom only three reached adulthood. The other young ones died, probably of tuberculosis.

Sandra Djwa wrote a biography of my father, and did some wonderful research that did not end up in her book. It was her theory that my grandmother must have had tuberculosis. As long as she was healthy enough to nurse the children, they all contracted it and they all died. Then, when she was too ill, my grandfather was not nursed by her; and along with the next two children he survived.

Freeman: Early in this section, you say, speaking of the dream you had, that you were "not aware of terror, even guilt. It is more like a discovery."

Peter: Yes. In that dream.

Freeman: In the dream, yeah. I think in the poem too, earlier, when you make references to Donald, for example, and other examples of your brush with terror and complicity and death, there are those elements of terror and guilt and so forth. This section seems to be a little bit beyond that even. It seems to be more general, more generally tragic than simply the complicity and the violence of the human race.

Peter: Well, it's a double thing. On the one hand, we're seeing death and terror close up in the family. But on the other hand, as you rightly say, my relationship to it has somewhat changed. In all of this, perhaps I'm beginning to observe rather than suffer.

The dream that we're talking about here is a dream which occurred a long time after I had started to write the poem. It comes right here in the middle of the poem and is in fact part of the healing, I think, which the poem is giving me: the strength to, from a detached position, *recognize* all these factors that have borne in on me and my father and my grandfather.

Sandra Djwa's biography of my father was finally published in 1987. That horrible night in Watertown that begins the poem was right after Reagan had been elected in 1980.

This dream is six or seven years later than the early script that I wrote immediately after my bad night, and is one of the last things that got inserted into it. Does that make sense to you?

Freeman: It does. It's fascinating that in the course of writing the poem . . .

Peter: I'm changing.

Freeman: . . . you're changing, and then you're writing about it, and that's becoming part of the poem.

Peter: Right. Death is coming up closer, which is what we then get in the next section, where they reenact death in the *wajang koelit* and these trance plays.

Freeman: Right. Can you tell us a little bit about those rituals?

Peter: Well, there are two in section III.xii. The *wajang koelit* is a shadow play. I think a lot of people must have seen Indonesian puppets on sticks. They're two dimensional.

In the *wajang koelit*, the puppets act with a light behind them. There's a *dalang* or puppet master, the mastermind, makes these puppets act.

And people just see them as silhouettes, although they're quite brightly colored and so on.

The other ritual is these trance dances that are three dimensional and in the flesh. The actors become so involved in the play that they actually become entranced and have, as I say here, to be relieved of their krisses.

A kris is short, halfway between a dagger and a sword. It's kind of scary, because here are these people out of their skulls, moving quite violently with them. But it's said that if they're completely entranced, they don't get hurt. If they're not completely entranced, there's a risk that they will wound themselves.

The whole thing is fascinating. Anthropologists and psychologists have been interested, because it's a kind of collective frenzy which involves the audience as well as the actors. It's, in a way, really quite dangerous: we're reading here that some of the actors sometimes never completely recover.

You have to think of the country of Indonesia at the time when anthropologists, tourists, and cinematographers all come to record this. Before World War II Indonesia had a very long history, but not of victory. In the course of three centuries they had been completely conquered by the Dutch. It took a long time. Bali, which is one of the best places for *wajang koelit*, was only conquered in 1906, but it was conquered.

Bali to this day remains Hindu. The rest of the country, of course, is mostly Muslim. Java and Bali both have this memory of the great Hindu epic, the Mahabharata. It includes the Bhagavad Gita: very famous in the West, but only one part of that great epic. Ben Anderson also links the 1965 massacre to the Mahabharata, "the most loved part of Javanese mythology . . . which culminates in an orgy of bloodshed between close kinsmen."[51]

Arjuna, who is the central figure in the Gita, is an Indian hero. These are conquerors, but the Indonesians are not conquerors, so they mediate the story of the Barata Yudda[52] and these great Hindu conquerors, the Pendavas, the perfectly just, with people who represent themselves. And these people are clowns.

It's a way of adjusting to the presence of higher powers, human as well as divine. Then, their self-representation, in the form of Semar or the . . . who's the other? Toealen?

Freeman: Right.

Peter: They represent the less *macho* Indonesians in this play. By the way, when I say "Falstaffian" there, it's Clifford Geertz who made the comparison, that in "Henry V" you have—first of all—young Hal and then the old king. The energy is with the young Hal, but he's not the power. The king is the power.

Then, Falstaff becomes really the central figure, but he's a clown. All of this is recreated in Western drama by Shakespeare.

Freeman: Except Western civilization identifies with Hal.

Peter: Yes. Western civilization . . . and Hal, of course, becomes the king, so yes, Shakespeare in this play is focused on the exercise of power. Here, it's about manipulating those who exercise power, so that the clowns, by their comic deviousness, in a way get the upper hand over their bosses.

Freeman: Right. This is evocative of earlier in the poem, of how the victory of the Dutch was spun by the court poets.

Peter: Exactly. Right, yes. Exactly, exactly.

Freeman: It's the tactic, the necessary strategy of the oppressed.[53]

Peter: The first instance was for the sake of the court. This one is now for the sake of the people. But it's a very complex procedure, in which people are both being purged of their fear by acting it out, and also being given a sense that it's superior to be underneath, because you can make fun of these too serious characters, who are too obsessed with male power.

Freeman: Well, typically we've been ending these sessions with you rereading the very end of each session's text.

Peter: Right.

Freeman: It ends very powerfully with the great battle at a standoff, but I'm a little more interested in hearing the end of the previous section.

Peter: I was going to make the same suggestion. I also would like to explain that something happens here that happens two or three places in the poem. I think it happens at the very beginning. Yes. Usually, if it's italics, it's a citation and usually there's a little identification.

But at the very beginning, when I talked about the wind, "You, wind driven ghosts of snow," it's in italics but I don't have any citation, because that's a voice that comes up from inside me that I don't recognize as me.

That is what happens here at the end of this section. I am not rationally composing a poem here. I am writing down something that is coming to me from deep inside me, not from up here in the frontal lobes. From something that is not the rational part of my brain.

(In contrast the line "I see my father in the dying man," is what my father wrote about "his" father after "he" had died. I can use it perfectly to express what I think about my father, because each of us had this vision of a father that we respected but who was also a domestic tyrant.)

"It is all coming out," here continues the process initiated in I.iii, where I wrote,

> losing hold seems for one moment
>
> to be no threat
> but another beginning.

The process of recovering memory is becoming more and more overtly a process of expurgation, with a vision of health.

III.xiii–III.xv

Like giant doomed stars

> George is it possible
>
> I wonder speaking myself
> as a refugee third-
> generation Canadian poet
>
> that we are all victims
> of excessive inheritance

Freeman: We come out of the cosmic considerations of the last couple of sections about the struggle of good and evil, and of death, back into biography.

Peter: There is a segue because the two previous sections are about ancestries—my own personal ancestry and then the Javanese and Balinese seeing the shadow play about their mythical ancestors, the clowns.

Here, I'm quite obsessed with having met people with famous ancestors. I don't have to say too much about Jill who was a friend of my first wife in college. She was an Adams, and she wanted nothing to do with all that of Adams' heritage. It's an amazing heritage—John Adams, John Quincy Adams, Henry Adams.

Freeman: Oh, these are "those" Adamses.

Peter: These are those Adamses. Yes. Both Jill and George Homans are descended from them. I just looked up George Homans on Wikipedia. He is a great-great-grandson of John Quincy Adams and the great-great-great-grandson of John Adams. It was obviously quite a heavy load to carry there. Something is expected of you.

Jill just dropped out. She didn't want to be an Adams, and went off to the country. There's been a certain amount of forest-city and now female-male contrast in this poem: Jill went back into the country; George Homans became a professor at Harvard and President of the American Sociological Association, with very emphatic ideas about social behavior. And the good guys like himself are on top, according to his theory of social behavior.

Yes, it's those Adams. I'm trying to do something quite complicated in section III.xiii, because I'm contrasting the disempowered woman who drops out of society with the empowered male with status in that society. There I start quoting from Dante. It's not clear from these citations, but these two books mentioning Dante by Curtius and Auerbach are contrasting books that both discuss Beatrice and Virgil.

Dante talks a bit about style at the very beginning of the *Inferno*. Beatrice meets Virgil and they each compliment the other. Beatrice (like Curtius) compliments Virgil's *ornate* style, *parola ornata* (Inf. 2:67), a sort of cultivated lofty male style.

A little earlier, in a very famous passage, Virgil (like Auerbach) talks about Beatrice with her "sweet and plain style," her *dir suave e piana* (Inf. 2:56). And there's a contrast there between the male aristocratic element, and the female down-to-earth style—which is reflected of course with Jill being on the country and with George Homans being at Harvard.

You can contrast Curtius' emphasis on the importance of courtly pastoral poetry (a tradition which led to Marie Antoinette playing as a shepherdess at Versailles) with Auerbach's love of the forest romance Yvain which we talked about earlier.

I don't know if that comes across, but there's a kind of archetypal playing here of the two versions of power, bottom-up or top-down, Semar versus Arjuna, that are at work in society.[54]

[This contrast between male Virgilian reason and female Beatrician piety embodies, like my mother's argument with George Homans over the Vietnam war, the interaction of yang and yin which will become more and more overtly the underlying theme of the three long poems of *Seculum*.]

Freeman: These forest romances were commissioned by the wives of crusaders?

Peter: Yes, that's right. Marie de Champagne ran the court of Champagne because her husband wasn't there; he was off in the Holy Land. So you had a feminized culture: Chrétien de Troyes wrote his romances to please her, so they are the product of that feminine yin culture, with the male absent.

I wasn't present for this anecdote about George Homans; my mother told me about it. My mother helped me a great deal with this poem. She told me this really quite shocking tale where this professor behaved like a six-year-old, "We will win! We will win!"

He's loaded with the heavy, embarrassing weight of being an Adams. The need to dominate makes all these people go into a series of policies that are crazy, really.

I see something Oedipal happening in these two sections. At the beginning of the poem I think I was going insane and falling out of a sane society, but now I'm beginning to get strength. I am looking at these leading figures, Allen Dulles, Henry Cabot Lodge, George Homans, and seeing them as being more insane than I was and corrupted by the power I don't have.

Their problem is they have this power that they've inherited. I don't want to get too much into genealogy, but Henry Cabot Lodge has a huge load of genealogy too. His grandfather of the same name was the famous senator who was responsible for keeping America out of the League of Nations. There is a legacy with all of these people, and they're corrupted by it. I'm now beginning to see that I'm not uniquely crazy.

Particularly I was so disappointed with Henry Cabot Lodge, because the small subcommittee in the room was supposed to be reaching nuclear disarmament, and I came to believe that he was blustering and bluffing and delaying because he didn't want disarmament. There is something just sick about that.

Freeman: What exactly did he do?

Peter: In my episode here? Well, he was the ambassador of the United States to the UN. The French had a proposal. (As a second-level power, the French may have been more interested in disarmament, like the Canadians.) First of all, he mistranslated it. One of the things I did as a very junior diplomat was to correct his translation of French.

I don't remember the details, but what I do remember powerfully is the futility of this discussion. It was going nowhere. One reason it was going nowhere is that the Americans were in there to preserve their edge, their leadership in the arms race. And the Russians were doing something similar. Zorin was the Russian.

Then my mother made me rethink the section about George Homans. She reminded me how he was also very kind. When Maylie was pregnant with my son Mika and she had to be driven into hospital, George was the one who took it on himself to go down the lake, and get Frank from the camp and bring him back.

My mother is inserting all kinds of nuances. It's not just, in other words, a black-and-white portrait of an evil class. They're human beings, but suffering from, what do I say, "those unique degradations / which follow upon / any categorical assumption // of command."

Freeman: In itself a more nuanced expression of the common phrase that power corrupts.

Peter: "*All* power corrupts." Yes, right. Then I get into how power corrupted me as consul.

Freeman: Also typical of this poem, I think that there are no purely evil figures, and all of the evil you find in the world you also find reflected in yourself.

Peter: Right. Even my own role is not purely one of outsider. There was a time I briefly exercised a bit of power. It really was true that I began having sexual dreams about the young Polish women who would burst into tears when I turned down their visa applications.

These young women would tell me they wanted to visit the mining towns of Northern Ontario for a summer holiday. These towns were populated by large numbers of Polish-Canadian miners and there were very few women up there. The Canadian government insisted that these women visitors, if they were young and marriageable, should get an immigrant visa, because the chances (and perhaps the intentions) were they would meet someone there and get married.

I was not allowed to give an immigrant visa in Warsaw. They were hoping they'd come in, talk to me for half an hour and walk out with a nonimmigrant visa. I would have to tell them, "No, you have to apply to Ottawa for an immigrant visa, you have to get an X-ray, it'll take six months, it won't be this summer, with luck it will be next summer."

They would all weep, and some of them would get down on the floor and beg. They looked so beautiful. They had flowers in their hair; they were dressed in white folk costumes (*strój*); some of them would go down on the floor and throw their hands up on my desk. I started dreaming about this: the sexual advantages of power, the ability to make people weep.

I had no choice in what I did. I was under instructions.

In the end I did actually ask to be taken off the job, because I could feel it corrupting me. That may have been the moment when I finally decided not to continue in the Foreign Service.

Freeman: What was this bit about the new prime minister signing the NORAD agreement without realizing it?

Peter: That's a quite famous episode which I was an eyewitness to. I joined the Foreign Service in May of 1957 and nine days later—not because of me!—the Liberal government was voted out, after having been in power for thirty-two years.

We had a new government, a new prime minister who knew nothing about being prime minister, and a new cabinet. He appointed himself to be Secretary of State for External Affairs as well as Prime Minister, which meant he was the boss of the Foreign Service.

The Canadian equivalent of the Pentagon—the Canadian Joint Chiefs—had wanted for years to get a NORAD agreement where the defense of North America would be pooled with the Americans. It's in place now. There's one big center in Colorado and it commands all the posts in northern Canada.

It was going to happen. But the department I had just joined, External Affairs, had a lot of political concerns about preserving Canadian sovereignty, and we were still working on details of the agreement.

When the new prime minister came in, the head of Canadian defense just went to him and said, "The Liberals were about to sign this agreement but they didn't have time, and here it is; so you can sign it." He signed it. It should have gone first through External Affairs but it didn't, and we protested.

It was my little division, DL-1, Defense Liaison-1, that had the responsibility for this. When we protested the head of the army responded, "We went through External Affairs because the Prime Minister was the Secretary of State for External Affairs." But they completely cut out the Department.

It happened and it's since been written about. I wrote about it myself. This man George Ignatieff was an ambassador and wrote a memoir of his time, in which he described this episode.[55]

Freeman: Like Lodge's delaying act, this is an example of how the powers of the world . . . they're going to get what they want done.

Peter: Yes. They connive and they have all kinds of machinations. It's ugly, it really is. That's why I talk about "the curse of preeminence," "the hard edge nightmare // at the power center." I've obviously become quite alienated from all of this.

I had a lot of fun, I must confess, being a diplomat. I like drinking good wine and eating with interesting people in fine restaurants. But there was a kind of absurdity at the center of it. I don't think I emphasized enough in my prose that foreign affairs as presently conducted is kind of organized stupidity, organized silliness. Or organized craziness, and that the craziest are the ones who probably get to the top where they have the power to make us have wars and things like that. That's a very one-sided way of presenting the situation, but I think it's a side that isn't presented enough.

Freeman: I want to ask you about another figure you talk about, who, like you, proved himself unfit for that hard-edged nightmare.

Peter: Jake Beam, the U.S. Ambassador in Poland. He came from what we call the Main Line aristocracy of Philadelphia, very well educated, very charming man to meet. Earlier I had had to deal with a number of Americans in power, mostly at the UN, where they would come and twist my arms when I was in charge of the Third Committee.

They would say, "This is how we all have to vote." First, I'd say, "No, thank you;" and then in the end I did vote their way. I was very impressed that Jake Beam was an ambassador, but not like the kind of people I had been dealing with at the UN.

The American Embassy in Warsaw was full of excellent people. I have to say that of the four who became my best friends in the American Embassy, it was about five or six years later that I realized they were nearly all CIA.

They were CIA, all very intelligent, knew a great deal about poetry, spoke excellent Polish. I learned from them. And Jake Beam, it's not like he was marginal, he went on to be the American Ambassador to the Soviet Union.

But he wasn't one of these people at the very top. He wasn't going to be. He wasn't driven enough. He was too much of a human being. You could just tell he was not going to reach the very top.

Freeman: "The talent for power // being almost certainly / a disqualification."

Peter: I want to make a comment on that because at first I didn't see the logic of what follows.

> just as governments
>
> that limit themselves
> with domestic restraints
> Athens Rome England even Spain
>
> almost immediately
> in an unfilled world
> explode into empires
>
> like giant doomed stars

I was trying to say that the governments who don't try to dominate, but try to restrain their powers and get a constitution that limits them, become powerful by that act.

As we see in the case of Britain and we see in the case of America. In America originally, Washington was warning against entangling alliances with the rest of the world. America had no ambition to dominate. It just wanted to have restricted government at home.

By that degree of sense, to have restricted power and restrained power, it joined those other governments that, as I say, "exploded into empires."

Freeman: I love the end of the earlier section: the analogy of driving along a road and what that entails in terms of . . .

Peter: Trust.

Freeman: . . . of trust in other human beings, flawed human beings.

Peter: I just read a poem by Tranströmer where he makes almost the same point quite independently.

Freeman: Using the same example.

Peter: I say, "Mountain clear driving on the freeway." It was coming in from a suburb on Long Island back to Manhattan. It was so easy: we could park right under the UN building. We had lots of privileges as diplomats.

Having been at a dinner with diplomats from four countries, now I'm on the freeway with who knows what's on my left. We are all risking our lives by trusting each other. And in this case it works.

III.xvi–III.xvii

The cool hissing of the bullets

> In accordance with Plato
> he kept to his station
> as the best of us have done

Freeman: We're beginning to enter into an area of the poem that is going to require a lot of background—explanations of historical, political figures and so forth. Let's start with Raleigh. Is he someone that we ought to know?

Peter: Yes. We encountered him early on in the poem. Raleigh Parkin is the man who talked in II.iii about the FFV, the First Families of Virginia, in North Hatley. What's happening here at the end of part III is about a changed perspective on power.

Section III.xv is the first time that I describe exercising power. I'm a consul in Warsaw, and I'm making all these young women cry. I'm thinking about power from inside, and not liking it, and deciding not to continue as consul.

Here, in III.xvi, I realized for the first time that my relationship to power wasn't just being a spectator of the Americans, the powerful Americans in North Hatley, but also to somebody who was actually my father's closest friend, just as his family was closest to our family. This led to the staged "marriage" when at the age of seven I "married" Elizabeth; and Raleigh dressed up in a morning jacket and a top hat.

If you met him, Raleigh seemed very gentle and not a dominating type of person. However, he moved great amounts of money for his employers the Sun Life Insurance Company, who were headquartered in Montreal, but sold life insurance all over the world.

He handled the investments of earnings in the countries where the premiums were paid, in order, as I say, to avoid creating balance of payments problems for the country. He was in his own way a small part of a huge system that was reinforcing and expanding corporate capitalism throughout the world. Just as I, in my small way in III.xv, was laying down the Canadian law in Warsaw.

Freeman: He was not in a position to be as affected by the probable results of his decisions, though, as you were.

Peter: Yes, that's true. He doesn't see. He just moves things on paper. I was quite surprised that he knew this man, Curtis Calder, whom I had already written about. There was a company called American and Foreign Power, and they owned power companies all over the world. Including in Cuba, where they were close to Batista and did a lot to fund the initial attempts to overthrow Castro, even before the CIA got involved.

They were also in Shanghai. They were global, just like Sun Life was global, and Sun Life investments handled by Raleigh were global.

The whole point of it is that Raleigh didn't really think about what it meant, in say Cuba, for these premiums to be helping American and Foreign Power to become even more powerful in Havana, in the rest of Cuba, than it had been already. That's the reason that I wrote this.

Freeman: He was just solving an accounting problem.

Peter: Yes, a book-balancing problem. In a way, I put it in here because it helps to redefine things. I grew up knowing Raleigh, but I never saw him as part of the global economic system. Later, after I'd done my research, I decided to go and talk to him. It turned out that he knew, at a very high level, some of the people I'd been writing about, who were mostly Americans.

It wasn't just a case of America doing something. Canada was complicit in what they did as well. The whole of part III is learning, as I said at the very beginning of part III, to see myself as part of the problem, not just witnessing it from outside.

Freeman: Can you provide a little bit more information about some of these other situations you write about here, such as Meyer Lansky's race track?

Peter: In Havana, the mob was well-placed and served as sort of enforcers to protect the interests of American corporations. They were well-located in the social system. For example, the National City Bank of New York owned the race track in Havana; and they leased it to Meyer Lansky.

This is very parallel to the situation that I'm talking about in the next passage, about Du Yuesheng's Green Gang, which was a gang in Shanghai that ran the dope trade. The people who originally made a deal with them were the French Banque de l'Indochine, the Bank of Indochina. It was very big in Shanghai as well as in Indochina.

When there are communists abroad, the reaction of foreign corporations is to make an alliance with some right-wing power, some local mafia. There was a famous massacre in 1927 that André Malraux wrote a novel about, *Man's*

Fate, La Condition humaine, which describes how the Green Gang and Chiang Kai-shek killed the communists in Shanghai.

This is what really catapulted Chiang Kai-shek into leadership in China, his successful alliance with the Green Gang. Not just to defeat the communists but to massacre them, which of course is very relevant to the massacre of the communists in Indonesia.

The massacre is described in the novel as being Chinese. But you had manipulators in Shanghai in the form of the American corporations and the Bank of Indochina. They all had their own deals with Du Yuesheng. There wasn't a massacre of the same proportions in Havana, but there is a similarity to the relationship that the American corporations in Havana had to Meyer Lansky, and to all of the mob figures who owned the casinos in Havana.

Freeman: Raleigh himself said that he was not aware of any of this.

Peter: Right. He had no idea.

Freeman: How did he feel when you told him about these things?

Peter: I wish I could say with authority. I had a more vivid memory of our talk when I wrote this, because I had the talk while I was editing *Coming to Jakarta*. I don't remember it very clearly now, but certainly he was not the kind of person who would accept massacres as being all in a day's work.

It wasn't in his little compartmentalized area of work. That's why I give the analogy of the Aswan engineers, not thinking about snails.

Egypt built this huge Aswan Dam on the Nile in order to provide a cheap source of power for the whole country. Also to control the flooding, which was until then an annual event.

Freeman: Just solving an engineering problem.

Peter: Right, but there were biological consequences, because the reservoir became an ideal water habitat for snails. Not only the Aswan area but the whole of Egypt became infested with snails. That makes me sound like I'm a complete conservative maybe who doesn't want any change. No, I do want change. But change of any category—it doesn't matter whether it's communist or capitalist—if it's not done ecologically with full considerations for the consequences, it can be harmful.

Freeman: You refer to the General Motors plant in South Africa. What were the political implications of that decision?

Peter: I have to speak for what I was thinking back then in the 1980s when I wrote this. I think it was the consolidation of corporate power in South Africa. South Africa was originally a rather agricultural country, farmers.

I remember Raleigh stressing to me that General Motors hadn't wanted to build the plant. It took not just Sun Life but other people to persuade General Motors that it was in their interest. Otherwise the Krugerrand would have been a weak currency because so much of it would have been going out of South Africa to Sun Life headquarters in Montreal and elsewhere.

In this way, they were reinvested in South Africa. And it looks as if that makes South Africa stronger, but it has a consequence of developing more and more of a corporate overclass above the original inhabitants. I think that's what I had in mind.

"In accordance with Plato / he kept to his station." He did his job. Plato praises that. The problem is if we all just do our jobs [or svadharma—cf. V.iii] then in the end forces are created which can result in massacres.

Freeman: From this section, which gives us a little glimpse at the casualness of the planners, the inadvertent way that these decisions are made, we go on to the next section. Even though it's separated by centuries, we get a glimpse on the ground at some of the consequences of these kinds of decisions.

Peter: Right. This is the way in which the Netherlands finally conquered Bali in 1906. This was in the lifetime of my father, for example. This whole episode is called a *puputan*, a mass suicide in the face of humiliation. It's interesting that Balinese has a word for mass ritual suicide—*puputan*. We don't know of very many, but there were actually two in the twentieth century within two years of each other. This was the first one, the big one.

Survivors talked about it later to a painter called Covarrubias, who lived on the island. We have a lot of very vivid description, perhaps not totally accurate, but certainly almost firsthand.

Freeman: Actually, before we go on, I want to clarify something. This is the historical situation referred to earlier in the poem. Is that correct? This is the situation that the court poets . . .

Peter: No.

Freeman: Is this not the court poets' situation?

Peter: The court poets in III.i were talking long ago about the very beginning of the Dutch occupation of Java, and we're given their mythical account. Here is a very factual account of the very last stage of the Dutch occupation, three centuries later, in Bali.

The first one was in the seventeenth century. This is 1906, which of course may sound very remote to younger people; but I was born in 1929. It was almost in my lifetime. The notion was "You don't have the power to defeat these people, so you just die in an appropriately formal way." They came out with armed with krisses and spears, not to attack the great Dutch but to kill themselves.

The objective account of *puputan* in Wikipedia says that the Dutch were watching and they just saw everyone start to kill themselves in front of them. Somebody fired a shot by accident and then things became more complicated.

It was a ritual suicide, very like Jonestown, and this tells us many things. It tells us that violence in the third world—perhaps particularly in this very controlled Balinese culture—that violence is not only an acceptable part of it, but at times what is expected. Mass deaths.

Freeman: It reminded me of the scene from the shadow play (III.xii), where the clown says, "Friend, I will kill myself."

Peter: Yes.

Freeman: It also suggests to me a people, a culture that has been psychically destroyed, that they have just been crushed.

Peter: I roughly agree. I'd say the whole of Third World history after the renaissance was about local cultures that had governed themselves adequately, even admirably, and then could not cope with the forces of Western Europe.

The big difference was that Western Europe had guns, cannons. They had specialized in modern weaponry, and there was no answer for that. You get something like this scene, where they stabbed themselves with their daggers because there is nothing they could do about the machine guns of the Dutch.

[The Balinese *puputan* of 1906 serves as a small and almost artistic tableau, epitomizing the confrontation of larger global and local forces in the last half century, that will be discussed next in part IV.]

IV.i

Beyond the mists

    Mégève   coming down
        beside a rainbow
        into a shower

    glissade 1000 meters
        on wet grass
        laughter at falling safe

    Think   married a Venezuelan
        and lives near Lausanne

Freeman: Today we are covering just a single section, because . . .

Peter: It's unlike any other. [laughs]

Freeman: It's unlike any other. It's the hardest section of the book for me.

Peter: Many people would say it's not poetry. But that's what some said about parts of Williams's *Paterson* and Ezra Pound's *Cantos*; and those poems have endured.

Freeman: There's something poetic going on here, with the framing device around the political content, which is one of the aspects of the section that has always confused me. Can you explain what the scenes are at the beginning and the end?

Peter: About Mégève. The first time I went to Europe as a nineteen-year-old, I was one of fifty Canadians who attended a student conference in Germany, together with fifty European students, and above all, most importantly, fifty non-Nazi Germans, carefully selected. It took place in a German (formerly Danish) castle, Schloss Plön, in the summer of 1948. That was the first summer that nonmilitary people outside the establishment could go into occupied Germany.

The conference was being paid for by NFCUS [cf. discussion of II.xiv] and the International Student Service (ISS). During it I hitchhiked and took trains without paying anything,[56] from Schleswig-Holstein right down through Germany to another ISS meeting in Mégève, which is in France looking over to Mont Blanc in Switzerland. This is a quite expensive resort, way beyond what I was used to. That's why I would say "uncomfortable luxury:" I was not used to it at all.

We had this meeting and other students were there, some of whom went on to be big in the World Assembly of Youth, which was something being sponsored by the CIA (as maybe the ISS was). Anyway, it was a glimpse I had at this sort of global network or roof that also involves the Bilderberg meetings—a network I have described in prose as part of what I call the supranational deep state.[57] It's far too simple to just say it's CIA-sponsored. The CIA is just part of it.

What becomes the big link, first of all to the massacre in Indonesia, and then later to Jack Ruby, is this web of Lockheed payoffs. The CIA would pick the people that they wanted money to go to, in a country that was buying Lockheed aircraft. All over the world, civil fleets were buying Lockheed aircraft.

Lockheed had a very intimate connection to the CIA because it made the U-2s for the CIA, so that there were CIA people in Lockheed and Lockheed people in the CIA. Lockheed sales created a huge global slush fund used to corrupt politicians everywhere.

Freeman: Before we go further, that initial stanza, "Coming down beside a rainbow into a shower," what specifically is that a memory of?

Peter: I was nineteen and I met an eighteen-year-old American girl there, and we climbed a small mountain together. As for this *glissade*: We literally came down maybe half a mile on our fannies on very steep grass. It was a bit dangerous because it was high speed and it was hard to stop. There were rocks every now and then, but we managed it. We laughed at the end of it when we were safe. She later "married a Venezuelan / and lives near Lausanne."

Freeman: So when you say, "Think," you're talking to yourself?

Peter: About her.

Freeman: You're searching your memory.

Peter: And at the very end, when I say, "Do you remember?," I'm saying that mostly to myself.

Freeman: I see.

Peter: "Yes // just for an instant," this glimpse of Mont Blanc. I don't know what it stands for, but a glimpse of something beyond what I had been talking about in the section. But also the glimpse of the mountain, the geographic roof of Europe, may have been linked in my mind with that conference, the roof of sandbox international student life.

Then I come in right after that woman and say, "tell me now you // with homes in the mountains / who are at hand / and know all things // where we hear only rumor."

That's a passage from Book II of the *Iliad* that introduces an extraordinary catalogue of ships. Four hundred lines describe, in all, 1,100 ships. The names of the captains of the ships are mentioned. So, I say here, "Tell me now . . . of the captains." I'm talking about the captains of industry and finance who meet at Bilderberg meetings organized by Prince Bernhard, a key figure in the network of Lockheed payments. They too are a kind of army that is controlling the world, all the way from Italy to Indonesia to Japan.

Freeman: You talk about the connection of this Lockheed network to the story of Jakarta, Indonesia.

Peter: Yes, and this is very important, one of the most important discoveries from my research for the poem. The CIA's position has been, "Well, of course we were happy that the army overthrew Sukarno, but we had nothing to do with it." But it's quite clear to me that Americans, collectively, did have something to do with it.

Four months before the coup, which Americans are supposed to not have known about then, the funds coming from Lockheed, controlled by the CIA, stopped going to someone who supported Sukarno, and started going instead to this General Alamsjah. Alamsjah was a supporter and ally of Suharto, the general who after the coup replaced Sukarno as the head of Indonesia for the next thirty years.

This is a poem about a massacre of perhaps a million people. And now we're talking about how that was paid for in part by an earlier shift of Lockheed money to the people who were about to take over the government and take it away from Sukarno. So that's one link to Jakarta.

Freeman: Up until now, we've heard about the training of military officers, we've heard about the encouragement, the general encouragement. Now we have a money connection.

Peter: To the actual event, yes.

Freeman: I'm curious about Prince Bernhard.

Peter: He was a son-in-law of the Queen of the Netherlands and an aristocrat himself, but he used his status and the aristocracy to gain political leverage. He was the right man to head the Bilderberg meetings and help set up this payments network, because he knew all kinds of people in different countries, who could then pass the money on to other people like the Italian premier.

Freeman: I was also interested in this Baron Edmond de Rothschild.

Peter: He was a friend of Tibor Rosenbaum of the International Credit Bank, which became notorious because of its connections to the Israeli Mossad, to Meyer Lansky of the American mob, and then to Robert Vesco.

Vesco was a millionaire with great political influence. A member of Nixon's White House staff, Richard Allen, used to fly around with Vesco in his private plane, going down to Costa Rica and places.

Vesco was involved in a major Wall Street stock scandal. But Vesco owned so much stock that if he was brought down as a criminal and all his stock had had to be sold, it would have taken the bottom out of the New York stock market.

Freeman: He was too big to fail.

Peter: He was an individual much too big to fail, yes.

You have to get the picture here. Prince Bernhard is at home in the overworld. One of the people that Prince Bernhard knew, or was introduced to by Baron Edmond de Rothschild, Tibor Rosenbaum, he is more underworld than overworld.

The Baron, Edmond de Rothschild, unlike most of the Rothschilds, got involved with casinos and all kinds of slightly off-color things. He was a man with connections to people like Tibor Rosenbaum, who was mainly an Israeli intelligence figure. But definitely, his bank linked with a bank controlled by Meyer Lansky.

All of this started to come out in America. That's why the baron, to protect himself, exposed what he knew about the ICB. But he had been working with the ICB closely before, probably for Mossad.

Freeman: There's powerful poetry in this section, because the density and impenetrability of the references kind of mirrors this world you're trying to . . .

Peter: Right, just like the catalogue of ships in the *Iliad*, which is of enormous interest to philologists. First of all, it's an example of very ancient poetry. This kind of catalogue of names is a particular style or kind of poetry. The oldest poem that we have in Anglo-Saxon, "Widsith," is very similar. It's just a list of rulers and their armies—dozens of them, no longer very memorable themselves. But you're looking into a distant other world.

I had that feeling when I read the Senate Hearing into the Lockheed scandals. All these names like Antelope Cobbler, and so on, had me looking into another world. Then we come to the world of the Bobby Baker payoffs.

We're doing this interview in 2012 and a volume of the Caro biography of Lyndon Johnson has just come out. It describes in great detail how the Bobby Baker scandals were just getting to be investigated by the Senate, but then Kennedy was killed and the Senate hearings stopped. Baker was also in a book by Ed Reid and Ovid Demaris that I quote from here, *The Green Felt Jungle*.

As I recall, that book was being serialized in *The New York Times* in the week that Kennedy was assassinated, and was beginning to expose all these links from the underworld through Ed Levinson to Bobby Baker to Lyndon

Johnson. Many historians believe that if those hearings had continued, Lyndon Johnson would have been taken off the ticket in 1964 and would not have become the President.

But of course, in that same week, Kennedy was killed. Two days later, Lee Harvey Oswald was killed by Jack Ruby who, in a funny way, connects through Lewis McWillie to Ed Levinson, too. It's one great cobweb covering the world.

> My book would have asked
>   as the Warren Commission staff
>   working for Allen Dulles
>
> was unable to
>   why Levinson's pit-boss
>   McWillie *gambler and murderer*
>
> from the old Binion gang
>   in Dallas and Fort Worth
>   who *had a fix with Mr. Big*
>
> *I don't think we'd better*
>   *go into that phase of it*[58]
>   twice brought to Havana
>
> *most likely as a courier*
>   his close friend
>   Jack Ruby

Freeman: . . . which connects back to another part of this poem, because this is the book that we discussed at the beginning of part II, that you had suppressed by the publisher.

Peter: Right.

Freeman: That was one of the triggers that set you off on . . .

Peter: Psychologically, it set me up. But I don't think I realized it fully until I wrote this section. Even Simon and Schuster. . . . I don't want to go into the details, but everything connects to everything else. I wrote a book about the Kennedy's assassination, which was accepted. It was announced; and literally there was a photograph of it in the Spring 1980 Pocket Books catalogue.

It was to be a first print run of 250,000, which would have been far more than any other book of mine ever. But it was not to be. Instead there were lawyers' meetings that went on and on for days. They kept assuring me, "Oh yes, it's coming out. It's coming out." It didn't come out.

Freeman: Why do you say it's a "dumb subject?"

Peter: I think it is "dumb" on two levels. First of all, it is a topic one is not permitted to treat seriously in the mainstream media. My book's suppression is only one example of this silence or dumbness. Later in the poem [IV.xiv] I recall how, at the very beginning of a discussion of possibly writing about the assassination with Gore Vidal for *The New York Review of Books*, my phone connection was promptly disabled; and the opportunity vanished.

So it's a "dumb subject" in another sense as well: You have to be a bit of an idiot to keep writing about a topic on which you are never going to be able to reach the general public, never going to be listened to.

Freeman: It's a hopeless situation to try. . . .

Peter: I am trying to expose all this. My prose hasn't been able to do anything. So, it was a "dumb subject" to write about. I may say that when I wrote this poem there were no American books about America's role in the massacre. None, except mine. I say a "book," because I wrote a manuscript book in 1982 (based on my research for the poem) that Noam Chomsky read and quoted from. That's another book that wasn't published.

Now at last a lot is getting published, and even a bit about how American bureaucrats picked some of the names to be assassinated.[59] That's the fallback story now, that after the "coup" U.S. Embassy personnel picked some of the leaders to be killed. But the true story is much bigger than that. It still hasn't been published in America, even though now it's a half century later.[60]

"Freeing me to write this poem."

[Since this interview, and by coincidence on the very day I first edited these remarks for this book, I learned by accident that in 2013 the *Jakarta Post* (an English-language daily) reported briefly on my version of what happened.

> Others, such as Peter Dale Scott, a former Canadian diplomat and a professor at the University of California, claim that a dalang (or puppet master)—maybe the CIA, maybe Soeharto—was manipulating the events that led to ... the bloodletting to come.[61]

This may be the first serious journalistic reference to my hypothesis anywhere—the more remarkable because Indonesia's president in 2013 was still a general.

In short the 1963 Kennedy assassination is just like the 1965 massacre in Indonesia: a forbidden topic as far as the big media is concerned. And it is also a related topic, as the elaborate fabric of connections in this section tries to show.

I suspect that the sense of hopelessness that briefly overwhelmed me in Watertown was inspired not just by the impossibility of discussing the Indonesian coup of 1965, but at least as much by the impossibility of discussing what some have called the American coup of 1963. The one may have in fact served in my mind, while I was writing the poem, as a screen for the other.

And what dispirited me so much about the suppression of my book was far more than the loss of a personal audience. I had written the book in the hope that the optimism of the 1960s, set back by the JFK assassination, the Vietnam War, and the election of Nixon, might still be revived by the incipient Congressional investigation of the JFK assassination. (I had worked hard in the 1970s with a group of much younger people, the Assassination Information Bureau or AIB, to make Congress to do this.) And so killing the book, reinforced by the election of Reagan, seemed to me like also killing this last residual hope.

And here in this section I have the solace of being able to suggest freely that behind the tragedies of Dallas and Jakarta there is this vast network of relationships between oil, drugs, the CIA, and the mafia—what I have called elsewhere the deep state. So maybe not as dumb a subject as I then thought—if pulling together the elements of this network, without precisely defining their function, helped me develop my ideas of deep politics and the deep state.]

IV.ii–IV.iii

The music changing

> There must be two of me
>   I remember the surge
>   of almost too vivid pleasure
>
> when the sheriffs lined up
>   their faces and numbers masked
>   the streetlights' reflections
>
> caught in the burnish
>   of their identical helmets
>   and we found we could hold our terrain

Freeman: This week we find ourselves in the 1960s.

Peter: We've obviously reached the Vietnam War, yes.

Freeman: There's a structure to this section, IV.ii, that leads up to "the music changing." I want to ask you if you could describe the nature of the change that you're writing about here. What was this shift? What was its significance?

Peter: That's a very personal line, because at the beginning I'm coming home from the San Francisco Opera (when I was the Peter Scott who entered the 1960s) and at the end (and the end of the 1960s) I'm going to all these rock concerts.

We had very good live rock music, of course, in those days. We had the Jefferson Airplane, the Grateful Dead, Janis Joplin, and so many bands. But what helped shift me from establishment opera to counterculture rock was this first public engagement with the Vietnam War I talk about. It was a very academic thing that I did at first, not an in-the-streets protest at all.

The New York Times, on July 22, 1965, had published an accurate report that the North Vietnamese precondition for negotiations with America (as part of its April 1965 "Four Points") was "United States *agreement in principle* on a withdrawal of forces from Vietnam, and not an actual withdrawal, as a precondition for negotiations." But on November 24, 1965, the *Times* now claimed, as it did regularly after that, that the "Four Points" program of North Vietnam "insisted that the Americans *must pull out before* a peace conference could be considered." A demand for prior withdrawal, as opposed to an agreement to withdraw, would of course have made negotiations impossible.[62]

But the second *New York Times* story, unlike the first, was not true. I knew it was false, because our library, a good library, was getting documentation directly from Hanoi, North Vietnam. So I could read in an official North Vietnamese publication that their position was that the United States had to accept (as it never had before) the Geneva Accords of 1954, calling for withdrawal of foreign troops; and "if this basis is recognized . . . it will be possible to consider the reconvening of an international conference."[63] And here was *The New York Times* lying about their position.[64] That was a big moment in my political education. It shook my entire belief system to realize that a leading newspaper would publish a falsehood, in order to reinforce an American determination to fight in Vietnam. It shook me again to learn that a letter pointing out the truth would be unacceptable.

For my letter to *The New York Times* pointing out their error was of course not published. But the letter expanded and became an essay; and in the end three of us (Franz Schurmann, myself, and Reginald Zelnik) developed it into a book, *The Politics of Escalation in Vietnam* (Boston: Beacon Press, 1967). At first this was released as a "Citizens' White Paper," and delivered to members of Congress as well as the President. The next year it became, I believe, the first anti-Vietnam War book to be published. In paperback it sold for 60 cents and SDS (Students for a Democratic Society) used it as an organizational tool, selling (I was told) 60,000 copies.

This was probably a bigger sales result, for this tiny little book I've forgotten about, than anything I've ever published since. That book was cautious, written in a style that hoped to persuade Congress. But my search for truth, and the realization that the U.S. power structure did not want the truth, contributed to my sliding into the counterculture.

Freeman: I didn't know about the existence of this book. I saw the end of this first page of this section here ("that letter never published") as an account of the effort failing, the effort coming to nothing.

Peter: It was never published in *The New York Times*, but its argument was published in this book.

Freeman: It did lead to something good.

Peter: Maybe, [laughs] in a small way, it contributed to the anti-war movement. Yes.[65]

Freeman: Within this shift, in this section, to the experience of the counterculture . . .

Peter: My camera eye as writer is now out in the streets seeing the first tear gas. That was quite a moment, you know. Almost none of us knew anything about tear gas, except that it existed and it was being used a lot in the South. There, suddenly, it was in Berkeley being used on us.

All these things happening at once, like The Beatles. "The Yellow Submarine" became a kind of metaphor. It was a Beatles' song and students sang it as a metaphor for the counterculture: that we were living in a yellow submarine.[66]

I never dropped acid myself, but I do describe my first marijuana experience. I still remember it very vividly, feeling "the difference // between the salt and the pepper / I felt being shaken / on my bare left arm." Only a little later on did it occur to me that there must be something slightly altered in my consciousness, to be aware of that.

The Human Be-In was in 1967. Timothy Leary, Allen Ginsberg, and thousands of people were there.

> Owsley by parachute
> at the Human Be-in
> Mika on Carole's shoulders
>
> on mine so they could see
> *the Brave New World*
> *worms in the rose*

That was, I guess, the beginning really of the Summer of Love. "*Worms in the rose.*"

Freeman: What is that? What was that from?

Peter: A comment about the 1967 "Human Be-in" by Michael McClure.[67] It's taken from a book by a friend, Martin Lee, called *Acid Dreams*. That was McClure's way of epitomizing the fact that, despite it all sounding so lovely, but there were things wrong about the Human Be-in, and even more about the following Summer of Love. In fact, I don't know where to begin with the things that were wrong. But one of them was that the U.S. government was apparently again testing drugs on unwitting people, like this STP from "Dow Chemical / and the Edgewood Arsenal."[68]

There were deep forces at work underneath the Summer of Love. Everyone was trying to be so naive and countercultural. But, in fact, the deep state had its claws into that process.

[In saying this I was thinking of Martin's words.

> According to a former CIA contract employee, Agency personnel helped underground chemists set up underground LSD laboratories in the Bay Area during the Summer of Love to 'monitor' events in the ghetto. But why . . . ? A CIA agent who claims to have infiltrated the covert LSD network provided a clue when he referred to Haight-Ashbury as a 'human guinea-pig farm.'[69]

My actual words to Freeman in 2012 were, "the dominant culture had its claws into that process," but in saying this I underestimated the deep divisions in high culture. The Summer of Love was conceived by conceptual artist Michael Bowen, the event's main organizer, and his mentor John Starr Cooke.[70] Both men were psychedelic occultists and Bowen at the time participated in the LSD experiments conducted by Timothy Leary at the New York mansion Millbrook, bought for Leary by William Mellon Hitchcock and his sister Peggy.[71] From one point of view, the aim at the Be-in was to create a mass psychedelic movement to alter American consciousness, in part through psychedelic drugs. (And in Bowen's opinion the event succeeded.)[72] From another, it was an old technique for promoting sales of illicit LSD, which at the Be-in "flowed like lemonade."[73]

I knew from *Acid Dreams* that Cooke (an heir to Castle & Cooke, one of the Big Five companies in Hawaii) was the brother-in-law of Roger Kent, prominent in the California Democratic Party, and Sherman Cooke, head of the CIA Board of Estimates.[74] Owsley Stanley, grandson of a U.S. senator, was responsible for the massive free distribution of LSD at the Be-in. (Stanley may have been involved in the distribution of STP as well. He made trial batches of STP but soon ceased producing it.)

I suspected (as have others) that the event was intended to expand the market for LSD, and that the CIA, as Lee charged, wished to study the consequences. I now suspect Stanley's motives were more ideological than financial. And whatever the position of the CIA, it is clear that the dominant culture as a whole was at first ambivalent and soon alarmed by the spread of LSD. Later in 1967, both Leary and Owsley were arrested.[75] In 1971 Cooke broke with Leary, while Peggy Hitchcock's husband at the time, Walter Bowart, later wrote a book, *Operation Mind Control*, attacking the CIA for its MK / ULTRA experiments.]

Freeman: That's definitely the feeling that I get from this section, particularly the way it ends, this sort of divorce between the cultural changes and the political machinations that are going on. Underneath, there's a kind of a separation. They ended up not having an effect. They sort of washed themselves clean of the political turmoil.

Peter: What I get out of seeing this is my concern that, on the one hand, I couldn't trust the system anymore. The system was lying to us. It was using lies to maintain a war that was totally wrong from the beginning. Of that I was sure from my very limited exposure to it when I was a diplomat.

But, on the other hand, I couldn't put my trust in the counterculture that was arising either. Although I was quite attracted by the prospects of freedom that opened up at the Human Be-in, I could also see that there were "worms in the rose."

I was much more distressed by "men with their Sunday morning / rifle range target practice." There was a friend of mine who had decided that the revolution was coming, and he should get ready for it. So he would go practice at a rifle range.

He said to me, "On my left-hand side, I had the Black Panthers; and on my right-hand side, I had the Ku Klux Klan. We were all getting ready for the day when we would shoot each other."

Well, I'm a Canadian. I'm not a fan of the NRA or the Second Amendment. I was getting a little lost between these emerging competing worlds, with which I could not identify.

Freeman: In a way, it's another form of detachment from the real issues of the day to decide that the only solution is violent overthrow.

Peter: Right. At the same time, also in this section, I think there is a bit of fascination with what's happening. Particularly, I met Ed Sanders at that time, and he did lead this band, The Fugs, that made music.

It's in Mailer's book, *The Armies of the Night*. Ed Sanders was up there with the Fugs on a flatbed truck, trying to exorcise the Pentagon—"Out, demons, out!"—and the crowd was all shouting it. Mailer's comment was that everybody was so caught up in this moment, there was no respect whatsoever "for the unassailable logic / of the next step."[76] I think that catches the mood quite accurately. People weren't thinking ahead. They were just caught up on the need to attack and challenge what was happening.

Peggy Hitchcock—I can't help but mention that she was a Mellon heiress. She was born into one of the richest families in America, but she became part of the LSD counterculture. She knew Timothy Leary and all these people. "Two hundred pounds of daisies . . . to skybomb the Pentagon." It was kind of exciting to be living among all of these exotic and somewhat extreme actions.

Freeman: Well, let me move on to another incident from that time, to an even greater level of engagement on your part.

Peter: Well, yes and no, both. I'm describing myself at the beginning, "There must be two of me" because at times I could feel all these surges of protest in myself.

"I myself wanted to reach / for a machine gun." That's not my normal self, that's something coming out of my interior that I don't know very well [cf. III.ii]. When push came to shove what's really being described here is an event in the story of People's Park which was in the spring of 1969. I guess I need to explain it to today's audiences.

The university had condemned a block where they wanted to build a housing structure. They tore down all the houses and then months went by, nothing happened to the area. Some organizers, a man called Mike Delacour in particular, decided that they would challenge the authority of the University, and build a park for the people in this wasteland which was being used to park cars and nothing else.

And Denise Levertov and a lot of people—there have been novels written about this, like *Changing Places* by David Lodge—all kinds of people, from faculty to small children, all converged on this block and started planting flowers, digging up the soil, irrigating it, putting in pathways.

It was of course a direct challenge to the university's ownership of the land. You can imagine the pressure on the university from Governor Reagan and the Regents of the university. All these people said, "Do something! Do something!"

Eventually, the university put up a fence around the lot and rooted up everything that had been planted. Then there was a huge rally on the campus and the student president at that time, Daniel Siegel, said to the crowd: "There are four things we can do. One is, tear down the fence." He never got to the second option because everybody drowned him out with applause.

About a thousand people went straight down to the People's Park, which was four blocks away; and the Alameda County Sheriffs were waiting. They were authorized to use birdshot in their shotguns but some of them put buckshot in, which was lethal. [Much later I read that they only used buckshot after they had used up all their birdshot.][77]

This was a kind of civil war inside the United States. James Rector was just sitting on the top of a building watching what was happening. He was killed and someone sitting beside him, also not doing anything, was blinded for life. At the time, there were rumors that other people had been killed that we weren't ever told about.

Anyway, again, it took things a step toward, shall we say, Kent State one year later, when four students were killed by the National Guard in Ohio.

Freeman: Were you literally watching from Wheeler Hall when James Rector got killed?

Peter: Well, I didn't see James Rector. I saw the crowd going out of the campus down toward the park. And then the white tear gas in the sky.... This was my opting out. I didn't want to go there with them.

I went up to that window alone. But I had met this man before through my teaching assistant. It's not that we were close or anything. He joined me there because he was so worried about his girlfriend Karen. It was an odd way to meet a mafia person.

Freeman: He's a mafia contractor who handled "the waterfront corruption." What exactly does that mean?

Peter: First of all, when I say he was mafia, he was not a gangster in the streets. Whether he was "made" or not I don't know. He had an Italian name.

He handled investments for the mafia. That put him very much in touch with businessmen. If you invest a lot of money, you become in a sense part of our capitalist society.

As he explained his job to me or explained it to Karen (I'm not sure which), "We invest in shopping malls and things like that. We do it with other investors—including the University of California."

He knew establishment figures. And the U.S. government had a terrible problem at the docks in Saigon, because a high percentage of the ammunition and arms and equipment that was being offloaded for the U.S. Army there went directly to the Viet Cong, who had bribed people on the waterfront. Apparently, John was hired by the U.S. government because of his mafia experience: he didn't know a word of Vietnamese but he knew quite a lot about dockyard corruption. He told Karen he was sent there by the USG to deal with it.

Freeman: This is another case, just to link this to our discussions about deep politics, of tapping the expertise of these criminal elements because they have experience with these illegal activities you want to engage in.

Peter: The textbooks like to teach you that there's society and then there's these criminal elements outside of society.

My view of America—no, of many societies—is that the underworld is an integral part of the dominant society, and survives and is tolerated because it serves various functions. This would be one rather exotic example of serving a function. A more usual function was to supply violent force to individuals and corporations like Henry Ford, who were fighting labor organizers.

Another usual function was to be a kind of police among criminals. Chicago once had many, many gangs and they all shot at each other and many other people got shot by accident. Once you got yourself into organized crime there was a central direction to criminality. Marginal criminals got arrested and put in jail and the top criminals became FBI informants. And a kind of peace was established in the streets of Chicago.

Freeman: As is your wont, you've humanized the mafia contractor.

Peter: Well, he was very human! [laughs]

Freeman: Yes.

Peter: Shall we say, I share with the reader the human features of him that were visible to me. His concern about Karen ("those distraught mafia knuckles") really was, as I write, the strongest memory I retain from that "supposedly historic day."

IV.iv–IV.v

Those baffled eyes

> I looked in his face
>
> forgetting all the others
> as if to say *Krech*
> *what does one do now*

Freeman: Today, we see two snapshots of former roles of yours, one as a Canadian diplomat, and one as a UC Berkeley professor.

Peter: And activist.

Freeman: And activist.

Peter: Right, for first time. Because in the section before these two, there was a protest, but I was just one of the people milling around.

Here, well. . . . Let's deal first with when I was a very junior diplomat at the UN. It was my job to write up the accounts of the speeches made in the UN Assembly. And I still share my later opinion that not one word of it "was worth being recorded."

The technology was quite amazing, because under instructions I would prepare these very long cables, and they'd be automatically put into code, and then transmitted to all these capitals.

So I felt very important at the time, but in retrospect I don't see what I did as being the slightest bit important.

Freeman: I love the quoted phrase, "*our NATO allies.*" I mean, three simple words that convey your innocence and naiveté at the time.

Peter: And the way we were all treating ourselves as important.

Freeman: Right.

Peter: Literally, I would put "TOP SECRET" on these cables. Most of the content was going to be the next day in *The New York Times*; but it was understood inside the Foreign Service that if you wanted to be read, the cable had to be at least "SECRET" or "TOP SECRET." Because if it was just "CONFIDENTIAL," nobody would be interested in it.

And then these odd words, "COMMIES" "KORCOMS" (for Korean Communists") "CHICOMS" (for Chinese Communists"). The Canadians never wrote that way, but the Americans did. I realized later, not at the time, that this was a way of dehumanizing the enemy. So that you could treat them as if they were not to be afforded the kind of rights and privileges that you would give to ordinary humans.

Freeman: The thing that fascinates me is that not only was it a way to dehumanize the enemy, but as you write here, it was apparently a way to make yourself part of the team, to follow the crowd.

Peter: Exactly, yes. You're in the club if you talk this way. But I don't think I ever was really very much in the club.

Freeman: It's interesting that this poem, as a whole, also raises the question of the extent to which people participating in an evil system are doing it for all kinds of human reasons, not necessarily for reasons of hate or destructiveness, or ...

Peter: Certainly not for that! And, of course, who knows? I cannot fully analyze what were my own motives. I tried to be a good member of the Canadian team, worked hard and long hours.

Was it because I was ambitious? Was it because I wanted to be liked by the other people? Because I liked doing a job well? I think that you probably can't really separate out these things.

But the point you're raising is a very important one: that the bureaucracy is a kind of tribe with its own culture. The longer you work and think as a bureaucrat, the less you're going to think like an ordinary human being.

Words, like KORCOMS instead of Korean Communists, just reinforce that kind of deviation into a special kind of bureaucratic universe.

I was shocked that people in State, who weren't even part of the plan to overthrow Sukarno, were all trying to show how they wanted to get rid of him, and had ideas how to get the Indonesian Army to go ahead and just take care of the communists.

The Communist Party in Indonesia was expected to win the next election. They were the largest party. I think quite considerably the largest party in Indonesia, and certainly the largest Communist Party outside the Communist bloc.

It was a little bit like the problem the CIA faced in Italy and France in 1948. America says it believes in democracy, but apparently not when people it doesn't like are going to win an election.

Though there was no talk of assassination in Europe, there was pretty overt language, in quasi-academic American texts, that called for "liquidating" of the Indonesian Communist Party (PKI), which is what happened.[78]

I was particularly discouraged by the role played by George Ball. I kept looking for the good guys in the State Department; and during the Vietnam War, George Ball was a relative dove.

He was somebody who became known as the devil's advocate: the man who was, in a sense, not on the team, because he always was warning—warning correctly, I think—about the folly of sending more troops to Vietnam.

But even he is saying, "We may be confronted . . . / with situation we have hoped for / i.e., a new government." In other words, a successful coup overthrowing Sukarno.

Then the response of the new Ambassador, Marshall Green, to the massacre:

> elimination continues apace
> party formally terminated
>
> in fourteen provinces
> only eleven more to go!
> continuing massacre Bali
>
> many headless bodies
> encountered on road
> tourists well advised
>
> to postpone pleasure trips
> to island of the gods

Freeman: Toward the middle-end of page 109, there's a phrase that's in italics, but there's no side note. I wanted to ask you about that.

Peter: "*Pour encourager les autres.*" It's only in italics because it's in French: *Pour encourager les autres.* You do something to set an example. For example, in World War I, in that horrible trench warfare, French soldiers started deserting.

They would make a point of catching the deserters and lining them up in front of the troops, and then shooting them, for everyone to see. *Pour encourager les autres* meant, to discourage them from doing what the deserters did.

My suggestion here is that *Time* was giving some publicity to the horror of the massacre and the clogging of the streams, to tell other people, in other parts of the world, "Don't think that it's a good idea to be communist. This could happen to you."

Freeman: Not as an exposé of our acts of violence.

Peter: No, quite different.

Freeman: But as a warning to . . .?

Peter: To other people not to be like the PKI, yes.

Freeman: What do you make of the *L.A. Times* take on the massacre? Was this deliberate propaganda? Was this . . .?

Peter: This is ten years later. In the *L.A. Times* summary of what happened, "The Communist Party // attempted to seize power / and subjected the country / to a national bloodbath." But the Communists were the "victims" of the bloodbath. The *L.A. Times* suggested that the Communists were somehow guilty of their own murder.

Freeman: Was this just journalistic laziness? Was there . . .?

Peter: I guess the thinking behind it is, if you believe the official version, which I don't, "They tried a coup against the government, and this is what happened to them. And so what they did subjected the country to a bloodbath." Bureauthink!

I don't think the party per se was involved in a coup at all. It's a complicated story, and maybe one or two people in the party got sucked into something. But to accuse the party of being responsible for their own horrible murder . . . I don't know what kind of audience we are supposed to be who could read something like that and not think about the inversion of it.

Robert Shaplen is a different case, because he was quite a good writer. I read his works a lot. But for him to talk about wearing white, which is associated with death in Indonesia, as if this had to do with their guilt. He doesn't quite say that, but it's almost as bad: "as if admitting their guilt."

Again, I was shocked at the assumption of these writers that you can get away with that sort of thing with the American public, which unfortunately is probably true. You probably could in those days and today.

Freeman: We move from there to a very different story, a very different case of group action, in your faculty protest.

But, before we talk about that, I want to ask you a little bit about the two events from your life that you refer to. You were once almost killed by a bouncing log?

Peter: No, no, no. I "threw" bouncing logs, short ones for pulp. I was at top of the pile. That was a summer I worked for something called Frontier College. Frontier College got me hired by the Quebec North Shore Paper Company, as a lumberjack (although I didn't really have the body for it), so that I could teach other lumberjacks in the off-hours.

Freeman: So the line, "The fluke by which I survived," is not attached to the previous lines but to the following lines?

Peter: It was the way that a fluke four-bounce end-over-end toss helped get me accepted by the other people, much stronger people.

Freeman: I see. It's an example of you fitting in with the group, looking up to others who are seniors in your group and that sort of thing?

Peter: Being part of that team, yes.

Freeman: So the next instance is this Canadian amendment?

Peter: Yeah. The so-called Second Congress of Vienna in 1961 picked up from the First Congress in 1815, after the fall of Napoleon, which, in addition to drawing the general outline of Europe for a century, also laid down rules for diplomacy and the rights of embassies and so on.

These had not changed in a century and a half. So, in 1961, diplomats were called to Vienna, and in the same hall in the Hofburg, which was the Imperial Palace, a very elegant hall with eighteenth-century mirrors on the walls, we were drawing up rules for the conduct of diplomacy.

At one point there was a bit of a stymie, because there were two competing groups of amendments, and I (with a couple of other countries, but it was formally a Canadian amendment) moved a kind of compromise text to get us out of the stymie.

I do remember the French, the very vehement French opposition to this amendment, but ours was backed by the Canadians, the British, the Americans, and maybe the Swedes. Usually, when you had the British and the Americans, there was a good chance something would pass, and this amendment passed. That was my tiny contribution as a bureaucrat. One tiny part of a clause in the 1961 United Nations Convention on Diplomatic Relations that now governs diplomacy.

It was something to do I think with the amount of immunity enjoyed by staffers who are not formally diplomats, but working inside the embassy.

Freeman: So it partly functions as a contrast to what these other diplomats were doing in the previous section.

Peter: I hadn't thought of that!

Freeman: And partly it's a contrast to this other kind of action that you're about to take in this section.

Peter: It's, also, I would say, immediately, a contrast to the example of me near the jackladder, at the Rivière aux Outardes. Indeed a contrast.

Then the third example, which I would like to think, is pointed in the direction of significant action, but doesn't get there.

It's the first time perhaps that I am in a protest that I helped design. But I don't commit to it with enough conviction, and self-control, and authority, to really make a difference, So it fails, but it's got a glimpse of light ahead in the future, where maybe something could happen.

We're on page 111 in the poem before I'm doing something like that.

Freeman: It's a beautiful poetry, by the way, a wonderful picture you paint of Sproul Plaza there.

Peter: And you know it, of course. You probably have seen that kind of day. A day rather like today, when it's gloomy and a little damp.

Freeman: It's a wonderful setting for an action piece.

Peter: Right. The action is all in slow motion, very slow motion.

Freeman: Exactly. It's very well rendered.

IV.vi

Truth and nonviolence

      and when he was *he Rama* murdered

      the new government
          needing to honor him
      gave him a military funeral

      transported his body
          on a flower-bedecked
      weapons carrier

      while overhead Dakotas
          of the Royal Indian Air Force
      dipped in salute

      with *showers of scented blossoms*

Freeman: My first question for you today is what is Gandhi doing in a poem about Indonesia and Peter Dale Scott?

Peter: We have to remember, among the threads of the poem, we now have the Bhagavad Gita. It's a section out of a war epic, the Mahabharata, which is a celebration of war, and Arjuna in the Bhagavad Gita is preparing himself for battle. Krishna is saying that anyone who sits "brooding / over his self-restraint / is called a hypocrite."

Freeman: Brooding over his self-restraint in time of war, at this point?

Peter: There are times when you have to go all out. I think Gandhi would have said the same thing, but all out for peace, not for war. The other main reason I want to talk about Gandhi is because this thing about this massacre in Indonesia happened in the middle of the anti-war movement in America over Vietnam. I saw the world as embroiled in a conflict between forces of violence and the truth-force of nonviolence. And writing about the craziness of violence created in me the desire to bring in the truth of nonviolence.

Initially, the anti-war movement was dominated by nonviolent people. Indeed one could say that the nonviolent movement launched the anti-war movement. But increasingly, there were people, among both the African Americans and also the whites, who said, "This is silly. This is war. We should be fighting. We have to get guns."

I heard it many times at rallies, people saying, "This is ridiculous. It's time to go and get our guns." Some of those people were obviously government provocateurs, because they wouldn't say anything else; but there were probably also people who sincerely believed it. The Black Panthers were a movement which took out guns and practiced out at the Chabot Rifle Range, believing, "We must get ready for the revolution." And so did the Weathermen in SDS.

These lines, for me, are very important, the left calling Martin Luther King an "Uncle Tom," That is what's Stokely Carmichael did say about Martin Luther King. In the whole of this part IV, I'm exploring how to act. No longer, "What is America?" (part II), or "Who am I?" (part III), but part IV: "What do we do?"

It seems very relevant, because I do believe in nonviolence, to start talking about the great exemplar of nonviolence in my century, the twentieth century, a very complex figure, and I explore some of the complexities in Gandhi.

Freeman: What was the incident referred to by Mailer?

Peter: He wrote this whole book, *The Armies of the Night*. That's where Allen Ginsberg came to levitate the Pentagon, and you had all kinds of people. Mailer was disappointed that it was so nonviolent, that people just lay there, "like a string of fish," to be picked up and carried away in cars.[79]

Mailer and Stokely Carmichael were both mocking nonviolence. So I think back to Gandhi and the criticisms made of him in his lifetime. For Churchill, it was just unthinkable that the British government would negotiate with a "half-naked . . . seditious fakir." On the Hindu side, they were saying he was interpreting the Gita badly because he was interpreting it for nonviolence. Of course, there were many Hindus at that time who believed that it really summoned Arjuna for war.

Freeman: These sacred scriptures are always so flexible.

Peter: And I find it fascinating that Gandhi's career started as a lawyer in London, getting his training. The only thing that was strongly Hindu about him at that time was that he was a vegetarian. It was hard to find vegetarian food in London.

He found it at this London Vegetarian Society, which was actually an offshoot of the Theosophists. So he read Madame Blavatsky and they introduced him to the Gita in an English translation. That's where he first explored the roots of what you might call his deep Hinduism.

Freeman: This quote about "exhausting all avenues" that were being forced on them, is this a defense of Arjuna, a pacifist defense or rationalization?

Peter: I don't remember the context exactly now, but it's certainly from the Mahabharata, which is much longer than the Bhagavad Gita. The Bhagavad Gita is just one book in this very, very long poem. It's hard to get a complete translation even.

Yes, the context in the poem is that the Pandavas are heroes. They're a bunch of brothers, they didn't seek war, but when they realized that war was the only honorable thing, they didn't shun it. This is what the Hindu scholars were using against Gandhi. They pointed to this quotation and said, "There are times where you have to fight."

I say this is what makes Gandhi more than his roots. From a Western perspective, we think of him as representing some kind of Indian philosophy in the East. I'm trying, in this section, to show that the sources of his thinking include Thoreau and Tolstoy. He is unique. He is one of the first world thinkers, because he was as much influenced by Thoreau and Tolstoy as he was by his Indian roots.

He's as much a product of the best of the West as of the best of the East.

Freeman: This "fasting for light," what was that about?

Peter: I think now we're in India. "Depressed Classes" was the legal British term for the Dalit, or what we in the West call the Untouchables. The response of the leaders of the Untouchables was, when they started talking about voting in India, and there would be an electorate, they wanted to have an Untouchable bloc.

The first time that Gandhi went into a fast to change things was not against the British. It was against these political leaders of the Untouchables (Dalit), because his vision of India was one in which inequalities of caste had disappeared. The last thing he wanted was separate electoral blocs. *"I would far rather / that Hinduism died / than that untouchability lived."*

Although he was a Hindu fighting for Hindu independence, he was also fighting for radical change. In fact, in theory, the Untouchables are not legally oppressed anymore; but socially they have not overcome their difficulties. For that reason, many Untouchables have converted, in the last few years, to Buddhism, because they're not getting satisfaction from Hinduism.

Freeman: This business of the new Indian cabinet and the new state of Pakistan, was he also defeating expectations there about the side that one might have expected him to take?

Peter: Yes. One thing I haven't mentioned so far is that throughout his career, although the political leaders of Indian independence movement (like

Nehru, the best example) needed Gandhi and worked with Gandhi, they didn't trust Gandhi.

They were trying to build a political movement working, essentially, with urban leaders. Gandhi was trying to rebuild a grassroots movement with some very primitivistic rural ideas. He wanted Indians to spin their own cotton, and make their own cloth and their own clothing, as a way of protesting the import of British cotton goods into India, which had impoverished whole classes of people in India.

This was not the way the modernizing political leaders were thinking at all. Then after the war, the separation into India and Pakistan was done independently of Gandhi. But when Gandhi saw that the new India was reluctant to give any money to the new Pakistan, he stepped in to say, "No, the treasury should be divided *per capita*," and that the Pakistanis should get their share.

Freeman: It's kind of an unpatriotic stance to take.

Peter: Yes, and it's interesting. The whole idea of patriotism is linked to states, governments, and flags. And Gandhi represented something more than that. He wanted peace in that subcontinent. He wanted different behavior on both the Indian and the Pakistani side. The first step would be for India to respect common equity and give the Pakistanis their share. He fasted for that. He had nothing to do with the London Conference.

Freeman: What was the London Conference?

Peter: That's where the politicians were working out the details. Meanwhile, he was dealing with this terrible crisis. Immediately after the division, both in Muslim areas and in Hindu areas, there were movements to expel those in minority and in many cases to kill them. So there were massacres.

Gandhi went to the Noakhali area of Bengal where the Muslims were massacring the Hindus, and attempted to pacify that area. When writing the poem, I believed from a book I had read that Gandhi was successful in this effort. But his success was very limited and temporary.[80]

He was the opposite of the kind of narrow sectarian fundamentalist that we see so often in the world today, particularly among fundamentalist Hindus and fundamentalist Muslims. He was trying to forestall that, prevent it from happening, and retain an idea of society that was larger than any narrower religion.

Freeman: I want to ask you about where, toward the end of this section, you typically, for you and for the poem, relate Gandhi's moment of doubt about his nonviolence. Was this an isolated moment, or was this a phase in his life when he . . . ?

Peter: It's some time since I've read a biography of him, but I remember the last months of his life as being very pained. So much was going in the wrong direction, particularly the massacres, the mass killings of Hindus and

Muslims, but also the arrogance and intransigence of the new Indian government and the Pakistan government toward each other.[81]

He could not have helped but feel he was missing the certainty of his power, because people were no longer listening to Gandhi the way they used to, in this situation—especially at the top. They felt, "Well, he helped us gain independence, but now we have to run an army and police. He is no use for this sort of thing."

He, to the very last day, was trying to maintain peace, nonviolently. There is still a Gandhi movement in India. Certainly, the movement had been very important and powerful in the gaining of independence; but it was cast to one side by the rulers—Nehru being one of them, even though Nehru was a personal friend of Gandhi.

Freeman: This section, once again like so much in the poem, ends on not necessarily a high note, on a note of foreboding.

Peter: Right, and irony. Actually, I always feel that my quarrel with contemporary culture, literature, and poetry, is the prevalence of irony, which I tend to dislike. But there is a pretty ironic close to this section. This man, who was nonviolent, anti-military, was given a military funeral. The highest compliment the new government of India, which he had helped to create, could give him was a military funeral, with the planes.

There are more ironies even in the military funeral. The planes fly overhead. What do they drop? Blossoms.

IV.vii–IV.ix

Its propensity to distance

> We talked for two hours
> and I think of him often
> as I read in the papers
>
> of Solidarność suppressed
> how those must be
> privileged moments
>
> one can so transcend history

Freeman: We have three sections today, two of which are set during your year as consul in Poland.

Peter: I had two years in Poland, and I was consul for a little less than a year.

Freeman: The first of the two sections is one that's always puzzled me a little bit, in terms of its internal logic. I want to try to put together the pieces in my mind, now that I have a chance to sit with you and talk about it. It begins with these engineers, in their excited talk about extracting sulfur, and in their concern about the fact that the peasants aren't willing to buy tractors.

Peter: That was a great problem, yes, because Poland was desperate to modernize after the socialists took over. They developed industry, and that meant that more and more people were living in the cities. So you had to increase the productivity from the farms in order to support the new urban population.

But the peasants didn't trust the government at all. This was a problem about which the Communists were actually consulting with the U.S. Embassy. Here the government was offering them tractors, and the peasants didn't want them, for the canny reason that if they stuck with their horses, they knew they could feed the horses from the land. If they got a tractor, then they were dependent on the government for gasoline. They suspected, and I think rightly so, that the government would control the price of gas as a way, in effect, of taxing the farmers.

This was a legitimate problem: You want to have a more urban country; you have to have increased productivity from the land. How do you persuade the peasants?

Freeman: These engineers who are discussing the problem, they're not thinking about the bigger picture that you present just below, the idea of growth distancing the planners from the people. They're just trying to solve this problem.

Peter: Exactly. They're technicians, and they're genuinely excited about their work. They had a vision. As a poet, I'm also having a vision of Poland's problem: of the gap between the peasants on the one hand, and the engineers on the other [or if you like, the land versus the city, a recurring yin-yang theme in this poem].

Freeman: I found myself thinking about them in terms of the Aswan engineers in Section III.xvi, similarly focused on the technical problems before them.

Peter: Right. Getting power. The Egyptians didn't even know, probably, that the snails would become an acute problem afterwards, yes.

Freeman: The next question I have is that there's another transition made. There's a preposition I want to ask you about.

Peter: "From?"

Freeman: ". . . from the Leninist autocritique . . ."

Peter: Because I'm doing a switch into talking about the massacre. *Coming to Jakarta* is always coming back to this appalling massacre in 1965, where I see the hand of the CIA. But before I come back to the large structure of the poem, let me talk about this Leninist auto-critique from Prague.

Freeman: Actually, even before then, could you point out the antecedent of the "from?"

Peter: Yes, "The philosophy of growth, with its propensity to distance the planners from the people," and then I switch it the other way around: the distance between the girl, who is a peasant, from the Prague Leninist auto-critique.

Freeman: Okay, got it.

Peter: In Eastern Europe, it was incredibly romantic to see these medieval landscapes. You would take a tram out of Warsaw. At the end of the tram, you would walk into the country and see villages to which there were no real roads, where the families had their geese and their cows and their sheep. A grandmother would be out tending a goat.

It really was like a painting by Brueghel. There was a distance between that kind of landscape with the peasant girl and this ideological Leninist thinking in Prague, which blamed the Indonesian massacre on the Chinese. Which of course, I don't.

Sukarno, before he was overthrown, was trying to balance east and west. He'd accepted American aid, but he also accepted a great deal of Soviet aid and some Chinese aid. After the massacre, the Soviets were not like me opposed to Suharto. They were hoping to stay in with Suharto.

The Soviets published analyses of the massacre, which did not, like me, blame it on the Army. No, they displaced the blame over to the Chinese, in the hopes that they and not the Chinese could continue to work with Suharto. It was quite interesting. You get to triangulate the different points of view of this massacre.

Then we go from the Leninist auto-critique, which was from some state-controlled journal in Prague, to this scholar, Rudolf Mrázek, who's very, very interesting. On the one hand, he was a student of Benedict Anderson at Cornell, who's one of the people in the West who, like myself, doubted the Chinese explanation.

Mrázek's a genuine scholar. But he was behind the Iron Curtain when he wrote this book I'm quoting from, which was published in Prague before the Czech revolt.[82] He had to conform to the party lines. He too was, in a sense—without naming me—refuting the point of view that I held, by saying *"No American // could claim that U.S. training / had strengthened Suharto."* That's exactly what I was claiming.

Mrázek was making a hero out of Suharto, "who tried to unify // under the spirit of *jago-satria*." We've talked about this earlier. *Jago-satria* is Bahasa Indonesia for the *ksatriya* of the Mahabharata: a warrior, inspired by the ideals of Hinduism.

Then, finally, I quote his explanation of why Suharto was not one of the generals murdered. The Suharto version of the coup is that it was a power grab by elements supporting Sukarno. But I wrote in refutation that all the generals who were murdered were pro-Sukarno, and none of the ones who were pro-Suharto, including Suharto himself, were killed. Mrázek's explanation was, "Well, that's because Suharto was 'not corrupted // and westernized.'" [laughs]

I think he *was* corrupted and westernized. This is actually very important for me. We are all conditioned by the social environment that we live in. Professor Mrázek was conditioned by his environment and came up with a pro-Suharto view of the massacre which was, from my point of view, very ideological, even though he was a good scholar.

It's a way of thinking about how the world we're in is extremely complex, and you and I here are just in one tiny little socioeconomic bit of it—luckily, one where we can criticize our own environment.

Freeman: That sheds a lot of light on the next section. I guess here then is another example of an extremely scholarly, intelligent man who had a certain point of view that you question the sources of.

Peter: I do indeed. Let me begin by saying that Clifford Geertz in the 1980s, when I wrote this critical poem about him, was an intellectual hero on my campus, including on the left. He didn't just collect facts in the narrow sense. He was a *cultural* anthropologist.

I read this essay by Geertz because I admired my colleague Stephen Greenblatt, who wrote about it, and also because it was about Indonesia. I was upset by Geertz's account of the massacre: his trying to reduce it to the cultural traditions of Indonesia and explicitly downplaying the role of the army. Of course, from my point of view, it is true that the army didn't by themselves kill everybody. They handed it over to others to kill. But this phrase . . .

Freeman: So he's writing about the violence of the cockfighting . . .

Peter: As a kind of explanation for the massacre.

Freeman: For how the people had this within them, and so there needs to be no further explanation in terms of external forces.

Peter: I was particularly annoyed his sentence explicitly downplaying the role of the army: "people were massacred // largely villagers by other villagers / though there were some / army executions as well."[83] The army wasn't just one tiny feature of this whole thing. They were the instigators of the massacre, even though it's quite true they didn't do all the killings themselves.

I'm doing a rather nasty thing. I'm putting his downplaying of the role of the army into the context of his research having been partly CIA-funded.

Freeman: Right. It's funny. It was kind of amusing almost how you asked these innocent questions of him. But earlier, as you're listing things that are not your complaints, you're actually providing what you believe were his motivations.

Peter: I don't want to come away from this with the implication that Geertz is not worth reading or that his research is corrupt because it was CIA-funded. No. He did good research. He just gratuitously involved himself in the question of the massacre in such a way as to massage the U.S. role in it. I was objecting to that, as I do at the very end, you know. When I ask him,

> how can you write
>
> about *the integrative revolution*
> in a book that is indexed
> to sixty-one countries

Paraguay the Soviet Union
but not the United States?

Sorry, isn't America part of the world? Sixty-one countries, but it doesn't occur to him to think of America, too? From his point of view, America is the island of objective sanity where you look at all the cultural irrationality in the rest of the world. No, we're part of the process too.

Freeman: We end with one of my favorite sections of the poem. I feel like, very shortly after this section, the poem, although it's been talking a lot about horrific events and the terrible state of the world, is about to get even darker in some ways and even despairing at one point.

Peter: We will come to that. [laughs] You may be right.

Freeman: I feel as though this little episode that you relayed with this Polish police officer functions in the poem the way it functions in your memory, as a kind of respite.

Peter: I think of it as an urban pastoral.

Freeman: [laughs]

Peter: There is so-called Cold War going on. He represents the police of the Iron Curtain countries. But he's a human being. I'm a human being. He persuades me to not press charges against someone who had stolen Cassie's toys out of our car. That was a period of relative calm in postwar Poland, after what had been a very bad time right after the war [when Czeslaw Milosz defected, fearing for his life, after one of his friends was killed].

Then there was the Polish Thaw in 1956. Gomułka was, first of all, let out of prison and then allowed to be the premier of Poland, although the Russians didn't trust him very much. I was there at the very end of the Polish Thaw, when you could still have this kind of discussion.

And the time I'm writing this in the 1980s was, again, a different kind of hopeful time, because it was in the wake of Solidarity. It was proving that the people could take on the army, the police, and, in the background, the Soviet Union. But the outcome was not clear when I was writing this. What was clear was that people were being killed, ordinary people, like the workers at Gdańsk.

Freeman: Makes those two hours all the more poignant.

Peter: Yes. It was a moment of respite, between the earlier bad time and the later bad time.

Freeman: In terms of the poem, I feel like there's a moment earlier in the poem that functions, for me, like these two hours. But there were no humans involved. It's you among the trees with the sap rising in them in the frozen night.

Peter: Oh, that's very poetic. Yes, that was a little escape. In the poem I wrote about the importance of escape, talking about Yvain, and so on.

Freeman: But there were no humans involved in that scene.
Peter: Right.
Freeman: Later in the poem [IV.xviii], there's going to be a scene with you and another person, at a party or something toward the end?
Peter: Yes.
Freeman: But though the genuine talk that might have happened doesn't actually appear in the poem, we're speculating on, "Could we have this kind of talk?" This is the one moment where, between two human beings, it happens in this poem.
Peter: Right. That's really beautiful, Freeman. I'd never thought of it, but those three moments are absolutely linked in the way you just said. Yes, beautiful . . .

IV.x–IV.xii

Portending deluge

        it is clear we must resist

      the black-shirted gangs
          some of whose own members
          experienced *recurring nightmares*

      in which their victims appeared
          before them like Banquo's ghost

Freeman: Last session we ended with one of my favorite sections of the book. This very moving conversation you had with the Polish police officer. One of those moments in the book when you make this genuine human contact with someone.

Peter: From the other side of the Iron Curtain.

Freeman: Exactly, yeah. There's a feeling of hope or the possibilities for the species, for the human race.

Peter: I know you said this last time, but it's the chance to be a little bit more than what we're born into being.

Freeman: Yeah.

Peter: That it is a characteristic of human beings that they can grow beyond those determining factors that shape them at birth.

Freeman: This week, however, I think we're about to enter what for me is the darkest part of the poem. We're about to enter a kind of a slide, a kind of a giving up or a kind of a desperation at the end of this section . . .

Peter: At least, a sense of danger.

Freeman: Yeah.

Peter: And this is where Wordsworth with the French Revolution comes into both of these next two sections. That freedom is a chance that you can be more than you were, but the consequences of freedom can be escaping from the limits of society in a crude way that comes to disaster.

And that was the great obsession in Wordsworth's *Prelude*, that he really believed in the freedom that he saw in the early days or the innocent days of the French Revolution. As he wrote, "Bliss was it in those days to be alive."

And I've quoted that more than once about being in Berkeley in the 1960s. There was that same sense of liberation and possibility. But also, the sense that things can get completely derailed in such a situation and then you run the risk of disaster.

For both these sections, the Wordsworth quotes are very important, I think. Wordsworth already knew that people had died in the revolution, but he still wanted to believe in it. Then, when the terror began and the guillotine was killing by the hundreds, he escaped. *The Prelude* includes his reflection later about what he had seen and what it meant.

I wrote *Coming to Jakarta* in the 1980s. At this point, I think I'm also reliving the Wordsworthian experience of having been through the 1960s in Berkeley, having seen a lot of lives ruined, and having to reassess everyone's earlier naive belief in freedom and change. We didn't have a terror, but blissful hopes turned violent; and a lot of people were also totally derailed on acid or heroin or other drugs. What did it all mean?

Just like Wordsworth, I'm sensing the risk of a world that doesn't really know where it's going and has the capacity to change rapidly; and that could easily mean another world war. I've always worried, in prose and poetry, how long could we maintain peace without going back to major war? Which is, after all, the history of the world.

Freeman: Both sections end with some form of the word *portent*. This section, toward the end, has a defiant "No!" to the option of giving up hope about these things.

Peter: Yeah, if I could say a bit more in prose about that. I entertained the thought that the overpopulation in Java was getting so extreme that, if there hadn't been a massacre, there would've been something else. It wasn't sustainable.

It wasn't an alternative between massacring a lot of people or just going on and being like before, because things were breaking down, as in this little food fact that rice production was beginning to give way to high-yield, low-nutrition cassava.

Java couldn't support itself anymore; there were too many people. In desperation people started growing cassava, which can feed more people but doesn't feed them as well. It doesn't give as rounded a nutrition as rice does.

Part of me pulls back and said, "Well, maybe everyone was going to die anyway, it doesn't really make much difference if they die by human effort or they die by starvation." That's where the "No!" comes in, because something very anti-human happened in this massacre.

Massacres! There are things about which you cannot say, "Well, it was a useful massacre" or "You just have to accept massacres." You have to resist massacres. That's what the point of that "No!" is. "It is clear we must resist the black-shirted gangs."

Then, the interesting thing that the gangs—this is from a prose account of what happened then—it's a westerner saying their victims appeared before them like Banquo's ghost, which is from *Macbeth*. Wordsworth, having seen the dead in Paris, says he seemed to hear a ghost that cried to the whole city, "Sleep no more" [Prelude, 10: 38–77], which is also from *Macbeth*.

It's just one of those neat little things that fit with each other. It fit very well for me in that I'm sort of committing to resist, which is to engage with this machine that is out of control, where you can't predict what the result will be, except that the risk of disaster is there.

Freeman: In the next section, you start off with this long account of the marinas in North Hatley being bought up. I'm curious; I didn't quite get how that was functioning in this section.

Peter: First of all, let's start with the drought/wetness thing. I wrote it in the year we had a very acute drought in California. I was just amazed that autumn to see the wetness of North Hatley—of course, Lake Massawippi keeps coming back into this poem. I went back at a time when they had an excessive amount of rain.

It wasn't the North Hatley I knew, because the land and many of the houses, the shops, the businesses in North Hatley, were being bought up wholesale by this in-law of the Saudi royal family, Saad Gabr. He wasn't a prince but he was married to a princess, and extremely wealthy. It looked as if he was going to buy the whole town.

My mother and my father disagreed about many things, and they disagreed about this. My father was objecting because he was always having to rent a boat to go down to his little camp, his cabin down the lake, and he was now having to pay far more to the Arab than he ever had to in the old days. My mother's saying, "But it's good, you know, for the French Canadians who will have more business," and so on.

If you like, this is an example of something bigger. I used Lake Massawippi and North Hatley at the beginning of the poem as an example of the pastoral endurance of things, in contrast to the change, decay, and danger of the city. But what's happening in the city is getting to the pastoral background. Even North Hatley is not going to continue to be what it was for me when I was a child, because of this Arab.

What do I mean by, "Arbitrage! to save the dollar / by monetizing oil?" Nixon took American dollar completely off the gold standard but devised a way with the Shah of Iran for increased oil prices to sustain the dollar's value; and also, among other things, help the Shah buy U.S. arms. Later, more importantly, America arranged to make the dollar the instrument of exchange for all OPEC oil purchases. That's still largely true to this day.[84]

If a country dares to break out of this system by saying they will sell oil for euros, well, that's what Saddam Hussein did in Iraq, that's what Gaddafi said he was going to do in Libya, and you saw what happened to them. And that is what the Iranians have been trying to do in Iran.

All this idea of monetizing oil destabilized the world and made major players of the Saudis, who were not really interested in the well-being and comfort of the world. One of them was Adnan Khashoggi, a half-Arab from Saudi Arabia who made millions on arms commissions that he used in political payoffs—"$106 million / in Lockheed commissions // to Khashoggi alone."

I mentioned Lockheed before [IV.i] as part of the story of the massacre in Indonesia, which is what we're really talking about always. Because the Lockheed commissions in Indonesia had once been paid to supporters of Sukarno. But in early 1965, before the coup. Lockheed switched them [to a Suharto supporter].[85]

The commissions were bribes. That's perhaps a better word than payoffs. And the commissions, instead of going to the supporters of Sukarno, started going to supporters of Suharto. That was a message to the Indonesian army that they had U.S. support to go ahead with the overthrow of Sukarno.

Today the relatively stable world of the 1950s is coming apart because of all these new arrangements to save the dollar. These new heroes in this world, Khashoggi, Bebe Rebozo, who was a money cut-out behind Nixon, and then Liem Sioe Liong, who was one of the people who got rich when Suharto took power because Suharto or his wife would invest in businesses with Liem and other Chinese-Indonesian businessmen.

This particular man, Liem, bought the Hibernian Bank in California, which had a branch on the Berkeley campus. It was all coming home to us. So "I thought of the Arab in Wordsworth's dream / *a loud prophetic / blast of harmony //* portending deluge."

In Book Five of *The Prelude*, Wordsworth remembers a dream in which an Arab in a sandy desert is carrying a stone and a shell. The stone (the Arab explains) represents reason, Euclid, elements, but there's more to life and humanity than reason. The shell is something irrational that is not defined, except that when Wordsworth listened to it he heard "aloud prophetic blast of harmony / an Ode, in passion uttered, which foretold / Destruction to the children of the earth / By deluge, now at hand" [Prelude, 5:95–98].

By this contrast Wordsworth, I think you could say, is trying to encapsulate the French Revolution in a line or two. The Revolution enthroned reason. They thought Reason was going to replace religion, but there was some kind of dialectic that answered reason with passion and destruction.

Freeman: I feel like we're on the verge of a kind of deluge in this poem as a whole. I feel like just a few sections ahead we're going to come. . . . Just the momentum of this world system is just going to kind of take over the poem and there are going to be some very unpleasant sections. But just before all that starts, there's this next section IV.xii, where you make a kind of a plea. You once told me that you had originally considered not putting this section into the poem.

Peter: It's different from any other section because it's more like a little sermon than poetry really. You could say, getting back to the Arab with the stone and the shell, that this is a kind of Euclidean voice of reason trying to insert itself and say, "Look here, the world is blowing up. . . .

Freeman: That's how I see it. I think you're trying to hold back the deluge that will be arriving in one more section here.

Peter: Right, but I'm not sure that it isn't a bit like, if there's a riot in the streets, somebody gets up on a car and says, "People, be reasonable." It's a bit late to be saying, "Be reasonable." I don't think I'm really saying what I say here with any conviction that it'll have any influence on anyone, that it will ever even be seen by the people who need to see it. But I believe in what I say.

I think it's reasonable. I don't remember this section with any particular affection. But when I saw what I'd said—"only by patrolling the world // could we have become so hated / only by fighting so hard / to preserve the dollar // could we have driven gold / to ten times its value / in eleven years"—I think that's good sense and it's worth saying. It's just that it's not going to make any difference to anything.[86]

IV.xiii–IV.xiv

If a sentence is left dangling

> or the bleary-eyed hippie
> > who followed me up Telegraph
> > into four or five bookstores
>
> and then back again (until
> > I shook him through a second exit)
> > saying over and over
>
> *we know who you are*
> > *I work with the FBI*
> > *sooner or later we are going to get you*
>
> and I could do nothing about it
> > the poor guy
> > was so obviously spacy

Freeman: What is the general theme of this section?

Peter: I think, actually, it is very lucky the two sections are together. In both we see the spirit of naïve rational ("yang") analysis that dominated part II of *Jakarta* begin to break down, and be interrupted by a kind of transcendental nonsense, [beginning to prepare us for *Listening to the Candle*, the more "yin" volume of *Seculum*. In the penultimate movement of the third volume, *Minding the Darkness*, I try to voice a kind of yang-yin synthesis.]

Thus section IV.xiii ends in a wild quoted burst *("the writing of Tryksara / A + U + M // on the surface of water")* of what the Platonists called *furor propheticus*.

The whole section is primarily about Java. Yava-dvipa, by the way, is the way the island of Java is referred to in the Ramayana.

I was fascinated that the same name turns up as Yava-dvipa in a Sanskrit text, and in an ancient Greek geography by Ptolemaeus as Iabadiou, and in a Chinese travel account by Fa Hsien in the fifth century as Yeh P'o T'i—all talking about this island. Whether it's Yava-dvipa, Iabadiou, or Yeh P'o T'i, it's Java.

It was famous as far west as Greece and as far east as China for its wealth. And even then it had this ability to absorb all cultures and unify them; so that in their mind, Shiva and Buddha are one. The god of violence and the preacher of nonviolence: the two are one in Java. Just as, later on, Marxism and God are blended by Sukarno into one ideology.

That's one pole of what we're talking about. And at the other pole are the oil companies. There should be a footnote or a side note explaining that Stanvac and Caltex are two joint ventures created in Indonesia—the first by Standard of New Jersey (later Exxon) and Standard of New York (Socony-Vacuum, later Mobil), the second by Standard of California (now Chevron), and Texaco (now gone).

They merged together to go into these other areas but also to really shake them up and bring them by the scruff of the neck into the twentieth century. They got involved with what I'm talking about in IV.xiii: how the oil companies funded the coup against Sukarno, which led to over half a million deaths. It's a tragic theme.

Then, in IV.xiv, I start by talking about Lee Harvey Oswald. It's much more about me and my feeble attempts to do something about all this chaos and so on, and I can't even complete a phone call. I mean, that's how powerless I am in this struggle with the great forces.

I really did have a lot of trouble with my telephone in those days. Less now, thank goodness.

One morning Bob Silvers invited me to coauthor an article with Gore Vidal for *The New York Review of Books*, of which Bob was the editor. Some higher authority didn't want that to happen, so they wouldn't let Gore and me complete even one phone call. After three or four tries, Gore gave up phoning me, and phoned Bob.

In the Canadian edition of this book, I had a bit more to say about what Bob Silvers reported to me, when he finally got through about five or six hours later on this phone, after being told my extension was not in service. (My extension was never out of service. I was phoning other people all this time; I just couldn't get a call from Bob or Gore Vidal.) And Bob then said, "Gore has had time to reflect / and has decided / to devote all his energy // to gay political rights."

In other words, I was used to phone disruptions, but Gore obviously wasn't. He was freaked. We had been going to write something about the Kennedy assassination, and he then decided that he had better things to do with his time. As I say in the poem, I didn't blame him. But I can't describe how powerless I felt after that fiasco. It definitely contributed to my crisis in Watertown, which was I think a few weeks later.[87]

Is there any way of linking these two seemingly very disparate cantos? I think there is, because the key to it is at the very end. I say, "I can't blame anyone / except maybe the advice / to Odysseus from the blind man."

Tiresias says, "You may reach home, though in evil plight, if you will curb your own spirit and that of thy comrades" [Odyssey, 11: 105–06]. This was the whole point of the visit to the underworld, for Odysseus to learn he must curb his spirit (θυμός, *thumós*).

Tiresias has given some revolutionary advice which will change Odysseus from being the kind of hero you had in the *Iliad*, where everyone is full of spirit, goes out, and slashes and kills, to becoming the cunning Odysseus who restrains his spirit, arrives back home in Ithaca disguised as a beggar, bears all kinds of insults thrown at him, and restrains his spirit, does nothing, until it is time to take his revenge. (His companions, in contrast, did not; and they drown in a shipwreck.)

This, I think, is an extremely important event, not in just the life of Odysseus, that he's changed into a new kind of hero with two levels in his character, the level of passion and the level of restraining thought, the difference between mind and heart.

There was no such distinction earlier on, but it became a very important distinction that we still have.[88] This is the way we live now: the way I live, you live. All of us have been taught in early school to restrain our *thumós*, our spirit or passions. [*Thumós* in modern Greek now just means "anger."] That characterizes our civilization, and we gain a great deal by that: Western civilization. We also lose that capacity for what's inscribed on the stone of Erlangga in IV.xiii (the king who went into the forest like Yvain and then came back richer from meditation, now able to conquer his enemy and unite the Kingdom of Java for the first time.)

And inscribed on his stone was, "Shiva Sogata rishi," "Shiva and Buddha are one," in which I see a kind of unity of spirit which takes us in a very different direction: of a less active, a less dominating direction, a more mysterious direction.

I see Iabadiou here, the Island of Java, as a kind of symbol for the so-called Third World which has been suffering from the depredations of Western civilization for five centuries now and has responded with spiritual powers, particularly in Asia, but not just there, to be able to deal with external forces from other sources that you cannot name.

Freeman: Essentially: "there have always been poets."

Peter: [laughs] It's a poet trying to cope with this situation. "If a sentence / is left dangling in the mind too long." I'm now actually naming the sickness that I've been suffering from, which led to a kind of breakdown at the beginning of the poem. And then, when I say later, "I see what I have to do," I have to write all this and complete the sentence that I wasn't able to complete in the phone call.

Freeman: At the end of that section, you're blaming the advice. You're blaming the advice for your inability to complete the sentence.

Peter: I am not rejecting civilization, but I am seeing that it has strengthened a yang-yin split in our psyche that needs somehow to be reconciled. The way to move forward is not to reject Western civilization—I have no interest in doing that—but in perhaps effecting some kind of reconciliation with this eastern spirituality in which the one-sided presentational "self" is reintegrated. This is the main theme of *Minding the Darkness*, the third volume of this trilogy.

Freeman: With that context, let's go through section IV.xiii again and begin to sort out some of these references.

Peter: I'll take the opportunity to complete my dangling sentence about the coup, and tell you something important. What happened was that I saw Noam Chomsky again—not the time I talked about in part I of the poem but about four years later. I told him that while researching for this poem I had learned how the oil companies had helped finance the coup. Instead of just buying from the State oil company (with money that went to Sukarno), they started buying from the oil company of the Indonesian Army, which according to *Fortune* magazine "played a key part in bankrolling those crucial operations."[89]

I told Noam this, and how at the same time Lockheed started giving payoffs to General Alamsjah, who was very close to Suharto. Noam said, "Oh! Give me a memo on that." I started writing away and my memo ended up as a manuscript book of about 120 pages. It's never been published. [And I've since lost it.]

And then I drew on that manuscript for this part of the poem. About the same time, I wrote a prose article summarizing that manuscript. It's basically the talk I gave before 1,200 people at the Association for Asian Studies in Washington in 1984, when Ralph McGehee and I debated William Colby, who had been the officer at the CIA East Asia desk when the massacre occurred. [It's now chapter 5 of this book.]

Colby said, "Oh, nothing like this ever happened." But it did. Among other things, money was passed. Most of it wasn't passed by the CIA, but by the oil companies, Lockheed, the Pentagon.

Anyway, I guess I'm getting a bit far away from Erlangga when I'm giving all these details. But this is the product of the Western mind. You know, conniving, cunning Odysseus who led to the cunning oil companies that paid the cunning Indonesian Army to kill off the Communist party. Clever corporate managers learn to plan without consulting their human feelings.

All this was connected to the Vietnam War. There was oil in the South China Sea and Mobil hired this man, William Henderson, to lobby everybody in Washington and in the Council of Foreign Relations, saying how it's important for us to fight in Southeast Asia.[90]

He never said it's important for us to fight in Southeast Asia because of the oil. He never mentioned oil at all, but oil was paying his salary. The end of this section grows slightly crazy: "To alert Washington / to Vietnam's crisis of confidence." In other words, Saigon was going to negotiate with Hanoi in 1963 if we didn't go in and stiffen them up.

Then I say "opening to opportunities / of creative destruction." Schumpeter saw capitalism as leading to more and more intense competition and violence, war, creative destruction: By destroying the old, create the opportunity for something new.

That's a very tragic view of history which I see as quite opposed to the Gandhian view of history. Which is, nonviolence is truth. Truth and nonviolence can, if properly, strenuously and energetically applied, change the world without violence.

Freeman: What is this quote at the very end of the section?

Peter: To be quite honest I don't exactly remember. The book is by Himansu Sarkar, the same book that from which the quotation "Shiva Sogata rishu" is from. It is a book about the influence of India on Indonesian literature.

The book is very mystical and I might say extra-rational or irrational. So for creative destruction I let madness in, to do something. These evocations of Hindu text are doing the same thing.

Freeman: The "A+U+M"?

Peter: . . . Well "Aum" is another spelling for "Om." Which is what you can say when you're meditating. "Ohhhhhhmmmmm." (That's not my kind of Buddhist meditation.) In Hindu meditation you do the "Om," and that activates your *chakras* up your spine. Anyway the important thing is that it's crazy. Doesn't make sense.

Freeman: Right.

Peter: The world doesn't make sense. History doesn't make sense. What I'm trying to cope with here is that I have gained enough sense to see that it all doesn't make sense.

Freeman: So we come down to the end, then, and we come down to this hippie following you up Telegraph Ave. You say that he was so obviously spacey, so you don't believe there was anything more to it than he was just nuts.

Peter: I don't know. What really made me wonder was that he picked me out. He came after me and he said, "We know who you are. I work with the FBI." Why would a complete stranger think that saying, "I work with the FBI," would mean anything to me? That made me think that maybe he knew who I was and he knew that I was having trouble with the FBI. I got my FBI file, you know, in 1978; and as I recall it contained perhaps 985 pages.

And this guy was obviously a nutcase. He looked like a nutcase. Does that mean he couldn't be an FBI informant? I'm afraid it doesn't. I think that the FBI often recruits as informants people who are really desperate.

They might have used this man just to scare me. (There were other ways I really was scared at that time, which I don't want to go into.) This man was also scary, even if he was just a lone nut, because I couldn't get rid of him.

Some people ask me, "Was your life ever threatened?" The answer is, "Yes." "How many times?" I don't know if this case would count for one or 200, because he must have done it well over 100 times in those ten or twenty minutes. Again, like the phone ringing, it gets to you. And it feels good to get rid of it and put it on a page.

"For if a sentence is left dangling / in the mind too long . . ."

IV.xv

¡Djakarta se acerca!

> But when you control
> > most of the world
> > you cannot stop
>
> it has been managed before
> > so you are expected
> > to manage it again
>
> the cunning plan
> > becomes in the streets of Santiago
> > a biblical whirlwind
>
> *Jakarta is coming*

Freeman: Today we come to the last of the sections of the poem that deal directly with the politics around the Indonesian massacre. I want to take this session to talk not only about this section but about the massacre in general. About its place . . .

Peter: Two massacres, including the one in Chile, which was modeled in its planning on the one in Indonesia.

Freeman: Let's talk about Chile first then. What was the story behind that?

Peter: In Chile the CIA had been trying in 1970 to prevent the election of a socialist president, Salvador Allende, first by putting lots of money into the Christian Democratic party, and then by getting the Chilean Army to intervene. But General Schneider, head of the Chilean Army, chose to observe Chilean law. So the CIA arranged for what they called Schneider's abduction, when in fact he was murdered with CIA weapons. The technique they used (and its climax in 1973) was an army coup, with the death of Allende in the presidential palace as the troops stormed the palace.

That was possible because of the earlier death of General Schneider who was a constitutionalist. He was replaced by General Pinochet who plotted with the CIA. A CIA-backed group used terror as a way of destroying peace in the capital, making the left believe that the right was going to get them, making the right believe that the left was going to get them.

To do this, they used this little card which they distributed by the thousands. *¡Djakarta se acerca!*, "Jakarta is approaching." [It was also posted on walls.] Everybody in Chile understood what this meant, because they were more aware of the massacre a decade earlier in Indonesia than most Americans were.

It made Chileans fear another massacre was coming. Indeed, a massacre did come. It was the massacre the CIA wanted, which was the right massacring the left, rather than the imaginary massacre of the left massacring the right which was a figment of CIA propaganda.

I quote David Phillips in the course of this section as denying "that CIA was behind the coup."[91] He said this in his memoir and he said it also on a TV program that I was also on myself. At least I think he said it on that program. [I was wrong: In his memoir, *The Night Watch*, Phillips denied CIA involvement in the Schneider assassination and the 1973 coup; but he did not mention Chile on the TV show.][92]

But I think the CIA was guilty of organizing all of this, and I have to add there is the guilt of David Rockefeller, that can be documented, actually, from David Rockefeller's own memoir.[93]

He talks about how he put pressure on the White House. He went directly to Kissinger, and he sent a friend to Kissinger, to get them to do something about the fact that a democratically elected government in Chile was going to nationalize various economic interests in which David Rockefeller and his bank owned a stake.

There was very little secrecy about it. We know a lot about the CIA role because of that special moment in American history, back home. It was the time of Watergate, and the end of the Vietnam War. There was great discontent in Washington, competition between different factions. The head of the CIA, Richard Helms, was exiled by Nixon to be Ambassador to Iran. This firing of a CIA chief was unprecedented. Helms was also having to go to Congressional committees and testify about what the CIA had been doing.

So all this documentation came out. We have much better documentation on Chile in 1970—the murder of Schneider—and in 1973—the coup—all that's much better documented than what happened in Indonesia back in 1965, eight years earlier.

¡Djakarta se acerca!

Freeman: This is an example of what you've spoken about before, which is how the different actors within the government often had different agendas and often opposed one another.

Peter: Right.

Freeman: It's not a unified conspiracy doing these things.

Peter: Especially under Nixon, because by the time of the events in Chile, the Pentagon Chiefs of Staff were spying on the White House. They had someone in there and they were bugging the president. Hoover died at this time. The FBI, itself, had competing factions. Mark Felt in the FBI helped [as "Deep Throat"] to bring down Nixon.

Nixon mistrusted the CIA with good reason. The CIA mistrusted Nixon with very good reason. It was a time of unprecedented imperial overreach—Nixon authorizing a break-in at the office of the psychiatrist of Daniel Ellsberg—but also, unprecedented openness, because there were hearings following that, and all these things came out.

These things go on in America to a greater or less degree; and really have been, I would say, since the great Red Scare of 1919. Usually, there's not much about them in the media. Those particular years, we got to know a lot about what Nixon was doing and a lot about what the CIA was doing—particularly in Chile.

Technically, Indonesia was a democracy. Sukarno had been elected. Chile was a much more authentically constitutional democracy than Indonesia. It was the model for democracy in South America. Nixon and the CIA subverted it and installed a military dictatorship, which lasted for years.

Freeman: I didn't know you'd been on the Susskind show! Was Chile the topic of the show?

Peter: No, actually it wasn't. It was a show about the Kennedy assassination. And if that could have been a CIA conspiracy, many people would suspect David Phillips might have been part of it.

He was in Mexico when Oswald allegedly went down to visit Mexico. Phillips, actually, made himself a suspect. He made a point of making different statements about the Kennedy assassination, not all of which could be true. He repeatedly contradicted himself. I've always suspected that two CIA officers or ex-officers, David Phillips and Howard Hunt, made it their job to be the pied pipers who drew attention away from what really happened.

Freeman: You didn't talk directly with Phillips about Chile?

Peter: No, I didn't. I may not even have talked directly with him about the Kennedy assassination. I do remember he said something which I was certain was a lie.[94]

What caught my eye (and this is in the poem) was David Phillips's eye. It began to twitch. It became a kind of meter for me when he was lying.

It seemed that the more he was lying, the more vigorously that eyelid was twitching.

Freeman: I love the line "murderer, liar or *even* chief of WH Division."

[laughter]

Peter: Yes, of course, being chief of WH Division meant that, beyond the shadow of a doubt, he was very responsible for what happened in Chile. He was planning the demise of its democracy by eliminating honorable people. I would say that demise is among the worst things that America has done. It has done many questionable things. It has done many good things. But among the most questionable things were these two overthrows accompanied by massacres.

The formula, in both cases, was get rid of the threat of a left-wing party by massacring the party. Again, I'm going back to stuff earlier in the book. I was very upset that I had a colleague, at the University of California, who was calling for the massacre of the left. He was not alone. There were a number of professors.

Usually, they would use more polite language. There was another quasi-academic who wrote of "liquidating the enemy's [i.e. the PKI's] political and guerrilla armies."[95] What does "liquidating" mean?

Freeman: "political armies" equals "civilians."

Peter: Yes, means "civilians." Exactly.

Freeman: This section ends in a way very evocative of the Indonesian massacre.

Peter: Yes, it's an echo. History echoed Indonesia. You're talking about the corpses in the rivers. That's not something that happened by accident. When you want to terrorize a country, this is an efficient way of doing it. General Lansdale and the CIA did it in the Philippines, in the 1950s. It was done in Indonesia in the 1960s. It was also done in Vietnam with Operation Phoenix.[96]

Freeman: Corpses are deliberately disposed of in the river?

Peter: It's in the poem at IV.x, where I quote from a survivor of that era explaining how corpses were "deliberately impaled // on bamboo stakes" to make sure they floated. They weren't just floating by accident.

Freeman: The final thing I wanted to talk about is that the title of the poem comes from this section, from the fliers that were handed out.

Peter: ¡*Djakarta se acerca!* "Jakarta is coming." I originally consciously intended to call the whole book, "Jakarta is Coming," which is a nice rational (I might say "yang") way of alluding to something in the poem.

My subconscious took over. I didn't even have a computer in those days; I had an office typewriter. What my fingers typed wasn't what I told my fingers to type. What came out was *Coming to Jakarta*, which I think is poetically a far superior title. (I guess a more organic sense of all the material I was integrating was slowly gathering in my subconscious.)

After all, the CIA and its assets in Chile themselves turned "Jakarta" from a historical event into a larger symbol for violence in general. From this point on to the end, the poem also enlarges to deal with violence in general, not just in other countries like Chile and East Timor, but since the beginning of history.

IV.xvi–IV.xviii

Whirr of low wings

> For so long
>   I have been sitting at my desk
>   and I tremble
>
>   in front of the terrible blank paper
>   the future from which it gathers words

Freeman: In the last session, we basically came to the end of the politics around the massacre. At this point, I think the poem itself broadens. It becomes almost cosmic, existential.

Peter: There's definitely a tonal shift in IV.xvi. I have to tell you I didn't foresee that coming. It's not like I planned a shift.

I don't want to say I had a vision. I fantasized. I suddenly found myself imagining Berkeley destroyed. Here we have the Radiation Lab (where the atom bomb was developed) and we've been agents of destruction.

Believing as I do that history is matter of action and reaction, and what goes around comes around—America having inflicted great destruction on Vietnam and Korea—then destruction could happen here.

It wasn't a vision exactly but it wasn't exactly my thought either. It was a thought that possessed me. It was very powerful and in the end I incorporated it into the poem. It happened as I was writing the poem and . . .

Freeman: Much like the occasional passage in italics that's not a quote from someone.

Peter: Right.

Freeman: Something within you comes out so strongly that it finds its way into the poem.

Peter: A line that I almost could have italicized but didn't: "The words must be terrible enough." That's not me so much deciding, "Oh I have to make the words more terrible." It's more like—I'm having this amazing thought and it's a terrible thought: The words have to be terrible.

[I had no idea in 1988 when this poem was first published, that three years later, in 1991, 2,000 to 3,000 homes in and around Berkeley would in fact be destroyed by fire, including the one I was living in with my soon-to-be wife, Ronna. I describe that shock in Part One of *Minding the Darkness*, the final volume of this trilogy *Seculum*.

It was an odd coincidence that this vision that possessed me came true. It would not be worth mentioning, except that my loss of home and belongings in the 1991 fire led to another momentary crisis of lostness, and a return to a Heideggerian state of *Dasein* or *being-there*, that recreated in a small way my crisis in Watertown a decade earlier. Each crisis constituted what medieval theologians called a "fortunate fall," an undoing of happiness, like Adams, that would lead to a fuller development—in my case, to the similarly structured poems *Coming to Jakarta* and *Minding the Darkness*.]

Freeman: The vision of fire broadens the poem to become about not just the violence inflicted on specific nations out there, but the world of violence, the culture of violence, the problem of human violence.

Peter: The nature of history itself, yes. As Aeschylus wrote, "violence breeds violence," and we've had so much violence that it has bred much more violence. There are allusions in this section to apocalyptic violence and destruction. The first is in Latin: *accipiens sonitum saxi de vertice pastor* (*Aeneid* 2:308).

Luckily, I have my *Aeneid* here. Aeneas is telling the story of the fiery destruction of Troy to Dido, who is his host in Carthage where he has escaped. He is now recalling, in a time of peace, the violence that he saw as he left.

He woke up and looked out and saw the city burning, and as he recalls it, "I shake myself from sleep and stand with straining ears even as when fire falls on the cornfield . . . spellbound, the bewildered shepherd hears the roar from the rock's lofty peak."

In other words, the shepherd is on a peak, like I'm up on a crag. There are just such crags above the Rad Lab. That line in the *Aeneid* is not exactly a prophecy, because Aeneas is recalling the burning of Troy in the past (which leads to an ominous funeral pyre in *Aeneid* 4). But the *Aeneid* as a whole is another instance of a "fortunate fall," of a loss of Troy through fire leading to the building of a new and better Rome.

The next one is from Zechariah 14:12. Zechariah is perhaps a book by more than one author. It refers to Greece, which makes it a very late book in the Old Testament.

In it Zechariah predicts that God will destroy the enemies of Jerusalem in such a way that "their flesh shall consume away while they stand upon their feet."

That is Zechariah in the fifth century BC. I think that, when I wrote it, I was not just thinking about Hiroshima, but maybe thinking also about the AIDS epidemic that in the 1980s was afflicting all of America, and perhaps the Bay Area in particular, without any sure sign of a cure at that time. It was an affliction that had come, and you couldn't see the end of it.

The third allusion is "Eniwetok the atoll gone." Perhaps only people my age will remember this. America was testing H-bombs. They were getting bigger and bigger. I think this was perhaps the last H-bomb test. They put it on an atoll in the Pacific. The test was so successful that when it was all over, there was no more atoll. It had vanished.

Finally, these quotations from the "Bhagavad Gita." I'm going to try and do this quickly, but it's quite a meaningful allusion. I'm getting into nuclear notions here. By another coincidence, the end of my completed poem was finally revised at Los Alamos, where the atom bomb was developed.

One of the best early popular books about the A-bomb was called *Brighter Than a Thousand Suns*, which is the source here for a quotation from the Bhagavad Gita that Robert Oppenheimer, often called the "father of the atomic bomb," uttered after the bombing of Hiroshima and Nagasaki.

> If the radiance of a thousand suns
> Were to burst at once into the sky
> That would be like the splendour of the Mighty One...
> I am become Death,
> The shatterer of worlds.[97]

He sort of saw himself as a victim of history the way that Arjuna in the Bhagavad Gita is assigned a role to go out and kill, which he doesn't really want to do. Krishna as the god has come to tell him that he must to do it—and that the process is going to happen whether he does it or not. When Arjuna sees Krishna, he sees his face "brighter than a thousand suns"—the title of the book about Los Alamos.

In the following lines "The mouths" ("jaws" perhaps would be a better translation for our purposes) of Krishna he sees are going to devour and mangle the bodies of the warriors. He sees this before it has actually happened; again, it is a prophecy.

It is a vision of the future, as it is explained in the Gita to Arjuna. This is what is going to happen. Your choice is not whether you are going to make it happen or not, but whether you're going to be the agent of destiny, of fate, and be a significant person, or to opt out of destiny and fate.

Oppenheimer was ambivalent about the bomb and particularly very ambivalent about dropping it on Japanese cities. He may have rationalized it by saying, "Well this was something that was going to happen anyway, whether I supported it or whether I opposed it." In other words, he may have seen himself as being like Arjuna in the Bhagavad Gita. This issue is very pertinent to what I will discuss about Achilles in part V—the importance of being in the right relationship to the irrational.

I don't know actually what was going through my mind when I wrote this section because it was so long ago. I suspect at this point I felt I was writing something that had to be written, to come out. Not something that I was making up, if you can see the difference.

Freeman: "The words must be terrible enough."

Peter: "The words must be terrible enough."

Freeman: Going to the next section where you discuss East Timor.

Peter: That's a bit easier. [laughs] Let me say very quickly that 1977 was the bloodiest year of the Indonesian invasion of East Timor. Which only happened after Kissinger and President Ford actually set down in Jakarta for a few hours in 1975, and gave a green light to Indonesia for the invasion.

The East Timorese were throwing off the Portuguese and they wanted to be independent; but no, that was not to be allowed. East Timor had never been part of Indonesia, ever. For centuries it had only been some tribes; and then it became a colony of the Portuguese. The Portuguese left suddenly in 1975, after a revolution in Lisbon. So here was a little vacuum, a little place that wasn't dominated.

Kissinger gave the go-ahead to fill the vacuum. The Indonesians went in. Eighty thousand people were killed. Was that news in *The New York Times*? No, the exact opposite. *The New York Times* had reported a lot about East Timor a year earlier, when there was a debate about what was going to happen to it.

But it stopped reporting when, after Kissinger's approval, Indonesia invaded. Then you had this whole-scale massacre—a repeat actually of the massacre in 1965. And, like the one in 1965, almost zero coverage in the American press until it's over.

[The radio journalist Amy Goodman gave broader dimensions to the silence of the U.S. media about the slaughter in East Timor:

Through this period of 22 years, [the Indonesians] killed a third of the [East Timorese] population—700,000 people. In 1979, when the killing was at its worst, there wasn't one mainstream press article in the New York Times and the Washington Post—not one. ABC, NBC and CBS 'Evening News' never mentioned the words East Timor and neither did 'Nightline' or 'MacNeil Lehrer' between 1975, the day of the invasion, except for one comment by Walter

Cronkite the day after, saying Indonesia had invaded East Timor—it was a 40 second report—until November 12, 1991.][98]

Freeman: The coup in 1965 put in power the army that a decade later went into East Timor.

Peter: Yes. And before the army took over, Sukarno also was a bit of an Indonesian nationalist. He was up to some shenanigans against Malaysia on the island of Borneo which contributed to his downfall.[99]

But the really ruthless government in Indonesia was the Suharto regime. Ironically it was exposed in East Timor by two very brave American journalists, Amy Goodman and Allan Nairn.

A lot of people tell me I shouldn't like Amy Goodman because she doesn't want people to talk about 9/11 on her radio show. But I have great admiration for Amy Goodman, because she and Nairn went in to East Timor at great risk to themselves, and filmed a massacre there. They got arrested and Allan Nairn's skull was cracked by the police with an M-16 stock, which gives you an idea of their behavior even with an American journalist.

Goodman and Nairn managed to save their videotape. They got it out. The American position for more than a decade had been that there were no massacres in East Timor. When these tapes got out, that not only led to the Indonesian withdrawal from East Timor, but I believe it was a factor in the withdrawal of American support for Suharto and eventually the fall of Suharto.

It makes you feel that sometimes journalists and seekers for truth can affect history.

Freeman: Within the poem there's no sense of that at all at this point.

Peter: The attack and videotape hadn't happened yet, when I wrote. At that time, the future for East Timor looked very bleak. Let's say it contributed to my depression that these terrible things could happen without retribution. Once again: not only did they happen, but almost nobody was thinking about them. I knew about it and couldn't tell Americans what I knew. It just made me feel worse.

Freeman: We now come to the final section of part IV, IV.xviii. It's another personal section. It's another story of your encounter with someone and another story of the natural world touching you. Only it's different from before.

Peter: In a way it's a reconciliation, unlike two earlier male-female scenes in North Hatley. [One is in II.xv when I meet the stepdaughter of Walter Lippmann and gave her a little lecture about Germany. Then another scene in III.xiii where I was not present but heard about it from my mother—this American sociologist George Homans losing it and shouting to my mother about Vietnam, "We will win, we will win."]

Here is a kind of reconciled section, a mostly imaginary one, with this very fine woman. In an earlier draft of this I was just regretfully telling her that her ancestries have been involved in things that were less nice than she herself was. (Her name ironically was Hope.)

My mother had quite an influence on this poem. (It's not the first time I've mentioned this.) She said, "But you haven't written about how she played the piano."

So I tried to show Hope in the poem, not just as a passive auditor of my research into the OSS, but as a person, along with her French-Canadian husband Jacques. They lived in North Hatley.

I never had exactly this conversation in real life. It's more like another lecture than a credible conversation. But I did tell her elements of it. Hope was a Canfield, and I knew that the Canfields were important in New York. As I confess here, I made a mistake and thought that she was a cousin of Cass Canfield; but he was from a different family.

But what I want to say about her New York background still fits. So, "*in vino*, I speak truth."

Freeman: Yet, it was not as urgent for you.

Peter: Right.

Freeman: You've come to a kind of peace about it.

Peter: Yes. Let me expand on that a bit and say my imagined words to her had nothing to do with the time I'm writing the poem, in the age of Reagan. Anything that her ancestors did was back in the days when the old Wall Street, and the people in the New York Social Register, ran the Council on Foreign Relations and ran the CIA. They were in power. Under Reagan, there was a different America and these people were no longer in such complete power. I say there's a "new blood // from the Reagan entourage," and they're also plotting dominance, even more overtly.

It's a new crew with slightly different politics from the old crew. Carl Oglesby once talked about the Yankees and the Cowboys. Oglesby's Yankees aren't running America anymore. The Cowboys from the Southwest, Reagan being one of them, now dominate the country. So there's not much point now in lecturing her about what her parents and her grandparents did.

Freeman: It's a wonderful moment that ends the section. Is that . . . ?

Peter: When we go out of the room and down to the waterfront?

> As long as I haven't
> offended you let
> us step out on the lawn

> sloping down to where the
>   streetlight in the maples
>   at the edge of the water
>
> shines on the long-disused
>   lakefront bandstand

Freeman: Yeah.

Peter: There is one allusion here. It's not identified, but I have to tell you. When I say, "What is that whirr / of low wings in the darkness // of the ornamental pine? // *It is the owl*," do you know what I'm alluding to there?[100]

The owl was a symbol of Minerva or Athena, and of wisdom, and of understanding. Hegel once said very memorably, at the beginning of his *Philosophy of History*, that "The owl of Minerva takes wing only at dusk"—meaning that we don't understand things until after they've happened.

This is why history happens the way it does, because history is the product of rational beings, but they don't know what they're doing. It's the same pretty much with what I said in section IV.xvi here, that there's a process, and we are part of the process. [One could say that *Coming to Jakarta* (like the whole trilogy *Seculum*) has a Hegelian dialectical movement, from thesis—part II—to antithesis—part III—to synthesis—part IV.] Only after the process has crystallized and realized itself, then reason can understand what happened.

In part II I often sounded as if I were an authority on events. Here, by confessing my error and fallibility, I am taking a step toward a better relationship to the yin of the irrational. I begin in my ignorance to approach what Eliot in *The Waste Land* called "The Peace which passeth understanding."

On the one hand this section begins to prepare us for the closure of the poem *Jakarta*. But on another, by its tone of acceptance and not-knowing, inspired in part by my mother, it also begins to prepare us for the "yin" movement of *Seculum*, *Listening to the Candle*.

[On second thought, I would say that the owl represents a kind of inadequate closure to the quest for understanding in the earlier part of the poem. But that inadequacy makes it an open closure, reminding me of Virgil saying to Dante at one point in the *Inferno*, "it is time to go" (11:112)—"go" meaning both "leave" and "move on," to a different level of experience. I'm also reminded of Marx's implicit criticism of Hegel, "'Up till now, philosophers have merely interpreted the world; the point, however, is to change it.'"[101]]

It is time, in other words, for part V.

V.i–V.ii

The shadow play

*If you bring forth
what is within you
it will save you*

*if you do not bring forth
what is within you
it will destroy you*

Freeman: In the final part of this long poem we come back to a lot of things. We begin with a return to present-day Indonesian mythology, this shadow play.

Peter: Right, which is based on the Indian great epic, the Mahabharata, of which the Bhagavad Gita is one chapter, the subject of V.i. Arjuna is taught by Krishna how to liberate himself by rising above passion.

I think we already discussed this in the last interview, that the bad people are going to be killed anyway, so the only choice for him is whether he is to be part of the forces of Fate, or whether he is going, for personal reasons, to refuse to fight.

There is irony in the line that the true sage "will learn from *ahimsa* / to kill with detachment." Well, *ahimsa* is usually translated in modern English as "nonviolence"—it means literally not striking or not hurting, not wounding.

So, what Krishna is saying seems very paradoxical. He's saying that if you're going to be filled with the spirit and not do violence to fate, you will go out and kill: not out of a desire to kill, but with detachment. That's why Dan Ellsberg called the Bhagavad Gita Eichmann's bible; and in a way it was Oppenheimer's bible, because this helped Oppenheimer resolve his conflicts about the atomic bomb.

It was going to be made anyway. Should he be part of the process or not part of the process? It was not surprising that he took solace out of the Gita, as justifying what he was doing.

What is very surprising here is that Gandhi called the Gita his mother, because Gandhi was the man who made *ahimsa*, nonviolence, a really powerful force in the twentieth century.

The explanation is that Gandhi allegorized the Gita.[102] He understood it as not to be taken on the literal level of a battle between the Pendawas and their cousins. It's an allegory about the soul.

Arjuna represents the soul becoming detached from the passions of the battlefield. So, Gandhi turned it into an argument for *ahimsa* as he practiced it, which is *not-fighting, nonviolence*. This is the literal meaning of the word, which gets inverted in the Gita and then gets re-inverted to its original meaning by Gandhi.

Freeman: I've never been able to follow exactly what happens in this incident you relate in Saigon with Dan.

Peter: Oh, "leaving Germaine // saw Michel with a pistol"? Well, part V is talking about action, generally. There are some allusions here to the *Iliad* and the *Odyssey* we haven't got into yet.

I see Dan here as a man of action. He had been a Marine; but when he was in Vietnam, he was a civilian in the State Department. He was evaluating pacification, which led to his being out with an infantry unit in the field. When they came under fire, he crawled across a rice paddy and then threw a grenade into the machine-gun nest.

So, I'm respecting him as a man of action in that sense. The second example is when he and a Corsican were both lovers of the same woman, Germaine; and this Corsican Michel—I'm not quite sure of the details—was aiming a gun at Dan outside a Saigon café. When he saw Michel's gun aimed straight at him, he just, in a way that I would never think of doing, reached down to grab some sand to throw into the Corsican's eyes.

But all of that is to be contrasted with the nonviolent Dan, the Dan of enlightened action, *ahimsa*. I guess the main reason Dan is in here is because he is a leading practitioner of *ahimsa*. He is a former Marine and public figure who was converted by Gandhi to nonviolence, to *ahimsa*; and decided that that was the way he would save the world, rather than by working in the Pentagon.

So the poem describes his sitting on the railroad tracks at Rocky Flats as an example of *ahimsa* in action, and contrasts it to the action of throwing a grenade.[103]

> you are free to call this
> either witness or theatre

> it was by all means play
>
> and in the final seconds
> the train stopped

It is the opposite of those actions of men in power done out of greed or ambition. I have told Dan that he is, even though an atheist, a man acting out of faith in things we cannot see. Correcting me, he has described himself as a man of hope; and these strangely contemporary words from St. Augustine would seem to support him: "Hope has two beautiful daughters; their names are Anger and Courage. Anger at the way things are, and Courage to see that they do not remain as they are."

[This courageous symbolic protest, by someone's sitting in front of a train, will be revisited at the same point (V.i) of *Listening to the Candle*, acting there (as here) as part of the transition to the next book.]

Freeman: We move on to the next section, the Gospel of Thomas.

Peter: Yes. In 1979 Elaine Pagels brought out an edition of the Gospel of Thomas, which was discovered in my lifetime. I allude very rapidly to how it was discovered.

Literally, a peasant found all these old papyri, brought them home, left them in the kitchen and his mother burned most of them because they were good fuel. And then by accident, one of them was saved.

Probably there were many, many gospels, like the Gospel of Philip, all esoteric sacred gospels. We call them "Gnostic," because they claimed to be on a higher level of *Gnosis* or knowledge than the Gospels for ordinary people.

At a certain point, the Church condemned them. And the theory is, or Elaine Pagels' theory is, that a monk in a monastery didn't want them to be lost, so he took them out and buried them in a big jar and they stayed there for 1,700 years until our own age, which needs them badly, or at least needs this message: "If you bring forth / what is within you / it will save you // If you do not bring forth / what is within you / it will destroy you."[104]

That's sort of a link between V.i and V.iii, because V.i is about the classics and the perils of interpreting them too literally, whether we are talking about the Bhagavad Gita or the Old Testament.

This leads to the idea that no, we have to bring forth a human reaction, out of ourselves, the way Gandhi did. Which I think is an important message for our time, and it's almost a reason to believe that there is a God: that this message buried for over 1,700 years, when it was too radical for the church authorities, should then be discovered and brought into public consciousness when we need it.

Freeman: It is itself an emblem of this saying.

Peter: Right. Just as Gandhi's voicing his need to allegorize the Gita would also be an example.

Freeman: We have a return now of the ghost of snow. This is the scary, night-time, nightmare vision you had as a child way back at the beginning of this book.

Peter: But I call her an angel this time, meaning that I see her as a messenger bringing a message. [The Greek ἄγγελος, ángelos, means "messenger".]

[Actually, we skipped the reference to the *Iliad* in V.i. I am going to draw attention to it in V.ii.

"The flared ghost // once fleet footed pursuing / down the black oak." That's a reference to the figure of Até (blind folly, rash action leading to ruin, madness) in the *Iliad* (9: 505, 512; 19: 92 is the spirit of the irrational that you encounter in heroic epics. Achilles in the *Iliad*, and later Odysseus in the *Odyssey*, escape ruin by a process of confronting the irrational in themselves, and establishing a more integrated relationship to it. For Odysseus in the underworld this will involve instruction from Tiresias in the underworld, as Dante will also be instructed by Virgil. In a sense, Wordsworth's experience of the Jacobin Terror in Paris, along with his recovery from it, was the same process; and if so, you might say that my experience of Terror, and recovery from it, is a kind of Everyman's recapitulation of that process too. "Jakarta"—as a metaphor for the gross violence of today's world—might be considered Everyman's underworld.

In the *Iliad*, Odysseus is the more rational figure, but he's not the great hero. By contrast the real hero Achilles in the *Iliad* is very irrational. In fact, the very opening line of the poem is, "Sing, goddess, of the anger of Achilles." It is by resolving his relationship to his anger (it's *mênin* in line one but it's related to Até) that he becomes a hero.]

I'm seeing here now that by the end of the poem, I'm really welcoming that ghost of snow, as having being there to alert me to the inadequacy of an overly rational reaction to the world we're in, that you have somehow to be exposed to the terror (because here I at last identify her as Até or Terror). Terror is an experience that in a sense reminds us of our helplessness at the deepest level, so she was a fortunate arrival even though it took another fifty years before she began to issue in poetry.

I pair the memory of the wind-driven angel with a sight I once saw in a small chapel above Lake Como: this grinning skeleton, also white. Underneath it was a quote so scary I thought (when I first saw it) that it wasn't religious.

Then I learned that it's actually in the Old Testament: "You will die and you will not live" [Isaiah, 38: 1]. We have these moments of truth, and I took it at the time as a moment of truth. What I recall from that summer is that skeleton, and not the overcivilized and irrelevant "scholars // rattling their teacups / back in the Villa Serbelloni."[105]

Freeman: Can you give a little background about these stories you end the section with, Steve Carr and then Jack Terrell?

Peter: I had read about Steve Carr as somebody who knew about Contras and drugs in Costa Rica. I'm simplifying it here. You can find Steve Carr in my book *Cocaine Politics* [pp. 154–156]. Steve was a witness to drug trafficking. He said, "They're going to get me." Lo and behold, he was suddenly dead of a cocaine overdose in Los Angeles. And then his death was used to threaten a second witness.

The second witness was Jack Terrill, who was told, "you'll be shot if you step off that plane." Terrell was a man in Washington with whom I investigated the cocaine traffic for a Congressional inquiry [in 1987, long after I had begun the poem in 1980. I have no reason to doubt Terrill's claim he was told this; this was a time of many deaths and death threats in connection with the cocaine traffic. Terrell was an important witness, and his accurate information about drug shipments led to repercussions described at length in my book *Cocaine Politics*. But in my poem *The Tao of 9/11* I tell how Terrell, after I finished the poem, not only lied but deceived me and others on unrelated matters.][106]

Then the third anecdote here is about Al McCoy, who in 1972 published a very influential book, *The Politics of Heroin*. In the same year, I also published a book, not influential at all, *The War Conspiracy*. In 1971, Al was on his way to Laos, and I was finishing up my book. We went together to interview somebody in Palo Alto who I had heard claimed that he had seen opium being loaded onto the CIA's Air America planes.

From my house here in Berkeley, we phoned him and said, "Will you talk to us about this?" He said, "Yes, no problem." The next morning (Al was staying with me in my house) the two of us got in a car very early and went down to Palo Alto. It's about 50 miles from here.

Now he wouldn't talk to us, because during the night someone who had been apprised of the content of our phone call committed an act of terrorism, which was to scare him into not talking, by blowing a hole a foot wide in the steel door of his MG.

He attached a lot of importance to the fact that the wooden floor boards weren't scorched. This meant that it was a professional application of an implosive device, which is what he and his people had done in the Special Forces, when he was fighting in the Vietnam War.

Now that's probably the closest that I have ever come to terrorism in action. It was done in order to dissuade him from talking to me and Al. You would think that would be very much on my mind.

The fact is that I repressed that memory. I use it as an example of how all of us repress memories that do not fit our everyday reality, even people like me, a researcher focused on researching drugs. I repressed this memory. So did Al. [For a closer analysis, see chapter 4 of this book]

I recovered it by writing this poem. There are a lot of memories in here that came back to me as I got more and more in the habit of going deeper into myself and coming up with what it was that was disturbing me. This is one of the very last, it's almost the last memory to come up.

I was pretty sure that Al didn't remember either, and it turned out he didn't. But as I fed him the details, it partially came back to him. In his book, the latest edition of *The Politics of Heroin*, he also alludes to this episode. But he does it by quoting this section of my poem.[107] It's the only part of my poem to get into a political science book.[108]

I start my own book, *American War Machine*, by talking about how—as I say, "We live by forgetting" [V.ii]. We stay sane by not dealing with "all" of the horror that is around us. I approve of that need to keep ourselves sane.

But from time to time, you have to recover disturbing things you have repressed. In this book, *American War Machine*, I start [pp. 1–5] with the same episode and with the fact that Al repressed it just as much as I did. Then I go on to lay out a whole agenda of repressed things that need to be dealt with.

[I'll talk later in this book about how writing *Coming to Jakarta* helped prepare me for writing *American War Machine*.[109] I really do believe that it's only because I wrote the poem that I was able then to write about repressed memory in prose. I believe that even the term "deep politics" may have first occurred to me as I was finishing this poem.]

V.iii

Let there be the courage

      for when the blind woman has seen

    the terrible beauty
        of energy come forth
      to destroy the worlds

O Apollo lord of
    the light you blind me
we cannot like children

    go back to duty and *svadharma*

Freeman: Now that we have been through the entire poem, there are a few topics that I'd like to discuss about the book in general.

One of them is the way in which your personal struggle reflects the human struggle with the political realities that you talk about. This integration is one of the most amazing things about this book.

Peter: As I was rereading this last section, I saw more clearly that the poem as a whole, particularly toward the end, moves from personal to *social* madness. This is represented in the last section by Cassandra and allusion to the McCarthy era which many people said was an era of collective insanity in America, looking for enemies and dangerous threats.

McCarthy was denouncing low-level army clerks and so on. It was insanity. The fact that this poem begins with a moment of near breakdown on my own part but that at the end I could see that it's not just me—that my own lack of mental health has to do with the lack of mental health in the world and specifically in America.

Leading to mass murder, the killing of over half a million people, many of whom were women, children, and school teachers.

Freeman: It's not just the descent into madness but the recovery from that that I think is a parallel between you and what you say needs to happen in the world.

Peter: I'm very struck by the change of tone toward the end. The act of writing the poem over almost a decade really did heal me in an important sense. Instead of just having something inside me that I couldn't even analyze, it was now more out in the open, and above all in a written product.

Of course, when I began the poem I had no idea it would ever be published. But after seven years of editing it a number of people had been reading it and liked it. I felt much more incorporated into a community of friends, poets, and scholars.

This poem was translated into Indonesian by the way, by the quite well-known Indonesian poet Hersri Setiawan. There was a project in 1985 or maybe 1995 to read the poem in Jakarta's Merdeka Square (Freedom Square) as an act of protest against Suharto. So that after my being very alone, very isolated, the poem became a vehicle for opening up to new friendships.

Freeman: The process of surfacing these memories is another aspect in which your personal experience matched what happens often in the world politically. Is this a way in which this poem was a recovery of a lot of your experiences, a lot of your memories?

Peter: Yes.

Freeman: I think part of your prose work in this world has been to help recover facts about connections about things that have been repressed by the world.

Peter: I hadn't been personally aware of the phenomenon of repressed memories until I wrote this poem. Then a lot of things that I had not thought about resurfaced.

The biggest was that memory, in V.ii, of meeting a witness to opium on CIA planes in Southeast Asia. He wouldn't talk to us, because somebody had burned a hole in his car door. (This should have been a vivid memory, but in fact Al and I had totally forgotten it.)

It is such a quintessential example of a repressed memory, because this was one of the most dramatic things that ever happened to me. Somebody was listening to a call from my home phone, and this resulted in an act of terrorism.

This section opens, "Where no vision is / the people die and yet / it is by imagination's failure // that we go on surviving." There's an immediate social function for the status quo in the repression of memory. There's also a higher social function for the future in the ultimate recovery of repressed memories.

My big prose book of 2010, *American War Machine,* opens with this same repressed memory.[110] In that book I talked about the importance of repressing memories to the whole phenomenon of deep politics, that there are levels of political activity, which we don't normally think about or talk about—in which it's considered bad form to discuss topics like the Kennedy assassination or 9/11. [Some observers refer to this as exclusion of topics from "the Overton window" of decorous discourse within the establishment.[111] See chapter II.]

There are certain circles where people will just walk away if you bring such topics up.

I think it's important to have those kinds of prose books. But as I said once in prose, I couldn't have written *American War Machine* if I hadn't already dragged these memories up in poetry, and become aware of them. [Cf. chapter IV].

Freeman: One of the most amazing things to me about this book and your work in general is that you don't consider the repression of either memories or political subjects to be simply bad. You say, "No. This is important too." Both the repression and the recovery are important parts of some kind of process for you. I think that really stands out in your work.

Peter: We are human beings by virtue of doing this. Our personalities develop by the way we forget and remember, and select between these. There is a pattern to the way the memory represses and recovers.

Freeman: You mentioned deep politics. That was another topic I wanted to discuss. Even though I guess you hadn't really come to that formulation of that theme at the time you were writing this book. The book nevertheless touches a great deal on deep politics.

Peter: Yes. You could say that the whole matter of the massacre in 1965 involved me, because of the fact that this was something being repressed in America as well as in Indonesia. I've read quite a lot about how people in Indonesia could not discuss the killings. Suharto came to power as a result of the massacre. He was there until 1998. So that's thirty-three years.

All that time, Indonesians risked their life if they talked about this massacre. [See below, chapter VI.] That had a very powerful psychological effect on the Indonesians. They are now aware of that.

Now they are trying to recover the memories, and also the evidence. For the first time now, they're looking for the mass graves, and so on. This is doing a great deal to help create a more sensible and democratic politics in Indonesia.

But in this colossal repression of the truth there is a bit of a metaphor for what happens in every country. In America, the newspapers just wouldn't talk much about the massacre until it was all over. Then eleven years later when there was another massacre in East Timor, and they repressed all reference to that.

Those events are some specific examples of how politics is conducted generally. That's why I believe deep politics is important, because as long as important truths are suppressed our politics will go on being irrational, and at times I would say even insane. The invasion of Iraq I think was insane [see section IV.xvii].

That will continue as long as we don't have a full consciousness of all the factors working on to generate our policies. So deep politics I say is important, and therefore writing this poem, for me at least, was also important.

There is a message that is reaffirmed in all three of the final sections. I'll go back to V.ii, where I quote from the Gospel of Thomas: "If you bring forth / what is within you / it will save you."

And I repeat most of it at the very end of V.ii: "If you bring forth what is within you. . . ." and then we go into V.iii, and V.iii has what we call an open closure. It doesn't close with a solid message, "Vote Democrat," or "Fight for peace!" or anything. It closes with what is really a reformulation of that quote.

Freeman: You told me that it once ended in an even more open-ended way, and that changed because of the intervention of your mother.

Peter: My mother restored the original ending, yes. I'd like to talk a bit, actually, about the two people who were so helpful to me, Roo Borson and Kim Maltman. It's very relevant to the tone of the end, because Kim was a theoretical nuclear physicist: he did mathematical equations. And the poem ends with many allusions to the first atomic weapon test in the desert in New Mexico, at Alamogordo (the Jornada del Muerto).

I did the next-to-final editing of the poem with the two of them at Los Alamos, in the midst of a violent thunderstorm, an absolutely sensational thunderstorm (like the thunderstorms just before Trinity and Oppenheimer's thought of Krishna).[112] However, the original ending was I think the right ending, and it is open-ended. It simply says that "we cannot like children // go back to duty and *svadharma*" (We can't just try to recreate the past); and then, "let there be the courage / not just to have seen // but to ease into the world / the unreal / breathing within us." And that is, I think, my message.

If everybody does what I did, and just gets their own internal self in more order, then what issues from them will be a contribution to the greater social order. And that a lot of what is wrong with the world now is that people don't do that, and that they come to tolerate intolerable situations. [For example, the unprecedented bombing of civilians in Guernica appalled the world in 1937, where the number of killed was then estimated to be 1,700 (estimated later as from 170 to 300). Now the United States bombs civilians year after year after year—in Fallujah, Mosul, Raqqa, and in regular drone attacks—and Americans barely notice.]

America's a great country and an example to the rest of the world of how different cultures can live together relatively peacefully. Having said that, there's a great deal inside America that is intolerable at every level, from the racism at the base, the way we incarcerate a higher percentage of our population than any other country, up to income disparity, the way that finance is handled at the top, and the way we let bankers "regulate" the banks. And we accept all this because we repress the fact that it's not tolerable.

The poem is written with the awareness that something needs to be done, but I am not going to make a fool of myself and sit down and write out the total formula. But to recognize the need to heal ourselves a little more, so we can try to heal the world a little more, I think is part of the message of the poem.

Freeman: This final section opens, again, with a repetition of motifs we've seen earlier about the unfitness of the human mind, the human soul for this world we live in. And it mentions Bisson and Chevalier.

Peter: "The nightmare / where Bisson and Chevalier were ousted / and they multiply bombs"—that is in general a reference back to the McCarthy period. Bisson and Chevalier were both victims, both lost their jobs, and were both in the shadow of larger figures.

Bisson was an associate of Lattimore, Owen Lattimore, who we talked about in the poem [II.vii, II.xii].[113] Lattimore was persecuted by McCarthy, and McCarthy attacked Bisson as an associate of Lattimore. Chevalier was an associate of Robert Oppenheimer, who was very much a topic in section V.i.

Chevalier was a lecturer in French literature at my University, the University of California, where Oppenheimer was a physicist. He was part of Oppenheimer's circle; and when Oppenheimer had to undergo a series of security checks, he was asked a lot of questions about Chevalier. And both these people lost their jobs, and Bisson was associated with the *Amerasia* case, which McCarthy kept talking about, although there were no major convictions. [*Amerasia* was actually not a case of espionage, but of stealing government secret documents which stayed in this country.]

[Chevalier was accused of trying to steal the secret of the atomic bomb, and when I wrote this poem, I thought I was writing about the injustice that these people lost their jobs. But since I wrote the poem, the Venona transcripts of decoded Soviet messages have been released publicly; and I now know what I didn't know then: that both Bisson and Chevalier were regarded by the KGB as assets for their espionage.

It was a more complicated case than I make it sound in this poem, but the idea that McCarthyism was a nightmare, I think few people would disagree with that now. Maybe I just didn't pick the best example of it.]

> and then by night
> the nightmare

If you don't deal with things sensibly by day, then they come up in nightmarish ways by night.

That takes me to Oppenheimer's first test and then "more than 1200 nuclear explosions / since the Jorñada del Muerto." (That, in Spanish, means "a day's journey of the dead man," but it's the name for the Alamogordo desert area in New Mexico, where in the Trinity test the first atomic bomb was exploded.)

Freeman: Which led, initially, to a number of physicists renouncing their clearance.

Peter: I believe that there was only one physicist who refused to continue working on the bomb. This was Joseph Rotblat, a remarkable man who refused to continue work on the project in 1944, when it became evident that Germany was not developing an atomic bomb.[114]

Freeman: Wow, and none since?

Peter: No. Now, of course, it's different. They only recruit the people who are willing to do it. But yes, there was a great deal of debate within the physicist community about the rightness of dropping the bomb, or how to drop it.

Even if you wanted to drop it, why not drop it on an atoll where there was nobody? Why did you have to pick a populated city, and so on?

Of course, the decision was not made by the physicists at all, it was made by the Army. And that, in itself, is a bit of the—I mean here was a decision of the greatest ethical significance. It was not made by people expert in thinking about ethics, it was made by army generals and Truman.

I think (it's just a personal judgment, but I want to stick it in here) that I wish, for the sake of Americans, for the sake of their conscience and relationship to the rest of the world, [and for the sake of their relationship to Até,] that they had not dropped it on to two densely populated cities.

Freeman: Well, we move on then to the passage that you already talked about, about this idea that we can't just go back to the simple past.

Peter: It's an allusion to the Bhagavad Gita, and the difficulty of the Bhagavad Gita as a text. Most enlightened Hindus read it allegorically now, how to deal with soul and conflict in the soul, and its emphasis on detachment.

But of course, the literal message was, to Arjuna, just get in touch with the fact that there is going to be a lot of killing, and you want to be active on the side of the people doing it justly, not just a victim.

Svadharma: I love it because I speak Polish, and *Sva* means your *own* dharma, your *own* assignment. In Polish, the word would be *swoje*, and *swoje* and *sva*, as so often in Polish and Sanskrit, are almost the same.

The idea is there's a general dharma, which is you don't kill. But Arjuna is a warrior, and so his *svadharma* is that he should kill. That raises the whole idea of caste, and the side note here says special or caste duty. Of course, from a Western perspective, caste duty sounds awful.

But caste probably was not the same when the Bhagavad Gita was composed as it is now, because it has come to mean a hereditary condition and nothing else. Whereas then it was really an ethical state, and they were more open, I think, to movement upwards or downwards depending on your ethical condition to be in the caste.

But the idea was that the noble, the *Arya*, were the fighters, the *Ksatriya*. (We find much the same notion in the aristocratic epics of Homer and Virgil, as opposed to the middle-class epic of Dante.) The warriors with their monopoly of violence were the top caste, and again that is something the world has to evolve away from.

The past, on many levels, whether it is the personal level or the social level, must not simply dictate what we're going to be. We have to change, to bring in to being a better condition of things in the world than the one that is around us.

You haven't allowed me to say something about "Apollo, Lord of the light, you blind me."

Freeman: I also want to ask about the blind woman.

Peter: Oh, the blind woman, yes. That was in New Mexico. I gather it's been exaggerated, but she's from the story as it was told at the time. Before people even knew this was an atom bomb, there was a story put out that there had been an accidental explosion of munitions. But a woman 50 miles away, who was blind, saw the flash. And that's the way it's told in all the early books about the first atomic test.

Now, it's a bit of an urban myth. The woman was legally blind, but first of all she was really a girl, a very young woman. And it was not a miracle that she could tell light from darkness. She was aware that there was a sudden flash of light, but her eyes were capable of doing this.

Freeman: And "Apollo, lord of light"?

Peter: That is from the *Agamemnon* by Aeschylus, and the person speaking is Cassandra. Cassandra is the woman who has been cursed by Apollo: to see the future and to be able to speak the future, but nobody will believe her. And in this special case of the quotation from the *Agamemnon* here, she is not just considered mad, but has gone mad.

Apollo, the god of reason, has possessed her and has made her insane; and that's what she's complaining about, "you blind me;" and she raves. But she's raving because Clytemnestra, the wife of Agamemnon, is going to kill her and Agamemnon, and she knows that it's about to happen, and nobody believes her.

It's a bit presumptuous, perhaps, of me to identify with this, but the prophetess at the end here is not being listened to, because she is speaking truth amid a social madness which corresponds with the madness of McCarthyism. And out of all this madness, I want to escape into a world where the unreal within us comes forth.

Freeman: On that note, let's do our final reading of the series.

Peter: I have one more thing to say before we do that. I think most people would see this, but in the last triplet,

> let there be the courage
> not just to have seen
>
> but to ease into the world
> the unreal
> breathing within us –

the last two lines can be read in two different ways. You can read it "the unreal" that is breathing within us, or you can read it "the unreal breathing" that is within us. And as very often in my poetry, it's ambiguous on purpose.

I want both those meanings about this formless presence to be possible. And of course it's an act of faith. I believe, like Thomas, that there is within us, human nature (our DNA) what will save us.

The trouble is that we're all so distorted by the painful world that we grow into, that it's very difficult for us to be aware of what our really human nature is. That's my act of faith—that yes, less damaged people are happier and closer to their potential than those who have been more damaged and respond in kind. That's why doing terrible things to children is so terrible, because it gets them off the track of their potential, and then we have the world that we have.

At the same time, a life without disturbance is also inadequate; we need a "fortunate fall" in order to grow. And we need somehow to become aware that we are damaged, and to heal ourselves by exploring this awareness. So, in my case, I am grateful to my crisis in Watertown for that.

II. Trauma, Poetry, Politics, and the Mystery of Hope

"Erschaffend wurde ich gesund [By creating I returned to health]"

—Heine, "Seven Songs of Creation"[1]

The first complete draft of *Coming to Jakarta* was written frantically in about six weeks, following an all-night panic attack in the wake of Ronald Reagan's election in 1980. In the course of a sleepless tossing, I became convinced for a few hours that I was on the point of becoming irreversibly insane. Worse, I was convinced that the three decades of efforts I had put into making America a more just society had been at best fruitless, or perhaps even counterproductive.

Such thoughts, always at the back of my slightly neurasthenic mind, had forced themselves on me before. But on this occasion, it was as if the back of my mind "took over" in a coup, pushing common sense and practical reason to one side. Then, starting a day or two later, this trauma was succeeded by an obsessive six-week period when I wrote poetry, often furiously, in most of my free moments. I covered pages and pages, often with little idea, and at first no idea, of what I was doing, other than recording suggestions from the same uncontrollable back of my mind, now somewhat calmed and imposing its own kind of order. Looking back, I see that I was often in a kind of trance, a mental state akin to dreaming and daydreaming, where I expressed what came to me, rather than what I rationally thought.

I have since realized that many poets can write in something like this trancelike, half-conscious way. This is why so many of them claim that their poems were often inspired, sometimes even dictated, by an inner Muse or (Czeslaw Milosz's term) *daemonion*.[2] A classic instance is the speech of Bernart de Ventadour in Dante's *Purgatorio*: "I am one who, when love breathes in me, takes note, and in that manner which he dictates within go on to set it forth" (*Purgatorio*, 24: 52–54).

In the final edits of this book I have had a further insight into the half-conscious, half-mesmerized condition of the poem's inception. I see now the link between the "doubleness" I kept discussing with Freeman in the text of the poem—between the yang or rational passages and the more mysterious yin passages—and the doubleness of the condition in which I often wrote.[3]

I am not in any way a neuroscientist, but I am utterly convinced of the doubleness of my own brain, with rational thoughts emanating from my frontal lobes and more mysterious utterances from somewhere deeper. Surely, we can see evidence of this doubleness in the near universality of dreaming: an irrational mental activity, distinct from and replacing Cartesian thought.

Since Eliot first wrote of doubleness in poetic drama,[4] it has become quite common to discuss doubleness in literature, but critics do so in different ways. Some (as did Eliot, or myself a moment ago) see doubleness as a lexical feature in texts.[5] Sometimes the doubleness is seen as sociological, as when the Canadian critic Linda Hutcheon, following Albert Memmi, grounds the doubleness of postcolonial literature in "the doubleness of the colonized in relation to the colonizer, either as model or antithesis."[6] Or doubleness can be seen as psychological, as when the critic Robert Langbaum suggests that mythic language draws on "a doubleness of language" that reflects "our doubleness of consciousness and selfhood."[7]

All these discussions of doubleness in their contexts share a common transcendence of common sense and the classical law of non-contradiction, as expounded for example by Aristotle: "It is not possible to say truly at the same time that the same thing is and is not a man" (*Metaphysics* 1006b, 35). In consequence, these meanings of doubleness also blend easily into one another. And I am struck how all of them help adumbrate the dimensions of my poem.

They overlap also with an often-quoted characterization of postmodern literature,

> in its ironic self-undermining critical stance and in its commitment to doubleness—that is, to the juxtaposition and equal weighing of such seeming contraries as the self-reflexive and the historically grounded, the inward-direction of form and the outward-direction of politics.[8]

Until I read this I had always considered myself one of the last modernists, in the tradition of Eliot and Pound. But I hear in this dense passage echoes of what Freeman in the interviews told me which he saw in *Coming to Jakarta*. So I now see why my friend James Schamus assured me, years ago, that I was really a post-modernist without knowing it.[9]

My own notion of doubleness is that serious poetry is disruption of the presentational self and the presentational world by messages from an Other within us. I see this Other, which I describe as "the back of the brain," as like the American Wild West, a source of lawless inspirations, which can be anything from uplifting to demoniacal.[10] I shall return later to my belief that our emergent core culture is a domain of dispute between these inspirations, and to my prevailing belief, which I myself cannot always subscribe to, that in the long course of time the better inspirations will prevail.

For now, let me just say that I do see my poem as exhibiting an "equal weighing of such seeming contraries as the self-reflexive and the historically grounded, the inward-direction of form and the outward-direction of politics." I was certainly guided while writing the poem by the sixties dictum that "the personal is the political." Starting with my own terror in Watertown, the poem felt its way gradually toward the massacre of Indonesian leftists in 1965.

The theme of bringing memory to consciousness is part of the process of unfolding in the poem itself. But this theme does not catch a deeper dialectic in the poem between what might be called the yang of consciousness and urban civilization, represented by my father and our politics, and the less definable forces of yin or mystery and primitive culture with which yang needs to find an equilibrium.

Interviewed about my poem by my friend Freeman Ng, I saw more and more clearly how my inability to share what little I knew about U.S. involvement in the bloody Indonesian massacre of 1965, reinforced by the collective resistance of North American society to listen to this, contributed to my brief but terrifying panic attack in November 1980, which led to my writing *Coming to Jakarta*.

As will be seen, there were other factors. The poem alludes (IV.i) to the suppression in the same year by my publisher of another book of mine, on the John F. Kennedy assassination, that had been planned for a first printing of 250,000 copies. That book, *Beyond Conspiracy*, had represented my last faint hope of converting what we then still called the movement to reopen the issue of who killed John F. Kennedy (a relatively small movement in which I had played an even smaller role), into a chance to revive so many hopes for America that died in the 1960s.

In editing *Poetry and Terror,* I have come to see my poem as also an elegy, not just for the dead in Indonesia, but for the decay of my first marriage, and for the passing of the Sixties era, when so many of us imagined that a Movement might achieve major changes for a better America.

CRISIS AND POETIC HEALING

The slow recovery and voicing of memories in the poem helped to heal my distorted mind. Much later I saw that this therapeutic response of poetry to psychological trauma characterized the other long poems that were important in it. After World War I, T.S. Eliot completed *The Waste Land* while being treated at a psychological clinic in Lausanne. After World War II, Pound notoriously wrote the *Pisan Cantos* (by far his greatest) after a breakdown from being caged by the US Army as a war criminal for six weeks in the open air.[11]

Perhaps, the best example is Wordsworth's *Prelude* of 1805. Seamus Heaney writes about Wordsworth's

> breakdown in the early 1790s because of emotional crises (the outbreak of war between England and France separated him from his French love and mother of his child) and political confusions (the reign of Terror had dismayed supporters of the Revolution) [followed by] the 1798 edition of *Lyrical Ballads*, the epoch-making volume that initiates modern poetry.[12]

Wordsworth experienced a second burst of creativity in March 1804, perhaps provoked by Napoleon's murder in the same month of the Duc d'Enghien.[13] In a few months, Wordsworth composed not less than eight books of the 1805 thirteen-book *Prelude*. In these so-called French books, Wordsworth for the first time dealt at length with his hopes for and disillusionment with the revolution, and even his breakdown itself—albeit still very obliquely with his love for Annette Vallon.

All of these works contain for me a haunting engagement with suffering that I do not find in other great long poems, such as Byron's *Don Juan* or *Paterson* by William Carlos Williams. Pound's *Pisan Cantos* have this additional feature in common: that after confessing to having inflicted great pain (*les larmes que j'ai créees m'inondent*—Canto 80), they also seem at their end to anticipate an alternative and different world (*out of all this beauty something must come*—Canto 84). They are in short examples of the "alterity" that Theodore Adorno sees in all literature, and what I call doubleness.[14]

They lack, however, what I see as the deeper archetypal movement in Wordsworth's *Prelude*, where alienation from the yang of overly urban civilization (Cambridge, London, Paris) is healed by a return to the yin of his childhood Lake District (reinforced by his sister). A similar movement can be seen in most of those modern poets I most admire (Yeats, Milosz, Levertov, Duncan, Heaney), just as its absence in other major poets (Zbigniew Herbert, Larkin, much of Ginsberg) helps explain what I see as ultimately limited about their worldview.[15]

The distinction I am making here is not one of purely "poetic" merit. Great poetry is as likely to arise from despair as from hope, from Larkin as from Milosz. And our poetic canon, in what Octavio Paz once called "a tradition against itself,"[16] is dialectical, enriched by disputes such as that which Milosz had with Larkin.[17]

POETRY AS "A KIND OF HIGHER POLITICS," AND THE MYSTERY OF HOPE

Coming to Jakarta is a process poem, one which slowly discovered its form, intention, and content through the act of being written. In the early sections I move from an account of a personal crisis to the discovery that I must write about terror; and then, two sections later, that this will be about the 1965 Indonesia massacre I have ceased talking about because no one will listen. This painful process is at first conscious, but this exploration of conscious memories leads unexpectedly in the poem's middle to a surprising recognition of my own tiny role in this global catastrophe. The resulting examination of my own limitations leads to more and more ignored memories, and these in turn to a special category of memories that are at once both the most striking and the most securely repressed.

The final and most striking example, as we have seen in chapter 1, was of an actual terrorist bombing (in response to a phone call I had made) of an MG sports car in Palo Alto, California (V.ii). This bombing was so outside my normal personal experience that one might logically have expected the memory to remain forever at the forefront of my consciousness. But in fact, my memory of it quickly disappeared, because it was not compatible with the assumptions by which I lead my life.

Writing the poem empowered me to recover far more repressed memories than the poem needed or could include. In editing it I limited myself chiefly to those for which, as in the Palo Alto incident, there was a corroborating eyewitness. I slowly became aware of the process which psychologists call homeostasis, a condition of equilibrium maintained by the reduction or elimination of a something (a tension, drive, or fact) disturbing it. The suppression of memory is a common way of sustaining the homeostasis necessary for survival. The recovery of memory, through poetry, can contribute to the disturbance of homeostasis that is necessary for change.

This psychological denial and suppression, even of truth, is easily seen on the collective level, where political concerns limit discourse to what has been called the "Overton window."

> Under this theory, put forward by public policy expert Joseph Overton, the public is willing to consider only a few ideas or scenarios as reasonable—those are the ones that reside within the window. Radical notions remain outside the window, unfit for serious debate.[18]

But it is inevitable on the personal level as well. "Human kind," as T.S. Eliot wrote, "cannot bear very much reality" (*Four Quartets*, 1: 43). Top-down power, in the past, has to a considerable extent been strengthened by our willing participation in the suppression of truth.

After the monstrosities of World War II, European writers slowly developed the notion of *travail de mémoire, Erinnerungsarbeit,* or memory work: the task of authors to correct falsified history.[19] In Toronto I once heard a German critic, invoking his own experience of Nazi Germany, introduce *Coming to Jakarta* as an example of memory work. This notion of memory work has stuck with me through the years. More and more, I have seen the cleansing and healing of the mind as a process that can go much further back than immediate past history, to our earliest experiences and aspirations.

Memory work, in other words, can lead, if pursued far enough back, to the peace that comes from living in truth.[20] And truth, the ultimate weapon of the nonviolent, needs to be recovered if domination by official lies and suppression becomes so oppressive that it must be diminished. The longer a society remains alienated from human needs, as in the Soviet Union, the more urgent the need for an alterity based on greater honesty about its ugly truths, as offered by writers like Solzhenitsyn and Pasternak.

But I regard my poem's obsession with the ugly truth of massacre as only the beginning of a deeper inner movement. In chapter 1, commenting on sections III.vii, I refer to "violent surges of energy which are inside us but not really ours because we don't control them"; and then I see their analogue in deep political behavior, In chapter 4 I call this the poem's "gradual confrontation with the disturbing reality that there is a gap between the visible yang world as we think we know it, and darker more inscrutable yin forces at work in the world, and also in ourselves."

This gap reflects my take on the doubleness in the human psyche and condition, currently represented internally in our brain, and externally by the doubleness of our human existence. I see humanity as not just as a present "condition" whose inadequacies we can try to understand; it is also a "process" toward an unknowable future we can only believe and hope will be better.

More succinctly, we both are human and, over millennia, are slowly becoming more human. In other words, I reject Aristotle's claim that "It is not possible to say truly at the same time that the same thing is and is not a man" (*Metaphysics* 1006b, 35). Our nature is given an initial determination by our genes at birth, but also slowly evolves toward what Edmund Burke called our "second nature," shaped by our cultural environment.[21] Burke's view of second nature was conservative, because he ignored the natural evolution of cultures.

My own is dialectical, perhaps even radical. Human birth-nature is evolving, if at all, very slowly, in geological time. Our second nature, in contrast, is evolving relatively rapidly, in historical time. For example, most of us no longer regard feeding slaves to lions as entertainment. Within just a century, lynchings have lost social approbation. And we as humans have not just experienced this change; we have contributed to it.

Science since Burke's time has come up with terms we can use to describe the evolution of cultures. One term is *ethology*, defined as the study of the evolutionary history of patterns of behavior.[22] Another, even more pertinent to this argument about doubleness, is *ethogeny*. These terms were used first to describe the development of habits in animals, but they are applied here by me (as by others) to the history of cultural evolution in humans. In short, I define *ethogeny* as the slow evolution of both our culture and our "second nature."

My own use of the term *ethogeny*, to denote the evolution of our cultural environment, makes no pretense to being scientific. Instead it is dialectical, recognizing that not only does environment contribute to our "second nature;" so also do some human creations contribute to it. In particular, I believe that a few really great poems, representing a major break with their prevailing mindset, can be called "root texts" in our cultural development. These are the poems Ezra Pound had in mind when he advised a young W.S. Merwin to "Read seeds, not twigs."[23] More narrowly, a poem which proceeds from a successful revolt in a poet's psyche, against an inadequate prevailing rationality, can contribute in the long run to a collective revolt against a failing system in society.

This has revived my faith, which was strengthened in me by my years of translating Polish poetry with Czeslaw Milosz, that poetry can contribute to political as well as personal healing. I am with those who consider the tacit republicanism of Milton's *Paradise Lost*, which can be seen as reflecting a nostalgia for the demise of the Cromwellian Commonwealth, to have been a source for the middle class culture that led to the American Revolution.[24] The debt acknowledged by the Solidarity movement to the poetry of Czeslaw Milosz is a clear vindication of Milosz's guiding conviction during World War II that his poetry was "a kind of higher politics, an unpolitical politics."[25]

In short, the narrative of our given nature and emergent nature cannot be separated from the narrative of our collective nascent humanity and emergent humanity. And root poems contribute to this narrative, as we see if we contemplate the new stages in cultural development represented by, say, the *Odyssey*, the *Aeneid*, the *Divine Comedy*, and Wordsworth's *Prelude*. Reading these poems as a sequence, one has to recognize that the sequence represents cultural progress, or what we might call an ethogenic metanarrative.

This enables a human evolution on the cultural level. One might even say, adapting Haeckel, that our cultural ontogeny recapitulates our cultural ethogeny.[26] Some of the patterns recapitulated may be transient, as when a few bearded Beatniks in the '50s were followed by a multitude of beards a generation later. But the inspired revulsion against slavery of Bishop Wilberforce and William Lloyd Garrison has now been internalized in the West, as part of our second nature.

As an example of how traumatic experience can produce poetry, which in turn can contribute to social change, I would like to mention what the soul music singer Nina Simone called her "first civil rights song," "Mississippi Goddam:"

> Alabama's gotten me so upset,
> Tennessee's made me lose my rest.

Her account of how the song came to her roughly parallels my experience with *Coming to Jakarta*:

> When I heard about the bombing of the church [the 16th Street Baptist Church, Birmingham, 1963] in which the four little black girls were killed in Alabama, I shut myself up in a room and that song happened. Medgar Evers had been recently slain in Mississippi.... When I sat down the whole song happened. I never stopped writing until the thing was finished.[27]

Simone performed her song at the 1965 Selma-to-Montgomery marches, where she met and engaged with Martin Luther King. Six days after the second march, on March 16, 1965, President Lyndon Johnson went on national television to pledge his support to the Selma protesters and for the passage of a Voting Rights Act. I don't want to exaggerate the limited successes of this process: three years later King was also murdered, and soon afterwards Simone, devastated, left America for Africa and Europe. But I can still claim that the story of "Mississippi Goddam" illustrates the dialectics of ethogeny. Few would deny that today in the South both politics and what Burke called the second nature of those living there have been irreversibly changed, from a process to which "Mississippi Goddam," born of trauma, contributed.

As I said earlier, I now see my poem as an elegy, not just for the dead in Indonesia, but for the passing of an era when many of us had hopes for major changes to America. Songs were so important to sustaining those unfulfilled hopes, which were expressed most succinctly in the spiritual, "We shall overcome!" But many other songs, often more quizzically, also focused on our hopes for change, such as Bob Dylan's "How many roads must a man walk down/Before . . . ?" Most of the songs I remember as popular in that very different era dealt, however mysteriously or obliquely, with our hopes for change.[28]

Dylan's lyric catches the mystery of our hope, in a way that helps me understand my poem. The link is not the explicit question about war, "Yes, how many times must the cannon balls fly?" This line, precisely because so sensible, is the least vibrant with that mystery. (Good poetry is not about arms control.) The link is in the first questions that expresses, albeit trapped in a sexist noun and pronoun, our belief that we are not yet what we must be to be human. Nor where we should be.

That belief was strongly reinforced in me in the 1960s, even after violence escalated on all sides. It was reinforced again by writing the poem, and now yet again by thinking and writing about the poem. I have come to believe that it is both human in our present condition to be violent, and even more human to hope and work for a process of diminishing violence.

As a young adult, I was taken with Sartre's notion that humans are existence without essence, in which case violence and nonviolence would be equally human. Even then I believed that we all live for the future as well as in the present: both assassins and victims cherish hope. And now I am convinced that Sartre was wrong: humanity contains within itself, as if encoded in our moral DNA, a slow but emergent bias, and thus process, toward nonviolence. This bias explains why, as I report in section IV.x of the poem, some members of the assassination gangs in Indonesia "experienced recurring nightmares."[29]

Here is the relevance of poetry: not to supply practical answers (what poets are not good at), but to reinforce the search within ourselves for what can prevail in our slowly developing history.[30] *Coming to Jakarta* quotes from the Gospel of Thomas, "If you bring forth what is within you, it will save you" (V.i). In this it recognizes both the need to be what we now are not, and also that the remedy to our fallen condition lies within ourselves.

In my poem, I write near the beginning of "the long voyage home // to where / we have never been" (I.iii). And at the end I pray, in the spirit of Thomas, for

...the courage
not just to have seen

but to ease into the world
the unreal
breathing within us (V.iii)

III. America's Culpability in Indonesia, and Why We Should Acknowledge It

"The possession of power is inevitably fatal to the free exercise of reason."[1]

In a September 2014 address to the nation, President Obama attacked ISIL (ISIS, the "Islamic State") as "terrorists . . . unique in their brutality. They execute captured prisoners. They kill children."[2] But of course such terrorism in the last half-century is hardly "unique." Nor is it unprecedented. Still less is it confined to America's foes. In fact, the first major Muslim extermination campaign against civilians, killed without trial for their "Westernness," occurred a half-century ago, on a far, far vaster scale. And it happened with active American encouragement and support.

I am referring to the Indonesian Army's massacre of leftists in 1965, as a prelude to the overthrow of President Sukarno. In that year, a rebellious cadre of anti-Communist generals, with U.S. encouragement, resolved the question of Indonesia's uncertain future, by killing and arresting members and sympathizers of the Indonesian Communist Party or PKI. (The PKI was the nation's largest political party and also the largest Communist party in the world outside of the Sino-Soviet bloc.) The total number of those killed will remain forever unknown, but was in 2016 was estimated by BBC News to have been somewhere between "at least half-a-million and up to three million people within a year."[3]

Although the Indonesian Army presided over the massacre, it mobilized major Muslim youth groups, chiefly Ansor, to carry out many of the actual murders.[4] A large number of people besides Communists and their families were summarily killed, including rural educators. The massacre has been commemorated, appropriately, as "The Forgotten Holocaust of Indonesia."[5]

In recent years, some British scholars and journalists have acknowledged candidly "that the British and American governments did not just cover up the massacre: they had a direct hand in bringing it about."[6] But it is still almost impossible to discuss this involvement in America itself. Two essays I wrote on the topic were published in Canada, Great Britain, the Netherlands, France, Germany, and four times in Indonesia—but never (except online) in the United States.[7]

My claim in chapter 5 is twofold: (1) that the United Kingdom and United States were actively involved in support for the massacre, and (2) before that, in the supposedly pro-communist false-flag coup attempt (later given the derogatory name "Gestapu," or "G30S"), that was the pretext for the massacre. Bradley Simpson, the American scholar who has supplied the best documentation for the first claim, says of the second claim only that "American historians . . . have spilled much ink" on it.[8] In this and other ways, it has been my experience that my argument, that Americans could have helped induce perhaps the largest massacre since the Shoah, remains very unfashionable in America, even among those otherwise sympathetic to my mode of political analysis.[9]

Since 1980 there have been increasing references in America to "postcoup" U.S. general assistance to the new Suharto military junta, during and after the massacre. Tim Weiner, for example, writes in his CIA history of "$500,000 of medical supplies . . . with the understanding that the army would sell the goods for cash."[10] However, there was active U.K. and U.S. encouragement and support for the massacre itself.[11] As documented in chapter 5, government-connected American academics, like Guy Pauker and William Kintner, urged their contacts in the Indonesian army, both directly and in print, to "to strike, sweep their house clean," while "liquidating the enemy's political and guerrilla armies."[12]

The support was not merely rhetorical. In July 1965, two months before the coup, and at a time when Congress thought it had terminated U.S. aid to Indonesia, Rockwell-Standard secured a contractual agreement to deliver two hundred light aircraft to the Indonesian Army in the next two months.[13] According to Bradley Simpson, the U.S. government also provided the Indonesian Armed Forces with covert monetary assistance, small arms from Thailand, and communications equipment.[14]

According to a Soviet commentator, Boris Vetin, "The CIA . . persuaded the top leaders of the [Indonesian] land forces . . . to enter into a *ralliement* with the Muslim Masjumi," a Muslim party which (a former CIA officer once told me) the CIA had backed generously in the previous 1957 election.[15] Vetin's claim is entirely consistent with what we now know about the army's "civic action" programs sponsored by the United States (see chapter 5). And it is consistent with CIA recruitment of the Muslim Brotherhood and other Muslim groups for anti-communist programs in the Middle East and elsewhere.[16]

One year earlier, a memo to President Lyndon Johnson from Secretary of State Dean Rusk, on July 17, 1964, made clear the importance of U.S. military aid to anti-Communist elements in the Indonesian Army: "Our aid to Indonesia . . . we are satisfied . . . is *not helping Indonesia militarily*. It is however, *permitting us to maintain some contact with key elements in Indonesia* which are *interested in and capable of resisting Communist takeover*. We think this is of vital importance to the entire Free World."[17]

Finally there is the admitted but still disputed fact, first reported by journalist Kathy Kadane in May 1990, that in the course of the massacre, personnel in the U.S. Embassy passed up to 5000 names of alleged PKI cadres to the Indonesian Army. Though an Embassy officer, Robert Martens, acknowledged to the *New York Times* "that he had passed the list of names," the *Times* nonetheless chose to run a belated and "balanced" story in which U.S. Ambassador Marshall Green dismissed the claim of Embassy involvement as "garbage".[18]

AMERICA AND VIOLENCE

Due to the recent rise of mass shootings, concern about U.S. violence within the United States is securely inside the "Overton window" of publicly acceptable discourse. But the situation is quite different with respect to American violence abroad. Americans, like the British before them, still tend to assume that their nation's actions are "clearly directed to others' benefit. . . . Where others push their national interest, the U.S. tries to advance universal principles."[19] Thus they pay almost no attention to the America's increasing international reputation for violence. (During the build-up toward the Iraq War, for example, "distrust of the U.S. overseas" (as Paul Krugman reported) "reached such a level, even among our British allies, that a recent British poll ranked the U.S. as the world's most dangerous nation—ahead of North Korea and Iraq."[20])

The English language has responded to the proliferation of violence in the world with new terms to deal with it, its effects, and its alternatives; and this facilitates a more civilized discussion of them.[21] One of the most recent terms is PTSD, or post-traumatic stress disorder (1982), a concept we owe to the Vietnam War. The U.S. Department of Veterans Affairs estimated in 2009 that PTSD at that time afflicted 20 percent of Iraqi war veterans.[22] But a more sensitive assessment might reach a far higher estimate. As a poet, I would say that for a very long time, violence has afflicted our whole culture, and most of us in it, with PTSD.

In general, however, America today seems to be hardly aware of how militarized it has become. In 2017, there was much talk of the Congressional inability to pass any domestic legislation. Almost no attention was paid when, "In a rare act of bipartisanship on Capitol Hill, the Senate [in September 2017] passed a $700 billion defense policy bill . . . with a Pentagon budget that far exceeds what President Trump has asked for. Senators voted 89-9 to approve."[23]

I see U.S. violence, and what might be called the violence-industrial complex, as a matter of urgent concern, not just for international comity, but for individual Americans as well. Violence and massacres are not healthy for a society, and they are not healthy for the individuals within it.[24] For the world to become less violent, American global leadership must become less violent; and the non-violence of so many of its people must become more powerful. And all this in turn will require narrowing the gap between U.S. acts of violence abroad, and Americans' awareness of them.

One small step toward this goal would be, I suggest, awareness of U.S. involvement in, and responsibility for, the holocaust of 1965.

I firmly believe that the health of America, and of Americans, will depend on greater recognition of, and alienation from, this country's continuous deep history of violence, both overseas and at home.[25] It seems obvious to me now that these two urges, to heal oneself and to heal the world, are ultimately one and the same.[26]

IV. "Gaps" of Consciousness; or, How Writing *Coming to Jakarta* Led Me to Deep Politics

"I think that the job of poetry, its political job, is to refresh the idea of justice, which is going dead in us all the time."

—Robert Hass[1]

FOREWORD

At the end of chapter 1, I recall a moment of violence that I should have remembered but in fact forgot: the terroristic firebombing of someone's car in peaceful Palo Alto. This chapter will explore, at great length, my two responses to that small encounter with violence, first by repressing my memory of it, and then recovering that memory through poetry.

But first, let me say a little more about that significant gap, between what happened and what I then remembered. That gap, between reality and consciousness, is what this chapter is about, what this book is about, what civilization is about. The event gave me a glimpse of forces not recognizable in the commonly shared awareness of America, and thus put me on a frontier between personal sanity and madness. By repressing the memory of that glimpse, I rejoined a society that was not sane. By recovering many such memories, I came to see contemporary America, for all its indisputable advantages and benefits, as also insane.

At present there is no society, just as there is no individual, that can be called fully sane. As Nietzsche wrote, "Madness in individuals is something rare; but in groups, parties, peoples, and ages, it is the rule."[2] But madness through the ages is not evenly dispersed. In eighteenth-century Europe, the times were quiescent, while poets like William Cowper and Christopher Smart experienced madness privately. This was followed by the Jacobin Revolution in France, wild carnage, a violent counter-revolution, and the great healing poetry (despite their mental illnesses) of Blake, Hölderlin, and Wordsworth. Their engaged poetry, unlike Cowper's and Smart's personal poetry, changed collective consciousness.

That dialectic between revolution and counter-revolution, still evolving and not resolved, has drawn America into an era of institutionalized violence that more and more observers are calling insane. One such observer is Daniel Ellsberg, whom I quote in *Coming to Jakarta* as asking "Are we not Jonestown?" (IV.x).[3] In *The Doomsday Machine*, Ellsberg is more explicit: in his words,

> any social system [that puts] first use of nuclear weapons in the hands of one human being . . . still worse in the hands of an unknown number of persons—*is in core aspects mad*. Ours is such a system. We are in the grip of institutionalized madness.[4]

Thomas Merton, when contemplating the horrors of nuclear warfare, came to refer to it as the "unspeakable," which James Douglass later defined as "an evil whose depth and deceit seemed to go beyond the capacity of words to describe."[5] But so many aspects of our developed class society, not just its nuclear policy, are unspeakable.

To have sanctioned the Indonesian massacre of 1965 is unspeakable. It is unspeakable that, at the time, McGeorge Bundy in the White House told LBJ that the massacre (which he chose to refer to as "Events in Indonesia since the abortive September 30th coup") was "a striking vindication of US policy." [6] Truly normal people cannot absorb this fact seriously and continue to live normal lives. And if we begin to open our minds to the realities of violence, much more comes into view, such as America's ruthless displacement of earlier inhabitants, or its treatment of slaves and their descendants.[7] And if we open our minds too far, we impair our ability to cherish what is good and precious in the world around us. As I say in a poem, "We are made schizophrenic / from loving America."[8]

I want to make it clear that I love America, believe in America, and above all believe in its ability to change. But there is one thing that unites all Americans today: the sense that, despite all that is right and good in this country, something is profoundly wrong. My own awareness of this wrong concerns violence: America, once the world's best hope for diminishing global violence, has now sustained for decades the most violent foreign policy in the world.[9] Writing *Coming to Jakarta* empowered me to see clearly how sick I had become by not confronting this expanding violence before.

DEEP POLITICS AND ENGAGED POETRY

This realm of unspeakable truths leads to two abnormal phenomena that would appear to be unrelated, but in fact are not: deep politics and engaged poetry.

IV. "Gaps" of Consciousness; or, How Writing Coming to Jakarta

Deep politics can be defined as politics which is not normally discussed in a corrupted society. And *engaged poetry* can be defined as utterances that raise issues with, or even rebel against, the normalcies of a corrupted society.

For most of my life I have felt split between two conflicting approaches to reality. As a political researcher, I have tried rigorously and methodically to understand American politics and its relation to violence in the world. Meanwhile as a poet, I have responded to the boundless complexities of reality with intuitive impulses to say what moved me. Sometimes, as in much of this poem, I have done so almost involuntarily (the way so many poets have been described as being "dictated" to, by a muse or daemon).

In recent years, I have come to realize the extent to which these two sides of my life have become synergistic. Each approach can be characterized as an attempt, using radically different methods but toward the same goal: to become more aware of forces in our life that are not easily discernible, and to express them in ways outside normal logic. Thus each approach for me has been an exploration, by different methods, beyond the frontier (and gap) separating the known from the unknown.

My awareness of this synergy arose primarily from writing my poem *Coming to Jakarta* and then decades later, encouraged by Freeman, reflecting on it. The awareness has meant a healing of my divided and occasionally tormented self. As I suggested in chapter 1, one way to describe this healing is to see my development from a rational but alienated anti-war journalist at the poem's outset, to someone more committed to nonviolence with all my being, intellectually, emotionally, and spiritually, at its end.

There are many ways one could illustrate this. Here I shall contrast my condescending lecture in II.xv to Walter Lippman's beautiful step-daughter Gregor, whom I tried ineptly to impress with irrelevant comments about Germany, and my reconciliation with another well-connected woman at the end of Part IV, to whom I speak fallibly (but "with complete decorum / not like with Gregor"), before suggesting that "we step out on the lawn" to where one can hear the "whirr / of low wings in the darkness . . . *the owl*" (IV.xviii).[10]

In this way, the poem increasingly becomes a process for the recovery of painful memories, some just put to one side, some actually repressed. And it is this cognitive process of recovering repressed memories that I see as particularly relevant to my parallel researches into deep politics.

In particular, I have come to recognize that my prose book *American War Machine*, beginning as it does with the recovered memory from Palo Alto in its opening pages, could not possibly have been written if I had not first, with some pain, written *Coming to Jakarta*. This poem is often presented (even by me) as my response on a conscious level in 1980 to the anguish of knowing facts I was unable to share, about U.S. involvement in the 1965 massacre by the Indonesian army of over half a million Indonesian men, women, and children. But the poem was also a gradual confrontation with the disturbing reality that there is a gap between the visible yang world as we think we know it, and darker more inscrutable yin forces at work, both in the world and in ourselves.

MY ENCOUNTER WITH VIOLENCE IN PALO ALTO

More and more, the search for relief and empowerment from voicing what was inside me led to the recovery of ignored or even repressed memories.[11] At first most of these were from childhood, and very personal. But the very last one was of the former Green Beret in Palo Alto who would not talk to us because his car had just been firebombed (V.ii). This event was mostly revealing about the world we live in. But the fact that I forgot about it revealed something very important about myself.

The memory, a decade old when I first recovered it, should have been unforgettable, but in fact it was swiftly repressed in my mind. I was not ready to adjust to what I later called "darker forces at work in our society than I would normally allow myself to admit."

> Perhaps the most powerful of these suppressed memories, and certainly the very last to be recovered, . . . was of a witness to opium flights in Asia who, after agreeing [on the telephone] with Alfred McCoy and myself to be interviewed, changed his mind overnight.[12]
>
> And for good reason: in those [fifteen or so] hours someone had warned him by burning a hole in the steel door of his M.G. with a sophisticated implosion device. One might think that such a vivid and incongruous message could hardly be forgotten. The fact was that I had totally suppressed my memory of it, even through the first two years of my determined poetic search to recover such memories![13]
>
> And so, as I rightly suspected, had Al. In the preface to the latest edition of his monumental classic, *The Politics of Heroin*, he writes in prose about his own suppression of the same facts. At the risk of seeming self-absorbed in the context of much larger tragedies, I will quote his prose account of an unforgettable event almost instantly forgotten.
>
> I landed in San Francisco for a stay with poet and Berkeley professor Peter Dale Scott. He put me in touch with an ex-Green Beret, just back from covert operations in Laos, who told me, over the phone, of seeing CIA aircraft loading opium. He agreed to be interviewed on the record. The next morning, we knocked at his door in an East Palo Alto apartment complex. We never got inside. He was visibly upset, saying he "had gotten the message." What happened?
>
> "Follow me," he said, leading us across the parking lot to his MG sportscar. He pointed at something on the passenger door and named a chemical explosive that that could melt a hole in sheet metal. It was, he said, a signal to shut up.

IV. "Gaps" of Consciousness; or, How Writing Coming to Jakarta

I looked but cannot recall seeing. The next day, I flew to Los Angeles, visited my mother, and then flew on to Saigon, forgetting the incident. I refused to recognize the reality of this threat until, 20 years later, I came across a passage in Professor Scott's poem, *Coming to Jakarta*:

> but that clean morning in Palo Alto
> the former Green Beret
>
> who just the night before
> had said he would talk to us
> about opium in Laos
>
> showing us the sharp black hole
> in his M.G.'s red steel door
> the floorboards hardly scorched
>
> and saying that hot
> an imploded thermal charge
> must have come from my old unit.[14]

"SOME HEAVIER UNNAMED AGENCY": *COMING TO JAKARTA*, DEEP POLITICS, AND THE DEEP STATE

What force or forces in America could have intercepted a phone call from me one late afternoon, and then responded with a small terrorist bombing in the middle of that night? When I first began to wonder about this, I assumed, without thinking, that it must have been the CIA. But when I reviewed this incident for the introduction to my long book about the CIA and drug traffickers, I saw reasons to suspect that a different "dark force" or forces might have been at work.

Writing [*American War Machine*] has enabled me to have further thoughts about the Palo Alto incident and particularly the importance of its date—September 1971. As we shall see, this was a time of a major change in the U.S. relationship to the Southeast Asian drug traffic.

In earlier versions of [*American War Machine*], I attributed the sanctioned violence of the Palo Alto incident, like the Letelier assassination I discuss next, to the CIA's global drug connection. But that statement does not solve a mystery: it opens one up. As a matter of description, it sounds more precise than terms I have used in earlier books: "the dark quadrant" from which parapolitical events emerge, or "the unrecognized Force X operating in the world," which I suggested might help explain 9/11. But the precision is misleading: in this book I am indeed attempting to denote and describe a deep force, or forces, that I do not fully understand.[15]

The more I pondered this mystery, the more I realized that the dark force or forces responsible for the incident, with the power both to gather communications intelligence and also to impose violence, must have been sophisticated, operating domestically in ways I do not normally associate with the CIA.[16] (This suspicion was in keeping with my having heard of, and reported, "the CIA or perhaps / some heavier unnamed agency," II.ii.)

After much reflection, I came to consider the Palo Alto bombing in *American War Machine* as a small personal analogue to

> what I now call deep events: events that are systematically ignored, suppressed, or falsified in public (and even internal) government, military, and intelligence documents as well as in the mainstream media and public consciousness.[17]

Over many decades, for reasons explored in this book, I was obsessed with deep events, from the John F. Kennedy assassination to Watergate and 9/11. Speaking poetically, these major events represent gaps in our collective consciousness, between whatever happened in each case and our awareness of the truth. They are like windows on to unknown realities, that for public safety have been boarded up. Alternative explanations, or even criticisms, remain (as we saw in chapter 2) outside the "Overton window" of socially acceptable discourse, "unfit for serious debate."[18] Externally, one merely risks being called a "conspiracy theorist." But internally, one suffers the psychic costs of alienation from normal daily life. Thus, as I write in my meditative poem "The Tao of 9/11," "There are things we don't think about in America."[19]

My poem and this book accept that there are deep events in which truths, precisely because they are important, have been covered up. Indeed, it would be hard to think of a more characteristic deep event than Gestapu or G30S, the 1965 alleged coup in the name of defending Sukarno, whose perpetrators in fact murdered the pro-Sukarno generals in the Indonesian Army, and thus supplied the needed pretext for the subsequent massacre. G30S was the foundational event of the Suharto era, during which a lying government-funded film about it "was compulsory viewing for school children, who were made to write a report about the evils of the communists once a year."[20] Thus the so-called Suharto Revolution was launched by a deep event.[21]

Following the Swedish author Ola Tunander, I have attributed American deep events to an American deep state; and I described back in 2007 how

> the American deep state has consistently used the resources of drug-trafficking terrorists, and more recently those of al Qaeda, to further its own ends, particularly with respect to oil, at the expense of the public order and well-being of the American public state.[22]

IV. "Gaps" of Consciousness; or, How Writing Coming to Jakarta

More recently it has become quite fashionable, starting three years before Trump, to refer to the American "deep state," even in the *Wall Street Journal*.[23] My 2015 book, The *American Deep State*, has since been joined by Mike Lofgren's *The Deep State: The Fall of the Constitution and the Rise of a Shadow Government* (2016). And though our two books have much in common, his book, in contrast to mine, pays very little attention to the interrelated topics of organized non-official violence, crime, drugs, and oil, topics that loom in the background throughout *Coming to Jakarta*.[24] Here I find his analysis more superficial, precisely because it does not venture into the zone of the unspeakable and undefinable that poets, and indeed all of us, need to be aware of.

POETRY, VIOLENCE, AND PROSE

In this book I have been dealing with the psychological and social functions of memory suppression and recovery: a topic of immense relevance to Indonesia's half-century of memory suppression with respect to the events of 1965.[25] There exists a vast literature on the widespread phenomenon of cultural trauma, and on psychological repression as a response to it. To quote Arthur G. Neal:

> The enduring effects of a trauma in the memories of an individual resemble the enduring effects of a national trauma in collective consciousness. Dismissing or ignoring the traumatic experience is not a reasonable option. The conditions surrounding a trauma are played and replayed in consciousness through an attempt to extract some sense of coherence from a meaningless experience. When the event is dismissed from consciousness, it resurfaces in feelings of anxiety and despair.[26]

When I first wrote about this some years ago I was fascinated by the fitness of this account to my own anxiety and attempt, in writing *Coming to Jakarta*, "to extract some sense of coherence" from my disturbing experiences—even though my personal experiences were minimally traumatic by today's standards. But now I wonder if it was not over-simplified to discuss the Palo Alto incident this way in the context of traumatic repression.

Al and I were witnesses to "someone else's" terror. I suspect we forgot the incident, not because for us it was immediately traumatic, but because at that time it would have required too much effort to comprehend it, and above all to adjust to it. Like the murder of my colleague Allard Lowenstein that I only thought of later (see chapter 1, Appendix to II.iv–v), the Palo Alto incident was an immediate threat, not to our physical well-being, but to our peace of mind. To have thought too much about its implications would have been costly, possibly inducing us to give up research and writing activities altogether.[27]

It is possible also that we did not remember the event, because to confront violence in any degree, even minor violence to which we were only witnesses, would have led (as it eventually did) to the much larger issue of violence in America as a whole. The consequences of considering this seriously can be life-changing. Consider the case of Nina Simone (see chapter 2) whose response in song to the murder of four little girls in a 1963 church bombing led her to compromise her successful commercial career as a soul singer, by becoming a major engaged poet, activist, and eventual refugee from America.

In various ways, I believe that poetry, by its own mysterious working, can be part of humanity's approach (or return) to truth. More particularly, my own poems are often an antechamber to a subsequent more engaged treatment in prose. For example, the wide-reaching research I did for *Coming to Jakarta* led four years later to the next essay in this book, which in turn was translated into Indonesian and circulated clandestinely in Jakarta while Suharto was still in power. And as just mentioned, this episode of the firebombed MG in Palo Alto, first recovered by writing *Jakarta*, now constitutes the opening episode (and containing metaphor) of my 2010 prose book, *American War Machine*.[28]

My responses to the massacre in Indonesia and the firebombing in Palo Alto are small examples of the social conditioning and repression that affects all of us all the time. In McCoy's and my repression of the discomforting bombing memory, and my eventual recovery of it in writing *Jakarta*, one can see clearly both how the phenomenon of deep politics—the sphere of the unspeakable—arises, and also how poetry and the imagination can be of use in recovering access to this sphere (the result in my case being *American War Machine*, which I might otherwise not have written).

In saying this, I am not privileging poetry as more veridical than prose. Nor am I suggesting that poetic intuition is a prerequisite for rational analysis. It is true that I had to write *Coming to Jakarta* before conceptualizing *deep politics* and *deep events*. But the long process that led to my Watertown crisis and the poem was triggered by earlier very prosaic events, like catching the *New York Times* in a public falsehood they would not correct (IV.ii), or learning that the CIA would take steps to falsify a minor truth discovered by me, when no one (as I then thought) had heard of me (II.xiii).[29]

In reconstructing the repressed Palo Alto memory I was extremely fortunate to have Al McCoy in particular as a corroborating witness; since Al, by writing and rewriting his classic *The Politics of Heroin*, was unusually aware of the forces at high levels in our society protecting the drug traffic, and thus more capable than most of recovering our shared memory.[30]

PSYCHIC REBELLION AS PSYCHIC HEALING

The first draft of my poem *Coming to Jakarta* was written in an intense burst of concentration in 1981, as, in a kind of altered state, I began to write myself out of a near mental breakdown. At the time the experience was painful; but in retrospect I am of course grateful for it. What felt then like a breakdown of my presentational self, sick from trying to survive in a sick society, was from a different perspective a breakthrough for something deeper in me, struggling to break free. One could say much more about this doubleness of shattering and liberation.[31]

A decade later, when the poem was honored in an issue of the literary review *Agni*, I attempted to analyze the diverse sources of my mental discomfort:

> The first was a growing self-hatred for carrying around a headful of horrors which most people (including my former editors and publishers) were less and less willing to hear about. An afternoon talk in 1980 with Noam Chomsky about our increasing difficulties in reaching audiences, right after each of us had had a book suppressed by its publisher, did indeed help trigger the very real personal crisis at the opening of the poem, the fear that I might be at the point of losing, like some close friends, my personal sanity altogether.
>
> But deeper than this external frustration with publishers was the sense that my own judgmental head was in some profound sense not right, my disgust (which can still haunt me) at "giving one last broadcast too many / about . . . the heroin traffic." Unlike many Americans whose prevailing discomfort in this era was guilt, my own nausea (I now believe) was from the poisonous facts I had assimilated and could not disseminate.
>
> The first eight sections of the poem record my search for the source of this nausea, and my delayed recognition (in II.iv), that it derived, not from knowledge reiterated, but from knowledge and emotions held back. By appealing to a more human and less compartmentalized audience, poetry, precisely poetry, allowed me to trace more inclusive relationships than those authorized by orderly prose analysis.[32]

Today I am more confident than before that my psychic rebellion against using prose to describe our society—and our world— was legitimate from the point of view of truth-seeking, an existential critique of the political science methods in which I had been trained at university. Section II.iv, to which I referred, was an autocritique for limiting myself to archival sources about the great Indonesian massacre of 1965, and the subsequent murder in Cambodia five years later of my friend Malcolm Caldwell (who had first encouraged me to research that massacre),

> no one will say by whom but I will guess
>
> > seeing as this is
> > > precisely poetry
> > > the CIA's and now Peking's Cambodian
>
> > assassins the Khmer Serai. . . .
> > so much for my balanced prose [33]

I should make it clear that today I have no evidence for, and also give no credit to, what my poetry proposed as a possible solution to the Caldwell murder mystery. However it was important to think for a while outside the evidence, for the archived evidence in our present civilization is, as I have written elsewhere, inherently biased.[34]

It is also important, when discussing politics, to be able to think holistically. But it is difficult to reconcile holistic thinking with the task of analysis. In writing poetry, one eschews method; and the neglected asserts itself.

Liberated from the need for rational documentation, my poem (using in Section IV.i the Homeric device of a catalogue) wandered freely through the manifold deep forces affecting American politics and my own depression, not excluding references to my suppressed prose book—which Pocket Books, in violation of a written contract, had failed to publish.[35]

All this leads to the current thinking about all art as a form of corrective "alterity", "reminding us" (as I have written in a lecture on Milosz) "that as humans we are more than settled furniture in the architecture of the status quo."[36] In that lecture I quoted from the social critic Theodore Adorno's account of a dialectical engagement between the other world of poetry and this tangible, secular world. In Adorno's words, "Even in the most sublimated work of art there is a hidden 'it should be otherwise.' As eminently constructed and produced objects, works of art . . . point to a practice from which they abstain: the creation of a just life."[37]

However (in the tradition of Schiller, Marcuse, and Milosz) I disagree that art, or at least poetry, always "abstains" from the creation of a just life. As a poet, I have tried to reinforce a tradition of socially engaged poetry. The poetry I taught as a professor, from Virgil's *Aeneid* to Wordsworth's *Prelude*, was poetry I taught as examples of how great poetry could exert leverage upon the world.

Coming to Jakarta reads in places like the chronicle of a nightmare. It is perhaps not a very brilliant example of showing a space ahead. The poem does however end prospectively:

> let there be the courage
> not just to have seen
>
> but to ease into the world
> the unreal
> breathing within us[38]

I do believe that the arc of the poem had led me to a glimpse of what Buddhists call original mind (or *anatta*), where we get back to the purity we begin with before experience, and that this glimpse, like Dante's passage through the very bottom of the *Inferno*, was the beginning of a return to a healthier view of life.

By the time these lines were written, I was already well embarked on the next volume of what would eventually become a trilogy, *Seculum*, continuing to explore the process to which I had been opened by writing *Coming to Jakarta*. The second volume, *Listening to the Candle* (1992), moved antithetically to some of the good things in life, and the third, *Minding the Darkness* (2000), to a reconciliation of the two first volumes—the nightmare and the joyous, and even more pointedly the yang and the yin—through the process of

> language and humans
> endlessly
> redefining each other . . .
>
> the earthway
> where we struggle to discover
> what has always been known[39]

I wish I could say that it has always been self-evident to me that a poet should love the world, and therefore should wish to change it. In fact, my vision has been frequently occluded by crises, like the one occasioning *Jakarta*, at which times it was a struggle to think even about changing myself. But it seems blatantly obvious to me now that these two urges, to heal oneself and to heal the world, are ultimately one and the same.[40]

Preface to Chapter 5

The following essay essay was first published in *Pacific Affairs*, 58, Summer 1985, 239–264. It arose from a discussion I had with Noam Chomsky about discoveries that I had made while researching for *Coming to Jakarta* (particularly about a switch in Lockheed payments before Gestapu to a Suharto supporter). He asked me for a memo; I responded with a 107-page MS (now lost). Condensed, that MS provided a text for a debate in which I and Ralph McGehee, at a Washington session of the Association of Asian Scholars, challenged former CIA Director William Colby.

This article is an edited version of that text. It was ultimately published in three languages in six countries, but never in the United States (except electronically on the Internet since 1995). It was reprinted in *Intelligence/ Parapolitics* (Paris), 79 (July 1986), 13–19. It was translated into Dutch as "De Verenigde Staten & Indonesie 1965," in *Indonesie: De Waarheid Omtrent 1965* (Amsterdam: Indonesia Media, 1985), 170–235. It was translated also into Indonesian, as (1) Peter Dale Scott, *Peranan C.I.A. Dalam Penggulingan Bung Karno. Buku ini dilatang beredar oleh KEJA-GUNG RI.* (West Berlin: Perhimpunan Indonesia, 1988); (2) *Peranan C.I.A. dalam penggulingan Bung Karno Konspirasi Soeharto-CIA: penggulingan Soekarno, 1965–1967* (Surabaya: Pergerakan Mahasiswa Islam Indonesia: Perkumpulan Kebangsaan Anti Diskriminasi, [1998]); (3) An anthology, *Gestapu, matinya para jenderal dan peran CIA* (Yogyakarta: Cermin, 1999); (4) Peter Dale Scott, *CIA dan penggulingan Sukarno* (Yogyakarta: Lembaga Analisis Informasi, 1999); (5) Peter Dale Scott, *Amerika Serikat dan penggulingan Sukarno 1965–1967* ([S.l.: s.n.], 2000); (6) Peter Dale Scott . . . et. al., ed. Joesoef Isak], *100 tahun Bung Karno: 6 Juni 1901–2001: sebuah liber* (Jakarta: Hasta Mitra, 2001), 278–316; (7) Peter Dale Scott, *Peran CIA dalam penggulingan Sukarno* (Jakarta: Buku Kita, 2007).

It is reprinted here in its original form, because after three decades the issues it raises have in my opinion not yet been seriously discussed in this country. See "Still Uninvestigated After 50 Years: Did the U.S. Help Incite the 1965 Indonesia Massacre?" *Asian-Pacific Journal: Japan Focus*, August 3, 2015, http://apjjf.org/2015/13/31/Peter-Dale-Scott/4351.html.

V. The CIA and the Overthrow of Sukarno, 1965–1967

In this short paper on a huge and vexed subject, I discuss the U.S. involvement in the bloody overthrow of Indonesia's President Sukarno, 1965–67. The whole story of that ill-understood period would transcend even the fullest possible written analysis. Much of what happened can never be documented; and of the documentation that survives, much is both controversial and unverifiable. The slaughter of Sukarno's left-wing allies was a product of widespread paranoia as well as of conspiratorial policy, and represents a tragedy beyond the intentions of any single group or coalition. Nor is it suggested that in 1965 the only provocations and violence came from the right-wing Indonesian military, their contacts in the United States, or (also important, but barely touched on here) their mutual contacts in British, German, and Japanese intelligence.

And yet, after all this has been said, the complex and ambiguous story of the Indonesian bloodbath is also in essence simpler and easier to believe than the public version inspired by President Suharto and U.S. government sources. Their problematic claim is that in the so-called Gestapu (Gerakan September Tigahpuluh) coup attempt of September 30, 1965 (when six senior army generals were murdered), the left attacked the right, leading to a restoration of power, and punitive purge of the left, by the center.[1] This article argues instead that, by inducing, or at a minimum helping to induce, the Gestapu "coup," the right in the Indonesian Army eliminated its rivals at the army's center, thus paving the way to a long-planned elimination of the civilian left, and eventually to the establishment of a military dictatorship.[2] Gestapu, in other words, was only the first phase of a three-phase right-wing coup—one which had been both publicly encouraged and secretly assisted by U.S. spokesmen and officials.[3]

Before turning to U.S. involvement in what the CIA itself has called "one of the worst mass murders of the twentieth century,"[4] let us recall what actually led up to it. According to the Australian scholar Harold Crouch, by 1965 the Indonesian Army General Staff was split into two camps. At the center were the general staff officers appointed with, and loyal to, the army commander General Yani, who in turn was reluctant to challenge President Sukarno's policy of national unity in alliance with the Indonesian Communist party, or PKI. The second group, including the right-wing generals Nasution and Suharto, comprised those opposed to Yani and his Sukarnoist policies.[5] All of these generals were anti-PKI, but by 1965 the divisive issue was Sukarno.

The simple (yet untold) story of Sukarno's overthrow is that in the fall of 1965 Yani and his inner circle of generals were murdered, paving the way for a seizure of power by right-wing anti-Yani forces allied to Suharto. The key to this was the so-called Gestapu coup attempt which, in the name of supporting Sukarno, in fact targeted very precisely the leading members of the army's most loyal faction, the Yani group.[6] An army unity meeting in January 1965, between "Yani's inner circle" and those (including Suharto) who "had grievances of one sort or another against Yani," lined up the victims of September 30 against those who came to power after their murder.[7]

Not one anti-Sukarno general was targeted by Gestapu, with the obvious exception of General Nasution.[8] But by 1961 the CIA operatives had become disillusioned with Nasution as a reliable asset, because of his "consistent record of yielding to Sukarno on several major counts."[9] Relations between Suharto and Nasution were also cool, since Nasution, after investigating Suharto on corruption charges in 1959, had transferred him from his command.[10]

The duplicitous distortions of reality, first by Lt. Colonel Untung's statements for Gestapu, and then by Suharto in "putting down" Gestapu, are mutually supporting lies.[11] Untung, on October 1, announced ambiguously that Sukarno was under Gestapu's "protection" (he was not); also, that a CIA-backed Council of Generals had planned a coup for before October 5, and had for this purpose brought "troops from East, Central, and West Java" to Jakarta.[12] Troops from these areas had indeed been brought to Jakarta for an Armed Forces Day parade on October 5th. Untung did not mention, however, that "he himself had been involved in the planning for the Armed Forces Day parade and in selecting the units to participate in it;"[13] nor that these units (which included his own former battalion, the 454th) supplied most of the allies for his new battalion's Gestapu activities in Jakarta.

Suharto's first two broadcasts reaffirmed the army's constant loyalty to "Bung Karno the Great Leader," and also blamed the deaths of six generals on PKI youth and women, plus "elements of the Air Force"—on no other evidence than the site of the well where the corpses were found.[14] At this time he knew very well that the killings had in fact been carried out by the very army elements Untung referred to, elements under Suharto's own command.[15]

Thus, whatever the motivation of individuals such as Untung in the Gestapu putsch, Gestapu as such was duplicitous. Both its rhetoric and above all its actions were not simply inept; they were carefully designed to prepare for Suharto's equally duplicitous response. For example, Gestapu's decision to guard all sides of the downtown Merdeka Square in Jakarta, except that on which Suharto's KOSTRAD [Army Strategic Reserve Command] headquarters were situated, is consistent with Gestapu's decision to target the only army generals who might have challenged Suharto's assumption of power. Again, Gestapu's announced transfer of power to a totally fictitious "Revolutionary Council," from which Sukarno had been excluded, allowed Suharto in turn to masquerade as Sukarno's defender while in fact preventing him from resuming control. More importantly, Gestapu's gratuitous murder of the generals near the air force base where PKI youth had been trained allowed Suharto, in a Goebbels-like manoeuvre, to transfer the blame for the killings from the troops under his own command (whom he knew had carried out the kidnappings) to air force and PKI personnel who were ignorant of them.[16]

From the pro-Suharto sources—notably the CIA study of Gestapu published in 1968—we learn how few troops were involved in the alleged Gestapu rebellion, and, more importantly, that in Jakarta as in Central Java the same battalions that supplied the "rebellious" companies were also used to "put the rebellion down." Two thirds of one paratroop brigade (which Suharto had inspected the previous day) plus one company and one platoon constituted the whole of Gestapu forces in Jakarta; all but one of these units were commanded by present or former Diponegoro Division officers close to Suharto; and the last was under an officer who obeyed Suharto's close political ally, Basuki Rachmat.[17]

Two of these companies, from the 454th and 530th battalions, were elite raiders, and from 1962 these units had been among the main Indonesian recipients of U.S. assistance.[18] This fact, which in itself proves nothing, increases our curiosity about the many Gestapu leaders who had been U.S.-trained. The Gestapu leader in Central Java, Saherman, had returned from training at Fort Leavenworth and Okinawa, shortly before meeting with Untung and Major Sukirno of the 454th Battalion in mid-August 1965.[19] As Ruth McVey has observed, Saherman's acceptance for training at Fort Leavenworth "would mean that he had passed review by CIA observers."[20]

Thus there is continuity between the achievements of both Gestapu and the response to it by Suharto, who in the name of defending Sukarno and attacking Gestapu continued its task of eliminating the pro-Yani members of the Army General Staff, along with such other residual elements of support for first Yani and then Sukarno as remained.[21]

The biggest part of this task was of course the elimination of the PKI and its supporters, in a bloodbath which, as some Suharto allies later conceded, may have taken more than a half-million lives. These three events—Gestapu, Suharto's response, and the bloodbath—have nearly always been presented in this country as separately motivated: Gestapu being described as a plot by leftists, and the bloodbath as for the most part an irrational act of popular frenzy.

U.S. officials, journalists, and scholars, some with rather prominent CIA connections, are perhaps principally responsible for the myth that the bloodbath was a spontaneous, popular revulsion to what U.S. Ambassador Jones later called PKI "carnage."[22] Although the PKI certainly contributed its share to the political hysteria of 1965, Crouch has shown that subsequent claims of a PKI terror campaign were grossly exaggerated.[23] In fact systematic killing occurred under army instigation in staggered stages, the worst occurring as Colonel Sarwo Edhie's RPKAD [Army Paracommando Regiment] moved from Jakarta to Central and East Java, and finally to Bali.[24] Civilians involved in the massacre were either recruited and trained by the army on the spot, or were drawn from groups (such as the army- and CIA-sponsored SOKSI trade unions [Central Organization of Indonesian Socialist Employees], and allied student organizations) which had collaborated for years with the army on political matters.

It is clear from Sundhaussen's account that in most of the first areas of organized massacre (North Sumatra, Aceh, Cirebon, the whole of Central and East Java), there were local army commanders with especially strong and proven anti-PKI sentiments. Many of these had for years cooperated with civilians, through so-called civic action programs sponsored by the United States, in operations directed against the PKI and sometimes Sukarno. Thus, one can legitimately suspect conspiracy in the fact that anti-PKI "civilian responses" began on October 1, when the army began handing out arms to Muslim students and unionists, before there was any publicly available evidence linking Gestapu to the PKI.[25]

Even Sundhaussen, who downplays the army's role in arming and inciting the civilian murder bands, concludes that, whatever the strength of popular anti-PKI hatred and fear, "without the Army's anti-PKI propaganda the massacre might not have happened."[26] The present article goes further and argues that Gestapu, Suharto's response, and the bloodbath were part of a single coherent scenario for a military takeover, a scenario which was again followed closely in Chile in the years 1970–73 (and to some extent in Cambodia in 1970).

Suharto, of course, would be a principal conspirator in this scenario: his duplicitous role of posing as a defender of the constitutional status quo, while in fact moving deliberately to overthrow it, is analogous to that of General

Pinochet in Chile. But a more direct role in organizing the bloodbath was played by civilians and officers close to the cadres of the CIA's failed rebellion of 1958, now working in so-called civic action programs funded and trained by the United States. Necessary ingredients of the scenario had to be, and clearly were, supplied by other nations in support of Suharto. Many such countries appear to have played such a supporting role: Japan, Britain, Germany,[27] possibly Australia. But I wish to focus on the encouragement and support for military "putschism" and mass murder which came from the United States, from the CIA, the military, RAND, the Ford Foundation, and individuals.[28]

THE UNITED STATES AND THE INDONESIAN ARMY'S "MISSION"

It seems clear that from as early as 1953 the United States was interested in helping to foment the regional crisis in Indonesia, usually recognized as the "immediate cause" that induced Sukarno, on March 14, 1957, to proclaim martial law, and bring "the officer corps legitimately into politics."[29]

By 1953 (if not earlier) the U.S. National Security Council had already adopted one of a series of policy documents calling for "appropriate action, in collaboration with other friendly countries, to prevent permanent communist control" of Indonesia.[30] Already NSC 171/1 of that year envisaged military training as a means of increasing U.S. influence, even though the CIA's primary efforts were directed toward right-wing political parties ("moderates . . . on the right," as NSC 171 called them): notably the Masjumi Muslim and the PSI "Socialist" parties. The millions of dollars which the CIA poured into the Masjumi and the PSI in the mid-1950s were a factor influencing the events of 1965, when a former PSI member—Sjam—was the alleged mastermind of Gestapu,[31] and PSI-leaning officers—notably Suwarto and Sarwo Edhie—were prominent in planning and carrying out the anti-PKI response to Gestapu.[32]

In 1957–58, the CIA infiltrated arms and personnel in support of the regional rebellions against Sukarno. These operations were nominally covert, even though an American plane and pilot were captured, and the CIA efforts were accompanied by an offshore task force of the U.S. Seventh Fleet.[33] In 1975 a Senate Select Committee studying the CIA discovered what it called "some evidence of CIA involvement in plans to assassinate President Sukarno"; but, after an initial investigation of the November 1957 assassination attempt in the Cikini district of Jakarta, the committee did not pursue the matter.[34]

On August 1, 1958, after the failure of the CIA-sponsored PRRI-Permesta regional rebellions against Sukarno, the United States began an upgraded military assistance program to Indonesia in the order of twenty million dollars a year.[35] A U.S. Joint Chiefs of Staff memo of 1958 makes it clear this aid was given to the Indonesian Army ("the only non-Communist force . . . with the capability of obstructing the . . . PKI") as "encouragement" to Nasution to "carry out his 'plan' for the control of Communism."[36]

The JCS had no need to spell out Nasution's "plan," to which other documents at this time made reference.[37] It could only imply the tactics for which Nasution had distinguished himself (in American eyes) during the crushing of the PKI in the Madiun Affair of 1948: mass murders and mass arrests, at a minimum of the party's cadres, possibly after an army provocation.[38] Nasution confirmed this in November 1965, after the Gestapu slaughter, when he called for the total extinction of the PKI, "down to its very roots so there will be no third Madiun."[39]

By 1958, however, the PKI had emerged as the largest mass movement in the country. It is in this period that a small group of U.S. academic researchers in U.S. Air Force- and CIA-subsidized "think-tanks" began pressuring their contacts in the Indonesian military publicly, often through U.S. scholarly journals and presses, to seize power and liquidate the PKI opposition.[40] The most prominent example is Guy Pauker, who in 1958 both taught at the University of California at Berkeley and served as a consultant at the RAND Corporation. In the latter capacity he maintained frequent contact with what he himself called "a very small group" of PSI intellectuals and their friends in the army.[41]

In a RAND Corporation book published by the Princeton University Press, Pauker urged his contacts in the Indonesian military to assume "full responsibility" for their nation's leadership, "fulfill a mission," and hence "to strike, sweep their house clean."[42] Although Pauker may not have intended anything like the scale of bloodbath which eventually ensued, there is no escaping the fact that "mission" and "sweep clean" were buzz-words for counterinsurgency and massacre, and as such were used frequently before and during the coup. The first murder order, by military officers to Muslim students in early October, was the word *sikat*, meaning "sweep," "clean out," "wipe out," or "massacre."[43]

Pauker's closest friend in the Indonesian army was a U.S.-trained General Suwarto, who played an important part in the conversion of the army from a revolutionary to a counterinsurgency function. In the years after 1958, Suwarto built the Indonesian Army Staff and Command School in Bandung (SESKOAD) into a training-ground for the takeover of political power. SESKOAD in this period became a focal-point of attention from the Pentagon, the CIA, RAND, and (indirectly) the Ford Foundation.[44]

V. The CIA and the Overthrow of Sukarno, 1965–1967

Under the guidance of Nasution and Suwarto, SESKOAD developed a new strategic doctrine, that of Territorial Warfare (in a document translated into English by Pauker), which gave priority to counterinsurgency as the army's role. Especially after 1962, when the Kennedy administration aided the Indonesian Army in developing Civic Mission or "civic action" programs, this meant the organization of its own political infrastructure, or "Territorial Organization," reaching in some cases down to the village level.[45] As the result of an official U.S. State Department recommendation in 1962, which Pauker helped write, a special U.S. MILTAG (Military Training Advisory Group) was set up in Jakarta, to assist in the implementation of SESKOAD's Civic Mission programs.[46]

SESKOAD also trained the army officers in economics and administration, and thus to operate virtually as a para-state, independent of Sukarno's government. So the army began to collaborate, and even sign contracts, with U.S. and other foreign corporations in areas which were now under its control. This training program was entrusted to officers and civilians close to the PSI.[47] U.S. officials have confirmed that the civilians, who themselves were in a training program funded by the Ford Foundation, became involved in what the (then) U.S. military attache called "contingency planning" to prevent a PKI takeover.[48]

But the most significant focus of U.S. training and aid was the Territorial Organization's increasing liaison with "the civilian administration, religious and cultural organizations, youth groups, veterans, trade unions, peasant organizations, political parties and groups at regional and local levels."[49] These political liaisons with civilian groups provided the structure for the ruthless suppression of the PKI in 1965, including the bloodbath.[50]

Soon these army and civilian cadres were together plotting disruptive activities, such as the Bandung anti-Chinese riots of May 1963, which embarrassed not just the PKI, but Sukarno himself. Chomsky and Herman report that "Army-inspired anti-Chinese programs that took place in West Java in 1959 were financed by U.S. contributions to the local army commander"; apparently CIA funds were used by the commander (Colonel Kosasih) to pay local thugs in what Mozingo calls "the army's (and probably the Americans') campaign to rupture relations with China."[51] The 1963 riot, which took place in the very shadow of SESKOAD, is linked by Sundhaussen to an army "civic action" organization; and shows conspiratorial contact between elements (an underground PSI cell, PSI- and Masjumi-affiliated student groups, and General Ishak Djuarsa of the Siliwangi Division's "civic action" organization) that would all be prominent in the very first phase of Suharto's so-called response to the Gestapu.[52] The May 1963 student riots were repeated in October 1965 and (especially in Bandung) January 1966, at which time the liaison between students and the army was largely in the hands of PSI-leaning officers like Sarwo Edhie and Kemal Idris.[53] The CIA Plans Directorate was sympathetic to the increasing deflection of a nominally anti-PKI operation into one embarrassing Sukarno. This turn would have come as no surprise: Suwarto, Kemal Idris, and the PSI had been prominent in a near-coup (the so-called Lubis affair) in 1956.[54]

But increasingly Suwarto cultivated a new student, Colonel Suharto, who arrived at SESKOAD in October 1959. According to Sundhaussen, a relatively pro-Suharto scholar: "In the early 1960s Soeharto was involved in the formation of the Doctrine of Territorial Warfare and the Army's policy on Civic Mission (that is, penetration of army officers into all fields of government activities and responsibilities)."[55] Central to the public image of Gestapu and Suharto's response is the much-publicized fact that Suharto, unlike his sometime teacher Suwarto, and his long-time chief of staff Achmad Wiranatakusuma, had never studied in the United States. But his involvement in Civic Mission (or what Americans called "civic action") programs located him along with PSI-leaning officers at the focal point of U.S. training activities in Indonesia, in a program which was nakedly political.[56]

The refinement of Territorial Warfare and Civic Mission Doctrine into a new strategic doctrine for army political intervention became by 1965 the ideological process consolidating the army for political takeover. After Gestapu, when Suwarto was an important political advisor to his former SESKOAD pupil Suharto, his strategic doctrine was the justification for Suharto's announcement on August 15, 1966, in fulfillment of Pauker's public and private urgings, that the army had to assume a leading role in all fields.[57]

Hence the army unity meeting of January 1965, arranged after Suharto had duplicitously urged Nasution to take "a more accommodating line"[58] towards Sukarno, was in fact a necessary step in the process whereby Suharto effectively took over from his rivals Yani and Nasution. It led to the April 1965 seminar at SESKOAD for a compromise army strategic doctrine, the Tri Ubaya Cakti, which "reaffirmed the army's claim to an independent political role."[59] On August 15, 1966, Suharto, speaking to the nation, justified his increasing prominence in terms of the "Revolutionary Mission" of the Tri Ubaya Cakti doctrine. Two weeks later at SESKOAD the doctrine was revised, at Suharto's instigation but in a setting "carefully orchestrated by Brigadier Suwarto," to embody still more clearly Pauker's emphasis on the army's "Civic Mission" or counterrevolutionary role.[60] This "Civic Mission," so important to Suharto, was also the principal goal and fruit of U.S. military aid to Indonesia.

By August 1964, moreover, Suharto had initiated political contacts with Malaysia, and hence eventually with Japan, Britain, and the United States.[61] Although the initial purpose of these contacts may have been to head off war with Malaysia, Sundhaussen suggests that Suharto's motive was his concern, buttressed in mid-1964 by a KOSTRAD intelligence report, about PKI political advances.[62] Mrázek links the peace feelers to the withdrawal of "some of the best army units" back to Java in the summer of 1965.[63] These movements, together with earlier deployment of a politically insecure Diponegoro battalion in the other direction, can also be seen as preparations for the seizure of power.[64]

In Nishihara's informed Japanese account, former PRRI/Permesta personnel with intelligence connections in Japan were prominent in these negotiations, along with Japanese officials.[65] Nishihara also heard that an intimate ally of these personnel, Jan Walandouw, who may have acted as a CIA contact for the 1958 rebellion, later again "visited Washington and advocated Suharto as a leader."[66] I am reliably informed that Walandouw's visit to Washington on behalf of Suharto was made some months before Gestapu.[67]

THE U.S. MOVES AGAINST SUKARNO

Many people in Washington, especially in the CIA Plans Directorate, had long desired the "removal" of Sukarno as well as of the PKI.[68] By 1961 key policy hard-liners, notably Guy Pauker, had also turned against Nasution.[69] Nevertheless, despite last-minute memoranda from the outgoing Eisenhower administration which would have opposed "whatever regime" in Indonesia was "increasingly friendly toward the Sino-Soviet bloc," the Kennedy administration stepped up aid to both Sukarno and the army.[70]

However, Lyndon Johnson's accession to the presidency was followed almost immediately by a shift to a more anti-Sukarno policy. This is clear from Johnson's decision in December 1963 to withhold economic aid which (according to Ambassador Jones) Kennedy would have supplied "almost as a matter of routine."[71] This refusal suggests that the U.S. aggravation of Indonesia's economic woes in 1963–65 was a matter of policy rather than inadvertence. Indeed, if the CIA's overthrow of Allende is a relevant analogy, then one would expect someday to learn that the CIA, through currency speculations and other hostile acts, contributed actively to the radical destabilization of the Indonesian economy in the weeks just before the coup, when "the price of rice quadrupled between June 30 and October 1, and the black market price of the dollar skyrocketed, particularly in September."[72]

As was the case in Chile, the gradual cutoff of all economic aid to Indonesia in the years 1962–65 was accompanied by a shift in military aid to friendly elements in the Indonesian Army: U.S. military aid amounted to $39.5 million in the four years 1962–65 (with a peak of $16.3 million in 1962) as opposed to $28.3 million for the thirteen years 1949–61.[73] After March 1964, when Sukarno told the United States, "go to hell with your aid," it became increasingly difficult to extract any aid from the U.S. congress: those persons not aware of what was developing found it hard to understand why the United States should help arm a country which was nationalizing U.S. economic interests, and using immense aid subsidies from the Soviet Union to confront the British in Malaysia.

Thus a public image was created that under Johnson "all United States aid to Indonesia was stopped," a claim so buttressed by misleading documentation that competent scholars have repeated it.[74] In fact, Congress had agreed to treat U.S. funding of the Indonesian military (unlike aid to any other country) as a covert matter, restricting congressional review of the president's determinations on Indonesian aid to two Senate committees, and the House Speaker, who were concurrently involved in oversight of the CIA.[75]

Ambassador Jones' more candid account admits that "suspension" meant "the U.S. government undertook no new commitments of assistance, although it continued with ongoing programs. . . . By maintaining our modest assistance to [the Indonesian Army and the police brigade], we fortified them for a virtually inevitable showdown with the burgeoning PKI."[76]

Only from recently released documents do we learn that new military aid was en route as late as July 1965, in the form of a secret contract to deliver two hundred Aero-Commanders to the Indonesian Army: these were light aircraft suitable for use in "civic action" or counterinsurgency operations, presumably by the Army Flying Corps whose senior officers were virtually all trained in the United States.[77] By this time, the publicly admitted U.S. aid was virtually limited to the completion of an army communications system and to "civic action" training. It was by using the army's new communications system, rather than the civilian system in the hands of Sukarno loyalists, that Suharto on October 1, 1965 was able to implement his swift purge of Sukarno-Yani loyalists and leftists, while "civic action" officers formed the hard core of lower-level Gestapu officers in Central Java.[78]

Before turning to the more covert aspects of U.S. military aid to Indonesia in 1963–65, let us review the overall changes in U.S.-Indonesian relations. Economic aid was now in abeyance, and military aid tightly channeled so as to strengthen the army domestically. U.S. government funding had obviously shifted from the Indonesian state to one of its least loyal components. As a result of agreements beginning with martial law in 1957, but accelerated by the U.S.-negotiated oil agreement of 1963, we see exactly the same shift in the flow of payments from U.S. oil companies. Instead of token royalties to the Sukarno government, the two big U.S. oil companies in Indonesia, Stanvac and Caltex, now made much larger payments to the army's oil company, Permina, headed by an eventual political ally of Suharto, General Ibnu Sutowo; and to a second company, Pertamin, headed by the anti-PKI and pro-U.S. politician, Chaerul Saleh.[79] After Suharto's overthrow of Sukarno, *Fortune* wrote that "Sutowo's still small company played a key part in bankrolling those crucial operations, and the army has never forgotten it."[80]

U.S. SUPPORT FOR THE SUHARTO FACTION BEFORE GESTAPU

American officials commenting on the role of U.S. aid in this period have taken credit for assisting the anti-Communist seizure of power, without ever hinting at any degree of conspiratorial responsibility in the planning of the bloodbath. The impression created is that U.S. officials remained aloof from the actual planning of events, and we can see from recently declassified cable traffic how carefully the U.S. government fostered this image of detachment from what was happening in Indonesia.[81]

In fact, however, the U.S. government was lying about its involvement. In Fiscal Year 1965, a period when *The New York Times* claimed "all United States aid to Indonesia was stopped," the number of MAP (Military Assistance Program) personnel in Jakarta actually increased, beyond what had been projected, to an unprecedented high.[82] According to figures released in 1966,[83] from FY 1963 to FY 1965 the value of MAP deliveries fell from about fourteen million dollars to just over two million dollars. Despite this decline, the number of MAP military personnel remained almost unchanged, approximately thirty, while in FY 1965 civilian personnel (fifteen) were present for the first time. Whether or not one doubts that aid deliveries fell off as sharply as the figures would suggest, the MILTAG personnel figures indicate that their "civic action" program was being escalated, not decreased.[84]

We have seen that some months before Gestapu, a Suharto emissary with past CIA connections (Colonel Jan Walandouw) made contact with the U.S. government. From as early as May 1965, U.S. military suppliers with CIA connections (principally Lockheed) were negotiating equipment sales with payoffs to middlemen, in such a way as to generate payoffs to backers of the hitherto little-known leader of a new third faction in the army, Major-General Suharto—rather than to those backing Nasution or Yani, the titular leaders of the armed forces. Only in the 1980s was it confirmed that secret funds administered by the U.S. Air Force (possibly on behalf of the CIA) were laundered as "commissions" on sales of Lockheed equipment and services, in order to make political payoffs to the military personnel of foreign countries.[85]

A 1976 Senate investigation into these payoffs revealed, almost inadvertently, that in May 1965, over the legal objections of Lockheed's counsel, Lockheed commissions in Indonesia had been redirected to a new contract and company set up by the firm's long-time local agent or middleman.[86] Its internal memos at the time show no reasons for the change, but in a later memo the economic counselor of the U.S. Embassy in Jakarta is reported as saying that there were "some political considerations behind it."[87] If this is true, it would suggest that in May 1965, five months before the coup, Lockheed had redirected its payoffs to a new political eminence, at the risk (as its assistant chief counsel pointed out) of being sued for default on its former contractual obligations.

The Indonesian middleman, August Munir Dasaad, was "known to have assisted Sukarno financially since the 1930s."[88] In 1965, however, Dasaad was building connections with the Suharto forces, via a family relative, General Alamsjah, who had served briefly under Suharto in 1960, after Suharto completed his term at SESKOAD. Via the new contract, Lockheed, Dasaad, and Alamsjah were apparently hitching their wagons to Suharto's rising star:

> When the coup was made during which Suharto replaced Sukarno, Alamsjah, who controlled certain considerable funds, at once made these available to Suharto, which obviously earned him the gratitude of the new President. In due course he was appointed to a position of trust and confidence and today Alamsjah is, one might say, the second important man after the President.[89]

> Thus in 1966 the U.S. Embassy advised Lockheed it should "continue to use" the Dasaad-Alamsjah-Suharto connection.[90]

In July 1965, at the alleged nadir of U.S.-Indonesian aid relations, Rockwell-Standard had a contractual agreement to deliver two hundred light aircraft (Aero-Commanders) to the Indonesian Army (not the Air Force) in the next two months.[91] Once again the commission agent on the deal, Bob Hasan, was a political associate (and eventual business partner) of Suharto.[92] More specifically, Suharto and Bob Hasan established two shipping companies to be operated by the Central Java army division, Diponegoro. This division, as has long been noticed, supplied the bulk of the personnel on both sides of the Gestapu coup drama—both those staging the coup attempt, and those putting it down. And one of the three leaders in the Central Java Gestapu movement was Lt. Col. Usman Sastrodibroto, chief of the Diponegoro Division's "section dealing with extramilitary functions."[93]

Thus of the two known U.S. military sales contracts from the eve of the Gestapu Putsch, both involved political payoffs to persons who emerged after Gestapu as close Suharto allies. The use of this traditional channel for CIA patronage suggests that the United States was not at arm's length from the ugly political developments of 1965, despite the public indications, from both government spokesmen and the U.S. business press, that Indonesia was now virtually lost to communism and nothing could be done about it.

The actions of some U.S. corporations, moreover, made it clear that by early 1965 they expected a significant boost to the U.S. standing in Indonesia. For example, a recently declassified cable reveals that Freeport Sulphur had by April 1965 reached a preliminary "arrangement" with Indonesian officials for what would become a $500 million investment in West Papua copper. This gives the lie to the public claim that the company did not initiate negotiations with Indonesians (the inevitable Ibnu Sutowo) until February 1966.[94] And in September 1965, shortly after *World Oil* reported that "indonesia's gas and oil industry appeared to be slipping deeper into the political morass,"[95] the president of a small oil company (Asamera) in a joint venture with Ibnu Sutowo's Permina purchased $50,000 worth of shares in his own ostensibly threatened company. Ironically, this double purchase (on September 9 and September 21) was reported in the *Wall Street Journal* of September 30, 1965, the day of Gestapu.

THE CIA'S "[ONE WORD DELETED] OPERATION" IN 1965

Less than a year after Gestapu and the bloodbath, James Reston wrote appreciatively about them as "A Gleam of Light in Asia":

> Washington is being careful not to claim any credit for this change in the sixth most populous and one of the richest nations in the world, but this does not mean that Washington had nothing to do with it. There was a great deal more contact between the anti-Communist forces in that country and at least one very high official in Washington before and during the Indonesian massacre than is generally realized.[96]

As for the CIA in 1965, we have the testimony of former CIA officer Ralph McGehee, curiously corroborated by the selective censorship of his former CIA employers:

> Where the necessary circumstances or proofs are lacking to support U.S. intervention, the C.I.A. creates the appropriate situations or else invents them and disseminates its distortions worldwide via its media operations.
>
> A prominent example would be Chile. . . . Disturbed at the Chilean military's unwillingness to take action against Allende, the C.I.A. forged a document purporting to reveal a leftist plot to murder Chilean military leaders. The discovery of this "plot" was headlined in the media and Allende was deposed and murdered.

There is a similarity between events that precipitated the overthrow of Allende and what happened in Indonesia in 1965. Estimates of the number of deaths that occurred as a result of the latter C.I.A. [one word deleted] operation run from one-half million to more than one million people.[97]

McGehee claims to have once seen, while reviewing CIA documents in Washington, a highly classified report on the agency's role in provoking the destruction of the PKI after Gestapu. It seems appropriate to ask for congressional review and publication of any such report. If, as is alleged, it recommended such murderous techniques as a model for future operations, it would appear to document a major turning-point in the agency's operation history: toward the systematic exploitation of the death squad operations which, absent during the Brazilian coup of 1964, made the Vietnam Phoenix counterinsurgency program notorious after 1967, and after 1968 spread from Guatemala to the rest of Latin America.[98]

McGehee's claims of a CIA psychological warfare operation against Allende are corroborated by Tad Szulc:

> CIA agents in Santiago assisted Chilean military intelligence in drafting bogus Z-plan documents alleging that Allende and his supporters were planning to behead Chilean military commanders. These were issued by the junta to justify the coup.[99]

Indeed the CIA deception operations against Allende appear to have gone even farther, terrifying both the left and the right with the fear of incipient slaughter by their enemies. Thus militant trade-unionists as well as conservative generals in Chile received small cards printed with the ominous words *Djakarta se acerca* (Jakarta is approaching).[100]

This is a model destabilization plan—to persuade all concerned that they no longer can hope to be protected by the status quo, and hence weaken the center, while inducing both right and left toward more violent provocation of each other. Such a plan appears to have been followed in Laos in 1959–61, where a CIA officer explained to a reporter that the aim "was to polarize Laos."[101] It appears to have been followed in Indonesia in 1965. Observers like Sundhaussen confirm that to understand the coup story of October 1965 we must look first of all at the "rumour market" which in 1965 . . . turned out the wildest stories."[102] On September 14, two weeks before the coup, the army was warned that there was a plot to assassinate army leaders four days later; a second such report was discussed at army headquarters on September 30.[103] But a year earlier an alleged PKI document, which the PKI denounced as a forgery, had purported to describe a plan to overthrow "Nasutionists" through infiltration of the army. This "document," which was reported in a Malaysian newspaper after being publicized by the pro-U.S. politician Chaerul Saleh[104] in mid-December 1964, must have lent credence to Suharto's call for an army unity meeting the next month.[105]

The army's anxiety was increased by rumors, throughout 1965, that mainland China was smuggling arms to the PKI for an imminent revolt. Two weeks before Gestapu, a story to this effect also appeared in a Malaysian newspaper, citing Bangkok sources which relied in turn on Hong Kong sources.[106] Such international nontraceability is the stylistic hallmark of stories emanating in this period from what CIA insiders called their "mighty Wurlitzer," the worldwide network of press "assets" through which the CIA, or sister agencies such as Britain's MI-6, could plant unattributable disinformation.[107] PKI demands for a popular militia or "fifth force," and the training of PKI youth at Lubang Buaja, seemed much more sinister to the Indonesian army in the light of the Chinese arms stories.

But for months before the coup, the paranoia of the PKI had also been played on, by recurring reports that a CIA-backed "Council of Generals" was plotting to suppress the PKI. It was this mythical council, of course, that Untung announced as the target of his allegedly anti-CIA Gestapu coup. But such rumors did not just originate from anti-American sources; on the contrary, the first authoritative published reference to such a council was in a column of the Washington journalists Evans and Novak:

> As far back as March, General Ibrahim Adjie, commander of the Siliwangi Division, had been quoted by two American journalists as saying of the Communists: "we knocked them out before [at Madiun]. We check them and check them again." The same journalists claimed to have information that ". . . the Army has quietly established an advisory commission of five general officers to report to General Jani . . . and General Nasution . . . on PKI activities."[108]

Mortimer sees the coincidence that five generals besides Yani were killed by Gestapu as possibly significant.

But we should also be struck by the revival in the United States of the image of Yani and Nasution as anti-PKI planners, long after the CIA and U.S. press stories had in fact written them off as unwilling to act against Sukarno.[109] If the elimination by Gestapu of Suharto's political competitors in the army was to be blamed on the left, then the scenario required just such a revival of the generals' forgotten anti-Communist image in opposition to Sukarno. An anomalous unsigned August 1965 profile of Nasution in *The New York Times*, based on a 1963 interview but published only after a verbal attack by Nasution on British bases in Singapore, does just this: it claims (quite incongruously, given the context) that Nasution is "considered the strongest opponent of Communism in Indonesia"; and adds that Sukarno, backed by the PKI, "has been pursuing a campaign to neutralize the . . . army as an anti-Communist force."[110]

In the same month of August 1965, fear of an imminent showdown between "the PKI and the Nasution group" was fomented in Indonesia by an underground pamphlet; this was distributed by the CIA's long-time asset, the PSI, whose cadres were by now deeply involved:

> The PKI is combat ready. The Nasution group hope the PKI will be the first to draw the trigger, but this the PKI will not do. The PKI will not allow itself to be provoked as in the Madiun Incident. In the end, however, there will be only two forces left: the PKI and the Nasution group. The middle will have no alternative but to choose and get protection from the stronger force.[111]

One could hardly hope to find a better epitome of the propaganda necessary for the CIA's program of engineering paranoia.

McGehee's article, after censorship by the CIA, focuses more narrowly on the CIA's role in anti-PKI propaganda alone (bolded text in the following quote was used in the original article to call out CIA deletions):

> The Agency seized upon this opportunity [Suharto's response to Gestapu] and set out to destroy the P.K.I. . . . [**eight sentences deleted**]. . . . Media fabrications played a key role in stirring up popular resentment against the P.K.I. Photographs of the bodies of the dead generals—badly decomposed—were featured in all the newspapers and on television. Stories accompanying the pictures falsely claimed that the generals had been castrated and their eyes gouged out by Communist women. This cynically manufactured campaign was designed to foment public anger against the Communists and set the stage for a massacre.[112]

McGehee might have added that the propaganda stories of torture by hysterical women with razor blades, which serious scholars dismiss as groundless, were revived in a more sophisticated version by a U.S. journalist, John Hughes, who was later the chief spokesman for the State Department.[113]

Suharto's forces, particularly Col. Sarwo Edhie of the RPKAD commandos, were overtly involved in the cynical exploitation of the victims' bodies.[114] But some aspects of the massive propaganda campaign appear to have been orchestrated by non-Indonesians. A case in point is the disputed editorial in support of Gestapu which appeared in the October 2 issue of the PKI newspaper *Harian Rakjat*. Professors Benedict Anderson and Ruth McVey, who have questioned the authenticity of this issue, have also ruled out the possibility that the newspaper was "an Army falsification," on the grounds that the army's "competence . . . at falsifying party documents has always been abysmally low."[115]

V. The CIA and the Overthrow of Sukarno, 1965–1967

The questions raised by Anderson and McVey have not yet been adequately answered. Why did the PKI show no support for the Gestapu coup while it was in progress, then rashly editorialize in support of Gestapu after it had been crushed? Why did the PKI, whose editorial gave support to Gestapu, fail to mobilize its followers to act on Gestapu's behalf? Why did Suharto, by then in control of Jakarta, close down all newspapers except this one, and one other left-leaning newspaper which also served his propaganda ends?[116] Why, in other words, did Suharto on October 2 allow the publication of only two Jakarta newspapers, two which were on the point of being closed down forever?

As was stated at the outset, it would be foolish to suggest that in 1965 the only violence came from the U.S. government, the Indonesian military, and their mutual contacts in British and Japanese intelligence. A longer paper could also discuss the provocative actions of the PKI, and of Sukarno himself, in this tragedy of social breakdown. Assuredly, from one point of view, no one was securely in control of events in this troubled period.[117]

And yet for two reasons such a fashionably objective summation of events seems inappropriate. In the first place, as the CIA's own study concedes, we are talking about "one of the ghastliest and most concentrated bloodlettings of current times," one whose scale of violence seems out of all proportion to such well-publicized left-wing acts as the murder of an army lieutenant at the Bandar Betsy plantation in May 1965,[118] And, in the second place, the scenario described by McGehee for 1965 can be seen as not merely responding to the provocations, paranoia, and sheer noise of events in that year, but as actively encouraging and channeling them.

It should be noted that former CIA Director William Colby has repeatedly denied that there was CIA or other U.S. involvement in the massacre of 1965. (In the absence of a special CIA Task Force, Colby, as head of the CIA's Far Eastern Division from 1962–66, would normally have been responsible for the CIA's operations in Indonesia.) Colby's denial is however linked to the discredited story of a PKI plot to seize political power, a story that he revived in 1978:

> Indonesia exploded, with a bid for power by the largest Communist Party in the world outside the curtain, which killed the leadership of the army with Sukarno's tacit approval and then was decimated in reprisal. CIA provided a steady flow of reports on the process in Indonesia, although it did not have any role in the course of events themselves.[119]

It is important to resolve the issue of U.S. involvement in this systematic murder operation, and particularly to learn more about the CIA account of this which McGehee claims to have seen. McGehee tells us: "The Agency was extremely proud of its successful [**one word deleted**] and recommended it as a model for future operations [**one-half sentence deleted**]."[120] Ambassador Green reports of an interview with Nixon in 1967:

> The Indonesian experience had been one of particular interest to [Nixon] because things had gone well in Indonesia. I think he was very interested in that whole experience as pointing to the way we [!] should handle our relationships on a wider basis in Southeast Asia generally, and maybe in the world.[121]

Such unchallenged assessments help explain the role of Indonesians in the Nixon-sponsored overthrow of Sihanouk in Cambodia in 1970, the use of the Jakarta scenario for the overthrow of Allende in Chile in 1973, and the U.S. sponsorship in the 1980s of the death squad regimes in Central America.[122]

Epilogue to Chapter 5 (2015)

My views on Sukarno's overthrow have evolved since the 1980s. In that era, seeing Sukarno in contrast to the repressive dictator Suharto, I described Sukarno as "an undeniably popular and reasonably constitutional civilian leader."[1] Today I recognize that in the last years of his rule the country was becoming more and more unstable, major economic problems were not being addressed, and Sukarno was culpable in seeking to placate public unrest by an ill-advised military campaign against his neighbor Malaysia.

Today I recognize that in the last years of his rule the country was becoming more and more unstable, major economic problems were not being addressed, and Sukarno was culpable in seeking to placate public unrest by an ill-advised military campaign against his neighbor Malaysia.

I also attribute greater importance to the fact that Sukarno's adventurism thus contributed unwittingly to his own downfall, since the secret army special operations unit OPSUS, a combat intelligence unit created by Suharto which handled a peace initiative toward Malaysia of which Sukarno knew nothing, evolved into part of the apparatus plotting for his removal, perhaps indeed the planning core of it.[2]

Although my 1985 article mentioned OPSUS only in footnotes 61 and 66, I now suspect more strongly than before that it may have supplied the milieu for a second coup-minded plot, piggybacked within the first plot to negotiate peace. I mean by this that there was at first an OPSUS plot, pushed by Suharto, sanctioned by Yani, and staffed with veterans of the 1958 CIA/Permesta coup plot, to negotiate peace with Malaysia against Sukarno's wishes.[3] But then some of the people conspiring may have had a second agenda, to purge (by means of the false-flag pretext of Gestapu) the army general staff of Yani and other overall Sukarno loyalists, thus clearing the way for the coup and the massacre. Such a sophisticated two-level plot, like the propaganda forgery of the *Harian Rakjat* "editorial," may have been beyond the capabilities of Indonesians acting alone.[4]

Piggybacked plots are however a staple of the CIA, and before them of the British MI6. And in 1965 the British Foreign Office, working with MI6, sent its top propaganda expert, Norman Reddaway, to Singapore. In 1998, shortly before his death, Reddaway went public, to describe how "the overthrow of Sukarno was one of the Foreign Office's 'most successful' coups, which they have kept a secret until now":

> A covert operation and psychological warfare strategy was instigated, based at Phoenix Park, in Singapore, the British headquarters in the region. The MI6 team kept close links with key elements in the Indonesian army through the British Embassy. One of these was Ali Murtopo, later General Suharto's intelligence chief, and MI6 officers constantly travelled back and forth between Singapore and Jakarta.[5]

Stephen Dorril's book *MI6* confirms that "In South-East Asia MI6 was working hand in glove with the CIA to 'liquidate' Indonesia's President Sukarno."[6]

In the same period Ali Murtopo, the head of OPSUS, also traveled back and forth, not just to negotiate clandestinely with the Malaysian government, but also to smuggle "rubber and other goods" to generate money for OPSUS and accumulate $17 million in banks in Singapore and Malaysia.[7] Yani had authorized Murtopo's clandestine MI6 contacts; he would have had no way of knowing if these talks had turned to plans to eliminate Yani himself.

Like his close ally Suharto (as I wrote in 1985), Murtopo rose up through the Diponegoro Division, the division which played a central role both in staging Gestapu, and also in putting it down. I would now suspect, admittedly without proof, that if one wanted to research CIA and/or MI6 input into the 1965 Gestapu plot, the MI6/Ali Murtopo/OPSUS/Permesta connection would be a good place to begin.

VI. Catastrophe and Hope
Art and Better Politics

The last century has been, unfortunately, a century of holocausts. The mass slaughter in Indonesia, although one of the greatest since World War II, is far from unique; it was preceded by the mass killings in India as that country became independent, and followed by mass killings in Cambodia and elsewhere.[1]

I now see that my focus on American involvement in the 1965 massacre, although pertinent, was also one-sided. It was a response to the equally one-sided tendency of the American media, including scholars like Clifford Geertz who should have known better, to blame this unrestrained appetite for violence only on the Indonesians.[2]

But one can find the same tendency among Indonesians themselves. In *Minding the Darkness*, the third part of my poetic trilogy, I revised my American perspective in *Coming to Jakarta*, by quoting the great Indonesian novelist Pramoedya Ananta Toer. Pramoedya, who had earlier been imprisoned by the Dutch from 1947–49, was not killed in the great slaughter; but he was imprisoned for fourteen years in its aftermath.

One of the conditions of his imprisonment was that he wrote a confession of his culpability, and here is part of his interesting response under this compulsion (as abridged in my poem ^):

> I myself am Javanese
>
> I was educated to Javanese ideals
>   guided by the Mahabharata
>   at whose climax they bathe

> in the blood of their own brothers
>> while other peoples who
> have managed to slip their shackles
>
> are the nations that rule the world
>> Even in the belly of Dutch power
> Java still glorified
>
> its narrow world culture
>> they bathed in the blood of their brothers
> right up through 1966
>
> And because Java was no longer
>> in the belly of European power
> the slaughter reached an unlimited scale
>
> without colonization my country
>> would have ceaselessly spilled
> the blood of its sons and daughters
>
> cultural integrity a bogey
>> for the countries stuffed with capital
> by which free peoples are enslaved
>
> the unemployed become murderers
>> with uniforms and badges of rank
> vast forests are torn apart
>
> It is necessary that I emphasize
>> the problem of power
> that tends to turn people into bandits
>
> above all if they have held it for decades
>> and without ever knowing Verlichting
> Aufklaerung remain in thrall
>
> everything that has happened
>> will live on for centuries
> Once more—my apologies.[3]

Pramoedya's analysis has great merit: the Javanese culture in its dances and shadow plays indeed draws on a cultural tradition honoring bloodshed, warriors, and their instruments. He faults this tradition for never having experienced an eighteenth-century Enlightenment (*Verlichting* in Dutch, *Aufklaerung* in German) to temper its traditions with reason.

But it might be said that if Indonesia represented traditional culture at odds with modern scientific Enlightenment, Washington represented ruthless modern Enlightenment at odds with traditional culture. It is now clearly part of the historical record that Washington assisted the violence, supplying needed infrastructure for it. Substantial evidence of Washington's critical role has been collected by history professor Bradley Simpson, in his important book *Economists with Guns*.[4] The record is devastating, and (in his word) "disgraceful" (p. 189).

At the time McGeorge Bundy in the White House told LBJ that the massacre (which he chose to refer to as "Events in Indonesia since the abortive September 30th coup") was "a striking vindication of US policy towards Indonesia in recent years: a policy of keeping our hand in the game for the long-term stakes despite recurrent pressure to pull out;" and that it was clear to the Indonesian army that "the Embassy and the US government are generally sympathetic with and admiring of what the army is doing."[5]

Bundy was not alone. As noted earlier, James Reston, in June 1966, wrote of the massacre in the *New York Times* under the headline, "A Gleam of Light in Asia".[6] What were Bundy and Reston defending? A process whereby

> paramilitary groups and assorted thugs deputized by the country's soon-to-be dictator, General Suharto, executed at least half a million people. Starving prisoners were dumped into rivers alongside corpses; women were molested and raped; victims were shot, beheaded with swords, and dismembered while still alive; thousands more, spared death, were forced [like Pramoedya] into concentration camps and prisons.[7]

This savage madness, though native to Indonesia, occurred also in the Philippines and elsewhere.[8]

To understand the attitudes of the Bundys and Reston, we have to recall the anxieties of the Cold War. All three of the world's greatest powers feared each other; and, perhaps rightly, all three regarded Indonesia, whose Communist Party (the PKI) was the largest outside the Communist bloc, as a country whose future could determine the Cold War's outcome.

Indonesia, with its oil and other raw materials, was a major factor in America's decision to launch a major war in Vietnam, and provide a shield against possible Chinese retaliation should the Indonesian Army move to destroy the PKI. As Bradley Simpson said to Errol Morris,

> [The U.S. Government's] covert operations accelerated in the summer of 1964 in ways that connect with the expansion of the war in Vietnam. Johnson's decision to sign off on expanded covert operations in Indonesia takes place right around the time of the Gulf of Tonkin incident. [In Washington] They were looking at all this as a piece.[9]

In the 1970s Washington used the techniques that overthrew Sukarno to assist a similar army coup against President Allende. In this coup, a CIA-backed psychological warfare group explicitly used the ominous words *Djakarta se acerca—Jakarta is coming*—to terrorize, destabilize, and polarize Chile, which once had been South America's most stable and progressive democracy.[10] Washington's approval of Indonesian violence was made clear again in 1975, when "Suharto managed to gain Washington's backing" for his invasion of East Timor, resulting in a "decades-long blood-bath."[11]

HOW ACADEMIC MODERNIZATION THEORY CONTRIBUTED TO THE KILLINGS

Chapter 5 discussed the role of the United States, including U.S. universities, in preparing for and encouraging the massacre. Simpson has more to say on why Washington's "best and brightest" accepted what he calls the "deeply flawed authoritarian development model" (p. 3) that was urged on Indonesia by U.S. advisers and social scientists, and eagerly adopted by the military in Indonesia and elsewhere. This derived from a fundamental deficiency in U.S. social scientific thought:

> By the early 1960s modernization theory dominated social science thinking about political and economic development in both the academic and political realms. Modernization theorists drew in expected ways on deeply embedded discourses that emphasized both the uniqueness and the appropriateness of America's developmental model for the rest of the world and the cultural superiority of the West in general and the Anglo-Saxon tradition in particular.[12]

He adds, correctly in my view, that

> Although modernization theory as a social science paradigm may have originated in the United States in the postwar period, it was part of a larger, widely dispersed fabric of thinking about the process of becoming modern, the origins of which stretch back to the Enlightenment.[13]

And he points out that, ironically, Washington, Moscow, and Beijing all had similar aid programs designed to promote modernization in Indonesia. The chief difference was that Moscow and Beijing emphasized industrialization whereas the U.S. regarded Indonesia above all as a source of needed raw materials, chiefly oil. Thus,

> U.S. officials and modernization theorists performed impressive acts of intellectual gymnastics trying to criticize the legacy of European colonialism while advocating development plans that continued colonial trade structures.[14]

Meanwhile modernization in Russia and above all Maoist China (which was about to be convulsed in 1966 by its Cultural Revolution) was (even more than in America) promoting a post-Enlightenment materialism destructive of traditional culture.

The United States, though far from Maoist, was wantonly destructive of Indonesian traditional culture. In 1953 alone, as part of the U.S. Information Agency (USIA's) cultural diplomacy program, "U.S. embassy officials estimated that 10 million Indonesians saw American films screened from the back of USIA trucks traveling around the country."[15]

There is, as I said earlier, an instructive irony here. Pramoedya lamented the failure of Enlightenment rationalism (perhaps represented in his mind by the Marxist PKI) to rethink a traditional Javanese culture (clearly represented in his mind by the Indonesian army) based on the *ksatriya* or warrior. Meanwhile Simpson sees the same Enlightenment as a source for an amoral social science paradigm that, by separating economics from ethical and cultural considerations, contributed to the massacre. (By the twentieth- century Enlightenment, like the church centuries earlier, had evolved from being a corrective for the status quo into being a reinforcement of it.) So I believe one can say that a debased Indonesian culture deficient in Enlightenment was being reinforced in the massacre by a debased Western Enlightenment deficient in culture.

I conclude that foreign policy, where it impacts on cultural evolution, is too serious a cultural matter to be entrusted to social scientists.

INDONESIA'S PASSAGE FROM CATASTROPHE TO HOPE

As late as 2012, when the interviews in chapter 3 took place, I had no reason to think that there was any hope that the truth about the massacre would ever be established. The lack of interest I sensed in the U.S. academy was enforced by law in Indonesia itself.[16]

Between 1984 and 1998, a lying government-funded propaganda film was required viewing for all schoolchildren.

> "Pengkhianatan G30S/PKI" ("The Betrayal of the September 30 Movement by The PKI") was played repeatedly in schools and on state-run television. The movie depicted the PKI as a group of bloodthirsty killers, men who tortured army soldiers—cutting off their genitals and gouging out their eyes—in a piece of Suharto-era propaganda. The lengthy film was compulsory viewing for school children, who were made to write a report about the evils of the communists once a year.[17]

With the fall of Suharto in 1998, the mandated screenings of this propaganda film ended, and Indonesia began a difficult transition from military dictatorship to a more open democracy. The first elected president, Abdurrahman Wahid, was someone I had already praised along with Pramoedya in *Minding the Darkness* (III.ix): although the Ansor youth of his mass Muslim organization Nahdlatul Ulama (NU) had participated in the 1965 massacre, Wahid later apologized for Ansor's involvement, and became a leader in a nation-wide campaign against sectarian violence. In 2000 another NU leader, Imam Aziz, established a civil society initiative for reconciliation between NU and the survivors of the 1965 massacre.

But the new civilian governments, still military-dominated, continued to limit discussion of the massacre. In 2007, for example, Indonesia's Attorney General ordered that all copies of fourteen school history textbooks be burned, on the grounds that they

> did not state that the Indonesian Communist Party (PKI) was responsible for the September 30th Movement (G30S in the Indonesian acronym), the murky coup attempt in 1965 which led to the downfall of Sukarno and the rise of Suharto. According to Indonesian law, school books must still refer to the September 30th Movement as "G30S/PKI" (or similar expression), pinning the blame squarely on the PKI.[18]

This blackout began to lift in 2014, after the release of Josh Oppenheimer's globally acclaimed film "The Act of Killing," a Danish-British-Norwegian production.[19] As the *Guardian* pointed out in March 2014,

> The Act of Killing may have lost out on this year's Oscar for best documentary, but it has instigated a spectacular change within Indonesian society. . . . Through a network of underground distributors and social media, The Act of Killing has now been viewed by millions of Indonesians. Government and anti-communist organisations continue to try to stop its distribution, but their efforts are ultimately futile in the internet age.
>
> It's a film that is impossible to ignore. Even people at the screening who didn't appreciate the [film], thought The Act of Killing would be ground-breaking in helping Indonesia break its silence about its history.[20]

One sign of the film's success in breaking this silence was that in 2014, Joshua Oppenheimer's sequel film, "The Look of Silence," was screened in Jakarta by two Indonesian government agencies: the Jakarta Arts Council and the National Human Rights Commission.[21] Later, in early 2016, senior Indonesian officials met with surviving victims "in an unprecedented meeting to discuss the killing of 500,000 communists and their supporters." At the meeting, "Agus Widjojo, a retired general, . . . called for the government to establish a commission for truth and reconciliation."[22]

The recent turnabout in Indonesia has revived my hopes for Indonesia, for America, and for the world. Indonesia, the largest Muslim country in the world, is a *carrefour* where eastern and western cultures have not just modified each other but shown signs of transcendence through the interaction. The blending of religious traditions there, as codified under a western-influenced constitution, has reinforced a version of Islam that has historically been moderate, and tolerant of other faiths.

But I would like to believe that this is just one example of the way that Indonesia, having been swayed in turn both toward both communism and capitalism, toward America, Russia, and China, has emerged with the possibility of playing a moderating role in the reduction of global conflict, just as Sukarno had envisaged at the Bandung conference of 1955.

Admittedly, this hope is based more on faith than on evidence. Many scholars fear that traditional Indonesian Islam, for the most part relatively moderate but unable to compete with Saudi wealth, may lose out in Indonesia to Wahhabi extremism.[23] But I take heart from the fact that Islamic terrorism, as witnessed for example in the major bombings of 2000, 2002, and 2005, appears for now to have been largely contained. Indonesia's apparent ability to contain terrorism is the more striking when we consider the continuing spread of violence in the Middle East, Libya, and sub-Saharan Africa.

CATASTROPHE AND GREAT LITERATURE

I am not comfortable in saying that good can come from massacre, but I have no problem saying that great literature can emerge from it. For the horrors of suppressing Sukarno's republic led to what has been rightly called "one of the great achievements of world literature":[24] the *Buru Quartet* of four prose novels written by Pramoedya while a political prisoner in Java. The four volumes supply a brilliant investigation of the historical clash in Indonesia between colonial attitudes and anti-colonial hopes for their overthrow.

In the volumes, Minke, the Indonesian protagonist, is heavily influenced by the writings of Multatuli (Douwes Dekker), a former Dutch administrator in Java who later, in his novel *Max Havelaar*, denounced Dutch colonialist practices that were impoverishing the Indonesian people. It is a measure of Pramoedya's capacious perspectives that in the novels Minke discovers that Joannes Benedictus van Heutsz, once the governor general of the Dutch East Indies, was also an admirer of Multatuli. Pramoedya's novels offer both an account of Dutch racist oppression and also a vision of reconciliation between western and native values, as the Dutchman Multatuli's ideas are assimilated and adapted in Minke's mind. Here Minke stands for Pramoedya himself, who later praised the novel *Max Havelaar* as "the book that killed colonialism."[25]

The title of the Quartet's second volume, referring to Minke, is *Child of All Nations*. I would like to think that Pramoedya's works, for which he received awards on four continents during his lifetime, will continue to inspire readers in the so-called First, Second, and Third Worlds.

Pramoedya's response to the fall of Indonesian democracy in 1965 replicates the responses of other great artists to catastrophe, from Virgil's *Aeneid* after the militarization of the Roman republic, to Wordsworth's *Prelude* after the demise of the nonviolent French revolution. A conspicuous, under-recognized case was that of the poet Rumi ("Dance, in the middle of the fighting"), whose native city of Balkh in Afghanistan, once so prosperous it was known as the "mother of cities," was leveled by the Mongols in 1220 and its inhabitants slaughtered, when Rumi (thankfully elsewhere) was only thirteen.

Shortly afterwards, Dante wrote his *Commedia*, in part a paean to world order under Pope and Holy Roman Emperor, after the unprecedented scandals of a chaotic imperial interregnum (1256–73) when for seventeen years there was no emperor at all, and also the so-called Babylonian Captivity (1309–77), when the papal court was moved under French influence from Rome to the papal enclave at Avignon, where it remained for the next sixty-seven years.

Another contemporary example besides Pramoedya of the power of art to transcend tragedy is Czeslaw Milosz, the Nobel-Prize-winning Polish poet whom Joseph Brodsky called "one of the greatest poets of our time, perhaps the greatest."[26] Milosz wrote some of his most stirring poems from what he later called the *Anus mundi* of occupied wartime Poland, while the city of Warsaw was being systematically demolished by the Germans.

Shortly after Milosz defected from his diplomatic post in the post-war Polish dictatorship, he wrote a short rhetorical attack against oppressors

> You who wronged a simple man
> Bursting into laughter at the crime . . .
>
> Do not feel safe. The poet remembers.
> You can kill one, but another is born.
> The words are written down, the deed, the date.
>
> And you'd have done better with a winter dawn,
> A rope, and a branch bowed beneath your weight.[27]

Milosz wrote this from abroad where his native Polish was not spoken, while his works back in Poland were banned. Later, from America, he wrote how he had once believed his writing

> would also be a messenger
> between me and some good people,
> even if they were few, twenty, ten
> or not born, as yet.
>
> Now I confess my doubt.
> There are moments when it seems to me
> I have squandered my life.[28]

He was unaware that his writings were keeping alive a spirit of resistance in Poland, so much so that when the Solidarity movement won in 1980 the right to erect a monument to shipyard workers killed a decade earlier, three Polish leaders were depicted: Lech Wałęsa, Pope John Paul II, and Milosz. Above them was the triplet from Milosz's poem "You Who Wronged":

> Do not feel safe. The poet remembers.
> You can kill one, but another is born.
> The words are written down, the deed, the date.

The monument, like the words on it, became part of a process in which Solidarity, in a non-violent revolution, eventually overthrew a government that did not represent the prevailable will of the people, by remembering its crimes.[29]

For forty years I had accepted that in Indonesia the great crime of the 1965 Indonesian massacre would not be revisited in my lifetime, still less that my poetry and prose would never have any impact on that appalling injustice.[30] Then, to my great surprise and pleasure, I witnessed the power of John Oppenheimer's two films to reopen the issue. Not just in America, but in Jakarta, his films converted the very intolerability of the catastrophe into an engine of hope.

And then, shortly after *The Act of Killing* was released, I received an unsolicited email from Oppenheimer:

> your writing about Indonesia has been an important inspiration for this whole project, and I have revisited it again and again. Above all *Coming to Jakarta*, but also your survey of American involvement in the genocide.[31]

I began *Coming to Jakarta* in a period when I was self-absorbed in pain and acute depression. But if my poem contributed in a small way to the vital global process of liberation, in Indonesia and elsewhere, I can only be grateful for my crisis with which the poem began.

POSTSCRIPT

Indonesia's outlook in 2018 is less hopeful than when I wrote this chapter two years ago. It seems more relevant today than before that, for example, in 2001 Christians and Muslims were slaughtering each other in Poso and the Moluccas, or that the Muslim killers (principally Laskar Jihad) had been armed by an element of the Indonesian Army (TNI). My optimism then was encouraged by Jakarta's success in tracking down and executing those responsible for the 2002 Al-Qaeda-backed bombing of tourists in Bali.[32] However, other militant Muslim groups were in fact proliferating in this period, and there are reasons to fear that Indonesia's tolerant Islam is now at risk.

In April 2017, the electoral defeat in Jakarta of progressive reformer Basuki Tjahaja Purna ("Ahok"), a Chinese Christian, followed by his imprisonment for blasphemy, alarmed progressives everywhere. Some in the west have attributed it to the increasing influence of Islamic extremism fueled by Saudi wealth. Others pointed to nativist resentment of Ahok's Chinese background. Allen Nairn attributed it in part to a deep-rooted campaign by the once powerful Indonesian military to oust Ahok's progressive mentor, President Joko Widodo (Jokowi).

According to veteran analyst Allen Nairn, the campaign against Ahok was part of a larger campaign by the once powerful Indonesian military to defeat Jokowi, Ahok's mentor in the fight against corruption. He claimed that the key figures in this larger campaign were "associates of Donald Trump in Indonesia, . . . army officers and a vigilante street movement linked to ISIS": the FPI (Front Pembela Islam, or Islamic Defenders Front)."[33]

One should not despair at this development. Indonesia took a major step toward a more open society when, in 2000, reformers separated the police from the military. This made it possible for those guilty of corruption or official violence to be convicted and punished; and violence in general has abated considerably since the thousand deaths in the 1998 riots.

Americans in particular should worry less about Indonesia and more about their own country, where since 9/11 the army, in violation of the Posse Comitatus Act, continues to play a significant police role in homeland security. This includes the surveillance of U.S. citizens, and the permanent deployment since 2008 of a U.S. Army Brigade Combat Team "to help with civil unrest and crowd control."[34] So far Americans seem to be less concerned about the risks of martial law than Indonesians, who still retain such bitter memories of it.

Hence the relevance of Milan Kundera's remark in 1979: "The struggle of man against power is the struggle of memory against forgetting." The Indonesians' memory of oppression in 1998 empowered them, just as the Polish memory of oppression empowered the Solidarity movement in the 1980s.

Americans, precisely because they have not been so obviously oppressed, would do well, I suggest, to learn from the experience of both peoples.

I return to my theme that, to comprehend America, we must also comprehend its role in the Indonesian slaughter of 1965. The future of both countries depends in part on this deepening of our consciousness. Moreover, I believe, because of both countries' rich experience in bridging diverse cultures, so does the future of the world.

Permissions

Excerpts from COMING TO JAKARTA, copyright ©1988 by Peter Dale Scott, used by permission of New Directions Publishing Corp.
Robert Hass, "Preface," in "Poetry and Terror: Some Notes on Coming to Jakarta," in Robert Hass, What Light Can Do (New York: Ecco/HarperCollins, 2012), 193–94.

Earlier versions of other portions of this book were published as follows:
My videotaped interviews with Freeman Ng were posted by him at www.ComingToJakarta.net.
Chapter III, "America's Culpability in Indonesia, and Why We Should Acknowledge It," as "Islam, a Forgotten Holocaust, and American Historical Amnesia," Asia-Pacific Journal: Japan Focus, April 15, 2015.
Chapter IV, "'Gaps' of Consciousness; or, How Writing *Coming to Jakarta* Led Me to Deep Politics," as "Coming to Jakarta and Deep Politics: How Writing a Poem Enabled Me to Write American War Machine (An Essay on Liberation)," Asia Pacific Journal: Japan Focus, June 27, 2011.
Chapter V, as "The United States and the Overthrow of Sukarno, 1965–1967" *Pacific Affairs* (Vancouver, B.C.) 58.2 (Summer 1985), 239–64.
"Epilogue to Chapter V," in "Still Uninvestigated After 50 Years: Did the U.S. Help Incite the 1965 Indonesia Massacre?" Asian-Pacific Journal: Japan Focus, August 3, 2015.
Part of Chapter VI, "Catastrophe and Hope: Art and Better Politics," as "North American Universities and the 1965 Indonesian Massacre: Indonesian Guilt and Western Responsibility," The Asia-Pacific Journal: Japan Focus, December 15, 2014.

Notes

FOREWORD

1. Previously published as Robert Hass, "Poetry and Terror: Some Notes on *Coming to Jakarta*" in *What Light Can Do* (New York: HarperCollins Publishers, 2012), 193–194.

I. INTERVIEWS WITH FREEMAN NG

1. In the course of revising, I found myself touching on matters usually dealt with separately in universities, under such categories as political science, literature, ethics, psychology, sociology, anthropology, and religion.

2. "The mean vaults at the back of my head" is a revealing line. Normally I would refer to the mean vaults in my frontal lobes. That I would write so angrily about the creative back of my head is a symptom of my psychic alienation at the time from my own sources of creativity—an alienation I would only become more conscious of in the early sections of the long poem I did not yet, at this time, have any idea I was going to write.

3. I have said almost since I wrote I.i that I considered it an example of "automatic writing." In so doing I was unaware of the degree to which that term has been appropriated by occultists like the wife of Yeats, who considered it writing channeled from a higher external source. (See, e.g., Anna Sayce, "How To Do Automatic Writing," www.annasayce.com/how-to-do-automatic-writing). I had in mind the "pure psychic automatism" that the poet André Breton used to define Surrealism, thereby inspiring the Automatisme of the Quebec artistic movement founded by the painter Paul-Emile Borduas. (I quote repeatedly from both Breton and Borduas in *Listening to the Candle*, the sequel to this poem.)

4. Peter Dale Scott, Paul Hoch, Russell Stetler, and Josiah Thompson, *Beyond Conspiracy: The Hidden Dimensions of the John F. Kennedy Assassination*. I no

longer have a copy of the page proofs, but the MS is cited as a book in a couple of published books, for example Gus Russo, *Live by the Sword* (Baltimore: Bancroft, 1998), 511.

5. The broadcast was actually to celebrate the publication of a book, *The Great Heroin Coup* (Boston: South End Press, 1980; reissued in 2015 by Trine Day Press), written in Danish by Henrik Krüger and translated by our mutual friend Jerry Meldon, to which I contributed a Foreword. This explains why Henrik and Jerry were with me in Harvard Square in "our Halloween Nixon masks."

6. One of them, "D," was the poet Daryl Hine, as recorded also by James Merrill's biographer: "Maintaining his composure was crucial to Merrill. As a reminder of what losing it might mean, there was Daryl Hine. This old friend has recently plunged into full-fledged mania: he had 'seen God in a parking lot,' 'taken off his clothes _ and been arrested.' Hine received treatment and recovered, but he resigned as editor of *Poetry* a short time later. The line between inspiration and insanity could be very thin" (Langdon Hammer, *James Merrill: Life and Art* [New York: Alfred A. Knopf, 2015], 608). The other friend may still be alive.

7. In his 1980 Nobel Prize lecture, Czeslaw Milosz recalled reading Selma Lagerlöf's *Wonderful Adventures of Nils*, "who flies above the earth and looks at it from above but at the same time sees it in every detail." In his words, this "This double vision may be a metaphor of the poet's vocation" (Czeslaw Milosz, *Beginning with My Streets: Essays and Recollections* [New York: Farrar, Straus and Giroux, 1991], 273).

8. Contemporary estimates are discussed by Robert Cribb, and compacted into an assessment of "as low as 200,000 or as high as one million" (Robert Cribb, "Unresolved Problems in the Indonesian Killings of 1965–1966," *Asian Survey*, July/August 2002, 559).

9. As noted in chapter 3, the journalist Kathy Kadane reported in May 1990 that during the massacre, personnel in the U.S. Embassy passed up to 5000 names of alleged PKI cadres to the Indonesian Army. My earlier essay in chapter 5 was unaware of this, but argues for a deeper and earlier U.S. involvement. And in Chapter VII, I note, citing Bradley Simpson in his important book *Economists with Guns*, that "it is now clearly part of the historical record that *after* the coup Washington assisted and paid for the violence, and supplied needed infrastructure for the violence." This too is an important argument, but a different one.

10. I had already dedicated an earlier poem to him, "Prepositions of Jet Travel," the title poem of my 1981 poetry chapbook.

11. Cf, the Wikipedia entry for "Malcolm Caldwell": "The motives for Caldwell's murder remain unexplained. An attack by a Vietnamese commando to discredit the Pol Pot regime on the eve of the Vietnamese invasion of Cambodia, is argued by Philip Short in his book as the most likely explanation. . . . Four of the guards at the guest house were arrested and two of them 'confessed' after torture at Khmer Rouge's infamous S-21 prison that the killers were subversives attempting to undermine the Khmer Rouge regime and that Caldwell was killed 'to prevent the Party from gathering friends in the world'. Alternatively, journalist Wilfred Burchett as well as some of Caldwell's family members believe that Caldwell was

killed on the orders of Pol Pot, following a disagreement between the two during their meeting."

12. At the time, I dismissed Pound's politics as crazy and therefore harmless. I now see them as more dangerous in a crazy world than I did then, having since learnt more about his influence on violent segregationists and anti-Semites like John Kasper. See Alec Marsh, *John Kasper and Ezra Pound: Saving the Republic* (London: Bloomsbury Academic, 2015).

13. My obsession with Pound at this stage was a little like Blake's obsession with Milton. We both see poetry as a source of truth, and we both therefore are obsessed with the errors we see in the work of these two great truth-tellers preceding us. This too is hopeful: by using our great but fallible predecessors as rungs on the ladder of truth, we hope to climb to a slightly better vision of the desirable.

14. Peter Dale Scott, "Greek Theater," in *The American Deep State: Big Money, Big Oil, and the Attack on U.S. Democracy* (Berkeley: University of California Press, 2017), 186.

15. For years I was suspicious of the circumstances in which Allard was killed by his former student, Dennis Sweeney. I am now quite satisfied that his murder had nothing to do with his questioning of Robert Kennedy's assassination. See David Harris's compassionate memoir, *Dreams Die Hard: Three Men's Journey through the Sixties* (San Francisco: Mercury House, 1993).

16. Herbert Foenstel describes William Bader as "a former CIA intelligence officer" (Herbert Foenstel, *From Watergate to Monicagate: Ten Controversies in Modern Journalism and Media* [Westport, CT: Greenwood Press, 2001], 82).

17. The essay can be read as Chapter V of *The War Conspiracy: JFK, 9/11, and the Deep Politics of War* (New York: Skyhorse, 2013), 178–215. The episode, too complex to be easily summarized, easily qualifies as a rebellious "deep event." Cf. Peter Dale Scott, *Dallas '63: The First Deep State Revolt against the White House* (New York: Open Road, 2015), 158ss.

18. See our collaborative volume, *Zbigniew Herbert, Selected Poems*, translated from the Polish by Czeslaw Milosz and Peter Dale Scott (Harmondsworth, Middlesex: Penguin Books, 1968; republished in America by Ecco Press).

19. Peter Dale Scott, "Letter to Czeslaw Milosz" in Peter Dale Scott, ed., *Crossing Borders* (New York: New Directions, 1995), 34.

20. For a prose account see my essay, "A Difficult, Inspirational Giant" in Cynthia Haven, ed., *An Invisible Rope: Portraits of Czeslaw Milosz* (Athens, OH: Swallow Press/Ohio University Press, 2011), 65–73.

21. After writing this Appendix, I see a deeper and more existential coherence in the movement of the poem from II.iv, with the loss of my friend Malcolm Caldwell, to II.v, with Pound isolated "in the wind and rain," and the mythic prophecy that seekers like Odysseus/Ulysses, in their exploration of "Kung and Eleusis," shall "lose all companions." Coming into perspective is the long-term pattern of an otherworld or yin balance to the yang of contemporary politics, a fitting segue to the pastoral memory of II.vi.

22. A personal note: When the Institute dissolved in 1960, publication of its journal *Pacific Affairs* was transferred to the University of British Columbia, in Vancouver,

Canada. Twenty-five years later, *Pacific Affairs* published my prose article that grew out of research for this poem, "The United States and the Overthrow of Sukarno, 1965–1967" (chapter 5 of this book). I was not aware of this IPR connection at the time of the poem, or of this interview.

23. The Co-operative Commonwealth Federation (CCF), now the New Democratic Party (NDP).

24. An Internet search confirms that the lines about banks are my own, but the critic Alec Marsh has seen in it an echo of Pound: "Pound would call this financial regime 'usura,' Scott does not use this term, but he does say, in *Coming to Jakarta* "EP however nuts / you may have been / in your Wagnerian way // you were right about banks / the problem of stored desire, which becomes no one's" (Alec Marsh, "Two Poets' Agenda in the Age of Terror (the 1980s): Adrienne Rich and Peter Dale Scott," *Bigbridge Reviews*, 17, www.bigbridge.org/BB17/index.html).

25. As the sidenotes make clear, it is a quote from *American Chronicle*, by Ray Stannard Baker, which I read in a biography of Lincoln Steffens.

26. For details, see David Talbot, *The Devil's Picture Book* (New York: Harper-Collins, 2015), 74–93; Peter Dale Scott, "How Allen Dulles and the SS Preserved Each Other," *Covert Action Information Bulletin*, 25 (Winter 1986), 4–14.

27. I now believe that a more serious motive for Allen Dulles was to preserve elements of the Nazi leadership, to counter Communism in postwar Germany.

28. R. Harris Smith, *OSS: The Secret History of America's First Central Intelligence Agency* (Berkeley: University of California Press, 1972), 116: "One director of that company [Italian Superpower] was *a Chicago banker, whose son,* New York banker James Russell Forgan, *was* a close friend of Allen Dulles." The italicized additions by the CIA in Langley turned a true statement into a false one: James's father, David Robertson Forgan, had no connection to Italian Superpower. James was also chairman of the two committees that prepared the planning documents for the creation of the Central Intelligence Agency.

29. Cf. IV.i: "It was at a Bilderberg / meeting that Prince Bernhard // was introduced by Baron / Edmond de Rothschild / to Tibor Rosenbaum of the ICB" (Clyde H. Farnsworth, "A Global Bank Tangle and Its Lost Millions," New York Times, April 9, 1975, http://www.nytimes.com/1975/04/09/archives/a-global-bank-tangle-and-its-lost-millions-behind-israeli-arrest-an.html).

30. Scott, *The American Deep State*, 170–171.

31. For Henderson, see Peter Dale Scott, *The War Conspiracy: JFK, 9/11, and the Deep Politics of War* (New York: Skyhorse Publishing, 2013), 324, 377.

32. Original text in Guy J. Pauker, *Communist Prospects in Indonesia* (Santa Monica, CA: RAND Corporation, 1964), 221–223.

33. Guy J. Pauker, "Indonesia: The Year of Transition," *Asian Survey*, VII, 2, 138–150.

34. See for example John Roosa, *Pretext for Mass Murder: The September 30th Movement and Suharto's Coup d'Etat in Indonesia* (Madison: University of Wisconsin Press, 2006), 186.

35. Peter Dale Scott, "Exporting Military Economic Development," in Malcolm Caldwell ed., *Ten Years' Military Terror in Indonesia* (Nottingham: Spokesman

Books, 1975), 233–234; David Ransom, "The Berkeley Mafia and the Indonesian Massacre," *Ramparts*, October 1970, www.geocities.ws/mafiaberkeley/berkeleymafia.html.

36. Ransom, "The Berkeley Mafia and the Indonesian Massacre."

37. Scott, "Exporting Military Economic Development," 254n40.

38. *Coming to Jakarta*, III.iv, 69; cf. Dante, *Inferno*, 1, 91; Homer, *Odyssey*, 10, 490, 563. The poem is beginning to shift, to a stage (parts IV and V) where it will no longer suffice to "look around / at so much visibility" (we must look within, to begin with). The poem is beginning to take on more and more the shape of a voyage.

39. The first four parts of the poem can be loosely compared to the four Buddhist Noble Truths: (1) "there is suffering" (part I), (2) "there is a cause of suffering" (part II), (3) "there is a remedy to suffering" (part III), and (4) "the eight-fold path of action" (part IV). But I knew nothing of the Four Noble Truths when I dashed off my first draft of the poem.

40. "Ballad for Americans" (Music: Earl Robinson / Words: John LaTouche), www.lyricsplayground.com/alpha/songs/b/balladforamericans.shtml.

41. Cf. Walter A. Kaufmann, "The Hegel Myth and Its Legend," in Jon Stewart, ed., *The Hegel Myths and Legends* (Evanston, Illinois: Northwestern University Press. 1996), 82–83.

42. The second volume, *Listening to the Candle*, incorporates memories of my experiences and readings at French monasteries, which eventually led to my being hired as an academic medievalist. One can see a foretaste of this dialectic in the female-male contrast of the two Adamses in III.xiii.

43. Cf. Francis Fukuyama, End of History and the Last Man (New York: Free Press, 1992), 61: "[A] reading of Hegel's historical works will reveal that historical accident and contingency play a large role in them."

44. My experience may not have been an unusual one. I now see affinities with Jonathan Edwards' account of when, "looking up on the sky and clouds, there came into my mind so sweet a sense of the glorious majesty and grace of God, that I know not how to express" (*The Works of Jonathan Edwards* [London: W. Ball, 1839], lv). Under the influence of Edwards and other preachers, soon hundreds were experiencing similar moments, in America's First Great Awakening of the 1700s (Frances FitzGerald, *The Evangelicals: The Struggle to Shape America* [New York: Simon & Schuster, 2017], 16–17).

45. William H. Davies, *The Autobiography of a Super-tramp* (New York: A. A. Knopf, 1917).

46. Michael Beresford Foster, *Mystery and Philosophy* (London: SCM Press, 1957). Cf. Cameron Wybrow and Michael Beresford Foster, *Creation, Nature, and Political Order in the Philosophy of Michael Foster (1903–1959): The Classic Mind Articles and Others, with Modern Critical Essays* (Lewiston, NY: E. Mellen Press, 1992).

47. Later, in the two succeeding volumes of *Seculum*, I composed analogous "pivots" for each: III,viii (to my daughter Cassie) in *Listening to the Candle*, and III.ix (to my second wife Ronna) in *Minding the Darkness*.

48. Robert Hass, "Poetry and Terror: Some Notes on *Coming to Jakarta*," in Robert Hass, ed., *What Light Can Do: Essays on Art, Imagination, and the Natural*

World (New York: Ecco, 2012), 201. Although Hass does not mention it, the future genealogy of Aeneas in *Aeneid* 6, 756–776 is a *topos* of epic echoing the genealogy of Aeneas' male ancestors in *Iliad* 20, 208–241, also dwelling on violence.

49. For years I believed it was Passchendaele, as one can read on the Internet; but in fact he was killed during the capture of Regina Trench, during the Battle of the Somme.

50. Frederick George Scott, *The Great War as I Saw It* (Toronto, F. D. Goodchild Co., 1922), 157.

51. Benedict R. O'C. Anderson, *Language and Power: Exploring Political Cultures in Indonesia* (Ithaca, NY: Cornell UP, 1990), 7.

52. In III.xii, I wrote, "the Barata Yudda or great war." Actually "Barata Yudda" means "Bharata war," Bharata ("The Cherished") being the common ancestor of the warring Kuravas and Pendavas.

53. Cf. chapter 2, where I mention Albert Memmi's discussion of "the doubleness of the colonized in relation to the colonizer, either as model or antithesis" (Linda Hutcheon, *Splitting Images*, 80; Albert Memmi, *The Colonizer and the Colonized* [New York, Orion Press: 1965], 140).

54. Scott, *The American Deep State*, 2–4.

55. George Ignatieff, *The Memoirs of George Ignatieff: The Making of a Peacemonger*, (Toronto: University of Toronto Press, 1985), 185–186. Cf. Alvin Finkel, *Our Lives: Canada After 1945* (Toronto: J. Lorimer, 1997), 111–112.

56. On the train, I would just flash my Canadian passport which looked quite official. No German conductor would dare challenge me, even though I was only nineteen.

57. Scott, *The American Deep State*, 16–17, 22–24, etc.

58. This is a revealing quote from one of Ed Reid's informants in Dallas.

59. Kathy Kadane, "Ex-agents say CIA compiled death lists for Indonesians," States News Service, 1990, www.namebase.org/kadane.html; cf. Tim Weiner, *Legacy of Ashes: The History of the CIA* (New York: Doubleday, 2007), 260.

60. See Peter Dale Scott, "Still Uninvestigated After 50 Years: Did the U.S. Help Incite the 1965 Indonesia Massacre?" *Asian-Pacific Journal: Japan Focus*, August 3, 2015, www.japanfocus.org/-Peter_Dale-Scott/4351/article.html.

61. Zoe Reynolds, "Putu Oka Sukanta and Poetry from Prison," *Jakarta Post*, July 25, 2013, www.thejakartapost.com/news/2013/07/25/putu-oka-sukanta-and-poetry-prison.html.

62. For the details, see Franz Schurmann, Peter Dale Scott, and Reginald Zelnik, *The Politics of Escalation in Vietnam* (Boston: Beacon Press, 1966), 71, 92; quoting from *New York Times*, July 22, 1965 and November 24, 1965. The question of the NLF ("Viet Cong") negotiating position is more complicated, obscured by contradictory translations of their "Five Points" statement of March 22, 1965, from on the one hand Hanoi and on the other Washington (*Politics of Escalation*, 70).

63. "Four Points" Statement of North Vietnamese Premier Pham Van Dong, as quoted in Franz Schurmann, Peter Dale Scott, and Reginald Zelnik, *The Politics of Escalation in Vietnam* (Boston: Beacon, 1967), 74.The CIA reported the North Vietnamese position accurately in a TOP SECRET intelligence analysis of 1966: "The

North Vietnamese made it clear in 1962 that they did not intend to make concessions. . . . In their concept, only the U.S. would make concessions: the U.S. would first agree to withdraw from the South, and in the subsequent negotiations the nature and timing of the U.S. withdrawal would be worked out." ("The Positions of Hanoi, Peking, and Moscow on the Issue of Vietnam Negotiations: 1962 to 1966," *CIA Intelligence Study*, ESAU ZZZI-66, 31 October 1966, www.cia.gov/library/readingroom/docs/esau-29.pdf.) Cf. Memorandum of Chester Cooper to President Johnson of May 25, 1965, *Foreign Relations of the United States, 1964–1968*, II, Document #315: "Mai Van Bo, Hanoi's representative in Paris . . . stressed that Pham Van Dong's four points were not to be considered as preconditions for negotiations, but rather as 'working principles' toward an ultimate settlement." Cf. also the explication of the "Four Points" by Luu Doanh Huynh in Robert S. McNamara et al., eds., *Argument Without End: In Search of Answers to the Vietnam Tragedy* (New York: Public Affairs, 1999), 231: "we were providing a way for the U.S. to withdraw without losing face."

64. Admittedly, the situation was somewhat complicated by the demand of the Four Points that South Vietnamese internal affairs be settled "in accordance with" the program of the more intransigent National Liberation Front, the so-called Viet Cong. See Paul R. Pillar, *Negotiating Peace: War Termination as a Bargaining Process* (Princeton, NJ: Princeton University Press, 1983), 110. But the *Times* characterization of the North Vietnamese position was simply false.

65. It was also the first step on the "other way" which led to the non-publication of my book MS fourteen years later (IV.i), that is, to my gradual separation from the dominant American mindset, and thus to the writing of this poem.

66. See for example, Robert Cohen and Reginald Zelnik, eds., *The Free Speech Movement: Reflections on Berkeley in the 1960s* (Berkeley: University of California Press, 2002), 153.

67. Martin A. Lee and Bruce Shlain, *Acid Dreams: the CIA, the Sixties, and Beyond* (New York: Grove Press, 1985, 1992), 162

68. Lee and Shlain, *Acid Dreams*, 187.

69. Ibid, 188.

70. Gene Anthony, *The Summer of Love: Haight-Ashbury at its Highest* (San Francisco: Last Gasp, 1995), 130.

71. In 1967 William Hitchcock decided to move to the West Coast. Here he joined forces with Owsley Stanley's colleague Tim Scully (Stanley being in jail at this point) and another chemist called Nick Sand to bankroll the production of large quantities of LSD for general distribution. This they achieved and by 1969 had manufactured over 10 million doses of acid, most of which was in the form of pills known as "Orange Sunshine" (OS)" (Richard J. Miller, "Timothy Leary's Liberation, and the CIA's Experiments! LSD's Amazing, Psychedelic History," www.salon.com/2013/12/14/timothy_learys_liberation_and_the_cias_experiments_lsds_amazing_psychedelic_history).

72. "When those who attended the Be-In saw for the first time just how many of them there were, they became empowered; something new had happened to them,

something profoundly uplifting, exciting, and transformative" (Michael Bowen, *My Odyssey: The First Human Be-In*, www.royalmaze.com/chapter-one-part-three).

73. Lee and Shlain, *Acid Dreams*, 161. Free initial distribution is of course the standard technique of creating new markets for illicit drugs.

74. Lee and Shlain, *Acid Dreams*, 157.

75. Owsley was arrested again in 1970, along with eighteen other members of the Grateful Dead, where Owsley worked as a sound engineer ("New Orleans Cops & the Dead Bust," *Rolling Stone*, March 6, 1970).

76. Norman Mailer, *The Armies of the Night: History as a Novel, the Novel as History* (New York: New American Library, 1968), 86.

77. Seth Rosenfeld, *Subversives: The FBI's War on Student Radicals, and Reagan's Rise to Power* (New York: Farrar, Straus and Giroux, 2012), 457, 656. The owner of a neighborhood gun shop (Berkeley still had such things in the 1960s) told me that, that afternoon, the Sheriffs bought out the entire retail stock of shotgun ammo in Berkeley.

78. See below, Chapter III, footnote 12; Chapter V, footnote 85.

79. Mailer, *Armies of the Night*, 276–277.

80. "Gandhi's failure to stop the violence that led to Partition is a haunting reminder that certain failures are far more valuable for upholding the principles of a civilized society than the violent, unethical birth of nations" (Manash Firaq Bhattacharjee, "Gandhi and the Trial of Noakhali," *The Wire*, January 10, 2016, www.thewire.in/69645/gandhi-and-the-trial-of-noakhali).

81. See James W. Douglass, *Gandhi and the Unspeakable: His Final Experiment with Truth* (Maryknoll, NY: Orbis Books, 2012).

82. Rudolf Mrázek, *The United States and the Indonesian Military, 1945–1966* (Prague: Czechoslovak Academy of Sciences, 1978).

83. Clifford Geertz, *The Interpretation of Cultures; Selected Essays* (New York: Basic Books, 1973), 282.

84. Discussion for example in Scott, *The American Deep State*, 78, 229n79.

85. See Chapter V at footnote 89: "Via the new contract, Lockheed, Dasaad and Alamsjah were apparently hitching their wagons to Suharto's rising star."

86. This was my pessimistic assessment from 2012 of my poetry in general, until two years after Freeman and I conducted this interview. But see chapter 6.

87. It was only in editing these interviews that I realized how much my 1980 Watertown crisis owed to the loss of my connections to first *The New York Review* (for whom I never wrote an article after 1970) and, much later, its editor Bob Silvers. With an opening phone call from Bob in late 1980 it seemed for a short while that this connection would be restored, but Bob's second phone call made clear that this was not to be.

88. Compare the argument of Bruno Snell in *The Discovery of the Mind* (New York: Dover, 1982), 1–22, especially p. 12.

89. *Fortune*, July 1973, p. 154, cf. *Wall Street Journal*, April 18, 1967.

90. William Henderson, "Some Reflections on United States Policy in Southeast Asia," in William Henderson, ed., *Southeast Asia: Problems of United States Policy* (Cambridge: MIT Press, 1963), 253–263. In addition to being an adviser on

international affairs to Socony Mobil, Henderson was an officer of American Friends of Vietnam. See Peter Dale Scott, *The War Conspiracy: JFK, 9/11, and the Deep Politics of War* (New York: Skyhorse Publishing, Inc., 2013), 324, 377.

91. At the time of the 1973 coup, David Atlee Phillips was the CIA's Chief of Western Hemisphere Division (C/WHD).

92. See transcript of the David Susskind show, October 24, 1977, www.maryferrell.org/mffweb/archive/viewer/showDoc.do?docId=8907&relPageId=59.

93. David Rockefeller, *Memoirs* (New York: Random House, 2992), 431–432; Peter Dale Scott, *The Road to 9/11: Wealth, Empire, and the Future of America* (Berkeley: University of California Press, 2007), 39–42.

94. See transcript of the David Susskind show, October 24, 1977, www.maryferrell.org/mffweb/archive/viewer/showDoc.do?docId=8907&relPageId=81, etc.

95. William Kintner and Joseph Kornfeder, *The New Frontier of War* (London: Frederick Muller, 1963), 237 (Cf. Chapter V, at footnote 43).

96. See Peter Dale Scott, "Atrocity and its Discontents: US Double-Mindedness about Massacre, from the Plains Wars to Indonesia," in Adam Jones, ed., *Genocide, War Crimes and the West: History and Complicity* (London: Zed Books, 2004), 146–163.

97. *Bhagavad Gita*, trans. Swami Nikhilananda (New York: Ramakrishna-Vivekananda Center, 1944), Chapter 11, txt 12 and 32, pp. 256, 261. Cf. Robert Jungk, trans. James Cleugh, *Brighter Than a Thousand Suns: A Personal History of the Atomic Scientists* (New York: Harcourt/ Harvest Books, 1958), 201.

98. Amy Goodman, "Exception to the Rulers, Part II," *Z Magazine*, December 1997, www.thirdworldtraveler.com/Foreign_Policy/Rulers2_GoodmanZ.html.

99. See Chapter V, "Epilogue".

100. "*It is the owl*" is italicized in the poem. I thought when writing I was quoting from a Jacobean drama I had seen performed at Oxford, but I have been unable to locate any such play. It is a sentence uttered in a Mexican-American novel, *Bless Me Ultima*; but I rarely read contemporary novels.

101. Karl Marx, "Eleventh Thesis on Feuerbach."

102. See Commentary on IV.vi.

103. In my oral interview with Freeman I actually called Dan Ellsberg's sitting on the railroad tracks "an example of *ahimsa* in action, and the better kind of action against these inferior kinds like throwing grenades into a nest." In a thoughtful response, Dan took issue (I believe rightly) with this oversimplified white-black contrast. In his words, "Almost everything, in my opinion (except participating in massacre) depends on circumstances. For a Russian soldier in Stalingrad, throwing a grenade at a German machine-gun nest in a building was not inferior as a kind of action." Writing more carefully as I am now, I have to agree that the moral contrast I drew in my interview was simplistic. At the same time my poetry, being "precisely poetry," was I think right to contrast these two modes of action without comment.

104. Since our interview, a Catholic has contested Pagels' translation, with the charge that "she has (probably unwittingly) modified the logion to accommodate it to psychological theory" (Mats Winther, "Gospel of Thomas, error in translation," Catholic Answers Forum, May 2015, forums.catholic.com/t/

gospel-of-thomas-error-in-translation/395315/1. But other translations are in the same spirit.

105. I saw the male scholars at the Villa Serbelloni (the Rockefeller Foundation Bellagio Center) as a guest of my then father-in-law, the Center's first Director. The Villa Serbelloni appears again in *Listening to the Candle* (III.x, pp. 93–94, quoting from a witness, Amy Clampitt) as the place "from which [my wife] Maylie's sister / drove off to become a nun". Years later after writing both volumes of *Seculum*, in 1997, I myself spent a month as a scholar-poet at the Villa, and was able to write of it ("when Ronna and I danced / naked . . . on the moonlit balcony / overlooking the lake") as I finished the final volume (*Minding the Darkness*, V.i-iii, pp. 233–243).

106. Peter Dale Scott, "Five Poems," *Jacket* 34, October 2007, www.jacketmagazine.com/34/scott-p-d-5p.shtml. Reprinted in Peter Dale Scott, *Mosaic Orpheus* (Montreal: McGill-Queen's University Press, 2009), 62–82.

107. Alfred McCoy, *The Politics of Heroin: CIA Complicity in the Global Drug Trade, Afghanistan, Southeast Asia, Central America, Colombia* (Chicago: Chicago Review/ Lawrence Hill Books, 2003), xii.

108. Actually, there are two instances. Cf. Tariq Ali, *The Clash of Fundamentalisms: Crusades, Jihads and Modernity* (London: Verso, 2003), 388.

109. Peter Dale Scott, "Coming to Jakarta and Deep Politics: How Writing a Poem Enabled Me to Write *American War Machine* (An Essay on Liberation)," *Japan Focus: Asia Pacific Journal*, June 27, 2011, www.japanfocus.org/site/view/3553. A heavily revised version follows as Chapter IV of this book.

110. Peter Dale Scott, *American War Machine* (Lanham, MD: Rowman & Littlefield, 2010), 1–5.

111. "Under this theory, put forward by public policy expert Joseph Overton, the public is willing to consider only a few ideas or scenarios as reasonable—those are the ones that reside within the window. Radical notions remain outside the window, unfit for serious debate" (Steven Levingston, "Glenn Beck's paranoid thriller, 'The Overton Window,'" *Washington Post*, June 15, 2010, www.washingtonpost.com/wp-dyn/content/article/2010/06/14/AR2010061405423.html).

112. Jungk, *Brighter Than a Thousand Suns*, 198, 201.

113. Owen Lattimore had been editor of *Pacific Affairs*, the journal published by the Institute of Pacific Relations which later first published what became Chapter V of this book.

114. "Joseph Rotblat," Wikipedia, en.wikipedia.org/wiki/Joseph_Rotblat. See Reiner Braun, *Joseph Rotblat: Visionary for Peace* (Weinheim: Wiley-VCH, 2007).

II. TRAUMA, POETRY, POLITICS, AND THE MYSTERY OF HOPE

1. Heinrich Heine, "Schöpfungslieder," in *Sämmtliche Werke*, vol. 2, 5th ed (Philadelphia: Verlag von John Weik & Co, 1860), 134.

2. In another book, I argue that Milosz's *daemonion* spoke to him most urgently after the traumatic event of being forced to flee a burning Warsaw, in 1944, with

nothing but what he could carry. See *Ecstatic Pessimist: Czeslaw Milosz as a Poet of Catastrophe and Hope* (forthcoming).

3. This balancing of yang and yin becomes more and more conspicuous in the complete trilogy *Seculum*, of which *Coming to Jakarta* is the first (yang) part.

4. "It is possible that what distinguishes poetic drama from prosaic drama is a kind of doubleness in the action, as if it took place on two planes at once" (T.S. Eliot, "John Marston," in *Selected Essays* (London: Faber, 1969), 229. The word "doubleness" dates back to Chaucer's "Ballad of Women's Doubleness"; but Chaucer uses it to mean "duplicity," with which doubleness today is contrasted.

5. Discussing Margaret Atwood, Linda Hutcheon refers to doubleness as "the need to keep literal and ironic meanings together" (*Splitting Images: Contemporary Canadian Ironies* [Toronto: Oxford University Press, 1991], 12).

6. Linda Hutcheon, *Splitting Images*, 80; Albert Memmi, *The Colonizer and the Colonized* (New York, Orion Press: 1965), 140.

7. Robert Langbaum, *The Mysteries of Identity: A Theme in Modern Literature* (New York: Oxford University Press, 1977). 89–90.

8. "Introduction," in Joseph P. Natoli and Linda Hutcheon, eds., *A Postmodern Reader* (Albany, NY: State University of New York, 1993), xi.

9. Similarly, I may have been a post-secularist without knowing it, or even being aware of the term. See discussion of III.vii of the poem in chapter 1. I would like to record here my gratitude to James Schamus for having, years before he became the CEO of Focus Features, walked on his own initiative into the offices of New Directions, and persuaded them to accept *Coming to Jakarta*.

10. My first book of poems, inspired by my very ambivalent fascination with the sixties, the Summer of Love, and People's Park, was entitled *Rumors of No Law*.

11. Eliot himself, according to John Worthen, was aware of this connection between illness and poetry:A few years later [Eliot] would describe how… "some forms of illness" could help imaginative writing. He quoted A.E. Housman's remark that "I have seldom… written poetry unless I was rather out of health" and commented "I believe I understand that sentence." During illness, "A piece of writing meditated, apparently without progress, for months or years, may suddenly take shape and word" (John Worthen, *T.S. Eliot: A Short Biography* [London: Hans Publishing, 2009], 108; citing T.S. Eliot, "Housman on Poetry," *Criterion*, 13:5 [October 1933], 54; *The Use of Poetry and the Use of Criticism* [London: Faber, 1933], 69).

I can understand Eliot's second sentence, except that I had not been consciously meditating the poem that burst out of me in the first six weeks of 1981, like water from a dam that has given way. Forces had been building up in me for years, but I don't think I had been conscious of them until this crisis.

12. *William Wordsworth: Poems*, ed. Seamus Heaney (Faber & Faber, 2011), 15-16. Cf. Matthew Arnold's lines on how Wordsworth's poetry can bring smiles and ease in "this iron time/ Of doubts, disputes, distractions, fears" ("Memorial Verses April 1850," www.poetryfoundation.org/poems/43594/memorial-verses-april-1850).

13. The French books of the 1805 *Prelude* were mostly composed between March and October 1805, but soon expanded to record disgust at Napoleon's coronation as emperor in December ("This last opprobrium, when we see the dog/Returning to his

vomit" [*Prelude*, 10:935-36]). Later Wordsworth wrote two poems that recalled the duke's murder, "Dion" and "Sonnet on the Disinterment of the Duke d'Enghien." Cf. *Prelude* (1805), 9:413–423; Lionel J. Sanders, *The Legend of Dion* (Toronto: E. Kent, 2008), 247–449.

14. In Adorno's words, "Even in the most sublimated work of art there is a hidden 'it should be otherwise.' As eminently constructed and produced objects, works of art ... point to a practice from which they abstain: the creation of a just life" (Theodor W. Adorno, "Commitment," *New Left Review*, I, 87–88, September–December 1974; in Terry Eagleton and Drew Milne, *Marxist Literary Theory: A Reader* [Oxford: Blackwell Publishers, 1996], 202).

15. I say more about this in *Ecstatic Pessimist* (forthcoming).

16. Octavio Paz, *Children of the Mire: Modern Poetry from Romanticism to the Avant-garde* (Cambridge, MA: Harvard University Press, 1974), 1. Cf. Michael Palmer, *Active Boundaries: Selected Essays and Talks* (New York: New Directions, 2008), 106, and so on.

17. E.g. Czeslaw Milosz, interviewed by Robert Faggen, "The Art of Poetry No. 70," *Paris Review*, Winter 1994, www.theparisreview.org/interviews/1721/czeslaw-milosz-the-art-of-poetry-no-70-czeslaw-milosz: "That emptiness and cruelty, which is the basis of Larkin's weltanschauung, should be accepted as a basis upon which you work *towards* something light" [emphasis in original].

18. Steven Levingston, Glenn Beck's paranoid thriller, "The Overton Window," *Washington Post*, June 15, 2010, www.washingtonpost.com/wp-dyn/content/article/2010/06/14/AR2010061405423.html.

19. See, for example Margarete Mitscherlich, *Erinnerungsarbeit: zur Psychoanalyse der Unfähigkeit zu trauern* (Frankfurt am Main: S. Fischer, 1987).

20. Truth is defined as that which is "in accordance with fact or reality." By truth here I mean not just what accords with the world of fact around us, but also what represents reality in a Platonic or Gandhian sense beyond what we can see.

21. "Man, in his moral nature, becomes, in his progress through life, a creature of prejudice, a creature of opinions, a creature of habits, and of sentiments growing out of them. These form our second nature, as inhabitants of the country and members of the society in which Providence has placed us" (Edmund Burke, ed. Peter J. Stanlis, *Edmund Burke: Selected Writings and Speeches* [New York: Doubleday, Anchor, 1963], 494).

22. Thomas Eisner and Edward O. Wilson, eds., *Animal Behavior: Readings from Scientific American* (San Francisco: W. H. Freeman, [1975]), 1. Their definition is actually "study of whole patterns of animal behavior under natural conditions, in ways that emphasize[d] the functions and the evolutionary history of the patterns." But since then social psychologists have appropriated the term: they recognize that "The scope of ethology is wide and includes all species (including man), living and extinct" (D.W. Rajecki, "Ethological Elements in Social Psychology," in Clyde Hendrick, ed., *Perspectives on Social Psychology* [Hillsdale, NJ: Lawrence Erlbaum Associates; New York: Wiley, 1977])

23. W. S. Merwin, *The Mays of Ventadorn* (Washington: National Geographic, 2002), 10.

24. See Robert Middlekauff, *The Glorious Cause: The American Revolution, 1763–1789* (Oxford University Press, 2005), 51, 136ss; Lydia Dittler Schulman,

Paradise Lost and the Rise of the American Republic (Boston: Northeastern University Press, 1992).

25. Czeslaw Milosz, *Native Realm: A Search for Self-definition* (Berkeley: University of California Press, 1981), 247. Cf. chapter 4; Peter Dale Scott, "Czeslaw Milosz and Solidarity; or, Poetry and the Liberation of a People," *Brick* 78 (Winter 2006); Peter Dale Scott, "Miłosz, Eliot, and the Generative Canon," *Sarmatian Review*, September 2017, www.ruf.rice.edu/~sarmatia/917/index.html. I say more about the role of the dialectical canon in this development in Peter Dale Scott, *Ecstatic Pessimist* (forthcoming).

26. See Stephen Jay Gould, *Ontogeny and Phylogeny* (Cambridge, MA: Belknap Press/Harvard University Press, 1977).

27. "Mississippi Goddam," Songfacts, www.songfacts.com/detail.php?id=14188; quoting Nina Simone, in LaShonda Barnett, ed., *I Got Thunder: Black Women Songwriters on Their Craft* (New York: Thunder's Mouth Press, 2007), 149.

28. An obvious example is Leonard Cohen's "Democracy Is Coming to the USA." Another, less easy to explain, is the Beatles' "We All Live in a Yellow Submarine."

29. On this important and widely observed phenomenon of killers' PTSD, cf. Geoffrey B. Robinson, The Killing Season: A History of the Indonesian Massacres (Princeton: Princeton University Press, 2018), 300: "The violence of 1965–66 also appears to have had deep and lasting psychological consequences for those who took part in it, whether as perpetrators or bystanders. The tortured behavior of the perpetrators highlighted in Oppenheimer's films The Act of Killing and The Look of Silence are cases in point, but the same symptoms – such as nightmares, physical illness, psychological disturbance, domestic violence, and substance abuse – may be observed in the memoirs, fictionalized accounts, and testimonies of perpetrators and bystanders. . . . [I]n Bali in 1994, for example, I met two men who as young boys had been splattered by the blood of PKI members whose execution by the army they watched. When I asked the men if they wished to share their story with me, they smiled broadly at first and then began to weep uncontrollably. Other accounts describe former killers who apparently lost their sanity, became un controllably violent, or suffered hallucinations of various kinds."

30. I say a little more about my notion of what is "prevailable" in Peter Dale Scott, *The Road to 9/11: Wealth, Empire, and the Future of America* (Berkeley: University of California Press, 2007), 270; *The American Deep State: Big Money, Big Oil, and the Attack on U.S. Democracy* (Lanham, MD: Rowman & Littlefield, 2017), 181.

III. AMERICA'S CULPABILITY IN INDONESIA, AND WHY WE SHOULD ACKNOWLEDGE IT

1. Immanuel Kant, "Secret Article for Perpetual Peace," in Kant, ed., *Perpetual Peace: A Philosophical Essay*, trans. by M. Campbell Smith (London: George Allen & Unwin, 1915), 160. https://courseworks2.columbia.edu/files/614995/download?download_frd=1.

2. "President Obama: 'We Will Degrade and Ultimately Destroy ISIL,'" *The White House Blog*, September 10, 2014, www.whitehouse.gov/blog/2014/09/10/president-obama-we-will-degrade-and-ultimately-destroy-isil.

3. "Looking into the Massacres of Indonesia's Past," *BBC News*, June 2, 2016, www.bbc.com/news/world-asia-36431837.

4. For details, see Nathaniel Mehr, *Constructive Bloodbath in Indonesia: The United States, Great Britain and the Mass Killings of 1965–1966* (Nottingham, England: Spokesman Press, 2009), 49–53, 100.

5. International Institute of Social History "1965: The Forgotten Holocaust of Indonesia," commemorative event of October 2005, www.socialhistory.org/en/events/1965-forgotten-holocaust-indonesia. A better word is needed for a campaign of mass political killing, a term analogous to genocide but explicitly highlighting political goals. As no such term currently exists, I will also use the awkwardly suitable term "Holocaust" here.

6. Isabel Hilton, "Our Bloody Coup in Indonesia," *Guardian*, July 31, 2001, www.theguardian.com/world/2001/aug/01/indonesia.comment. Cf. Matthew Jones, *Conflict and Confrontation in South East Asia, 1961–1965: Britain, the United States, and the Creation of Malaysia* (Cambridge: Cambridge University Press, 2002); Mehr, *Constructive Bloodbath in Indonesia*.

7. Chiefly Peter Dale Scott, "The United States and the Overthrow of Sukarno, 1965–1967," *Pacific Affairs*, 58, Summer 1985, 239–264; reprinted below as chapter 5.

8. Bradley R. Simpson, *Economists with Guns: Authoritarian Development and U.S.-Indonesian Relations, 1960–1968* (Stanford, CA: Stanford University Press, 2008), 173; cf. 311n6, where of the seven conspiratorially minded "American historians" named, two are actually Dutch, one (myself) is Canadian, another was born in Canada, and one was born to Anglo-Irish parents in Kunming, Yunnan. This leaves two native Americans, Ruth McVey and Lloyd Gardiner; and McVey has emigrated to Italy.

9. Since this book went to press two very important new books have opened up for further discussion both the massacre, and U.S. involvement in it: Geoffrey B. Robinson, The Killing Season: A History of the Indonesian Massacres (Princeton: Princeton University Press, 2018); and Jess Melvin, The Army and the Indonesian Genocide: Mechanics Of Mass Murder (Abingdon, Oxon: Routledge, 2018).

10. Tim Weiner, *Legacy of Ashes: The History of the CIA* (New York: Doubleday, 2007), 260.

11. See Jeremy Kuzmarov, "American Complicity in Indonesian Killings Runs Deep," *HuffingtonPost*, October 18, 2017, www.huffingtonpost.com/entry/american-complicity-in-indonesian-killings-runs-deep_us_59e81584e4b0153c4c3ec537. U.S. support was directed to the Indonesian police as well as army. Deputy CIA Director Robert Amory, Jr., recalled in 1966 that through "the mission of training police forces . . . a lot of excellent work has been done . . . . In some respects the groundwork done there, in Indonesia, may have been responsible for the speed with which the coup of last September, or whenever it was, was wrapped up" (Ralph E. Weber, ed., *Spymasters: Ten CIA Officers in Their Own Words* [Wilmington, DE: SR Books, 1999], 169).

12. Guy J. Pauker, "The Role of the Military in Indonesia," in John H. Johnson, ed., *The Role of the Military in Underdeveloped Countries* (Princeton, NJ: Princeton University Press, 1962), 221–23 ("strike"); William Kintner and Joseph Kornfeder, *The New Frontier of War* (London: Frederick Muller, 1963), 233, 237–238

("liquidating"). Other examples in Peter Dale Scott, "Exporting Military-Economic Development," in Malcolm Caldwell, ed., *Ten Years' Military Terror in Indonesia* (Nottingham, England: Spokesman Books, 1975), 227–232.

13. U.S., Congress, Senate, Committee on Foreign Relations, *Multinational Corporations and United States Foreign Policy, Hearings*, 94th Congress, 2nd Session, 1978, 941; cf. 955.

14. Armando Siahaan, "Historian Claims West Backed Post-Coup Mass Killings in '65," *Jakarta Globe*, January 9, 2009.

15. Roland Challis, *Shadow of a Revolution: Indonesia and the Generals* (Stroud: Sutton, 2001), 90.

16. Peter Dale Scott, *The American Deep State: Big Money, Big Oil, and the Attack on U.S. Democracy* (Lanham, MD: Rowman & Littlefield, 2017), 45–57; John Cooley, *Unholy Wars* (London: Pluto Press, 1999), 31–32, 87, 106, 169, 187, and so on.

17. *Declassified Documents Quarterly Catalogue*, 1982, 001786 [DOS Memo for President of July 17, 1964; italics in original]. This revealing document is not to be found in the once-suppressed volume of the *Foreign Relations of the United States, 1964–1968*, Volume XXVI, *Indonesia; Malaysia-Singapore; Philippines* (Washington: Department of State, 2000) at p. 124. The Preface to this controversial volume notes that Public Law 102–138 of 1991 confirms that "the published record should omit no facts that were of major importance in reaching a decision; and nothing should be omitted for the purposes of concealing a defect in policy" (p. iii, history.state.gov/historicaldocuments/frus1964-68v26/preface.) The controversy over the volume is partly discussed in the same Preface (p. vii). For a fuller discussion of the CIA attempt to recall the volume *after its distribution to university libraries and elsewhere*, see Thomas Blanton, "CIA Stalling State Department Histories," *National Security Archive*, July 27, 2001, nsarchive.gwu.edu/NSAEBB/NSAEBB52; Daniela Mohor, "UC Professor Spearheads Effort to Stop Book Recall," *Berkeley Daily Planet*, August 1, 2001, www.berkeleydailyplanet.com/issue/2001-08-01/article/6112?headline=UC-professor-spearheads-effort-to-stop-book-recall-By-Daniela-Mohor-Daily-Planet-staff.

18. Michael Wines, "C.I.A. Tie Asserted in Indonesia Purge," *New York Times*, July 12, 1990. Cf. the very misleading version of Tim Weiner, that Robert Martens, senior political officer of the embassy, gave the generals "an unclassified list of sixty-seven PKI leaders. . . . 'It was certainly not a death list,' Martens said" (*Legacy of Ashes*, 260). In fact, Martens himself wrote that his list comprised "a few thousand at most out of the 3.5 million claimed party members" (Letter to the editor, *Washington Post*, June 2, 1990; quoted in *Foreign Relations of the United States, 1964–1968*, Volume XXVI, Document 185, "Editorial Note," history.state.gov/historicaldocuments/frus1964-68v26/d185).

19. Jessica T. Mathews, "The Road from Westphalia," *New York Review of Books*, March 19, 2015.

20. Paul Krugman, "Behind the Great Divide," *New York Times*, February 18, 2003.

21. The Oxford English Dictionary provides dates for, among others, "non-violence" (2014), "conscientious objector" (to war service, 2016), "activist" (political, 1917), "non-interventionism" (2017). "satyagraha" (1920), "genocide" (1944),

"traumatize" (psychologically, 1949), PTSD (1982). Some of the OED's definitions record our cultural evolution or ethogeny: for example "war crime [1906] n. an offence against the rules of war, formerly excluding, but since the 1939–45 war including, any such act performed on the orders of a higher authority." Or, "passive resistance . . . 1928 V. G. Desai tr. M. K. Gandhi *Satyagraha in S. Afr.* xii. 172 None of us knew what name to give to our movement. I then [sc. in 1906] used the term 'passive resistance' in describing it."

22. "PTSD: A Growing Epidemic," *NIHMedlinePlus*. Winter 2009, www.medlineplus.gov/magazine/issues/winter09/articles/winter09pg10-14.html.

23. Sheryl Gay Stolberg, "Senate Passes $700 Billion Pentagon Bill, More Money than Trump Sought," *New York Times*, September 18, 2017, www.nytimes.com/2017/09/18/us/politics/senate-pentagon-spending-bill.html. A similar House vote was 356 to 70, with 127 Democrats voting in favor. See "Peter Dale Scott on Enlightenment Values in the Age of Trump," *WhoWhatWhy*, November 20, 2017, www.whowhatwhy.org/2017/11/20/peter-dale-scott-enlightenment-values-age-trump.

24. As already noted, some members of the assassination gangs in Indonesia "experienced recurring nightmares" (*Coming to Jakarta*, IV.x). Cf. Chapter 3, endnote 29.

25. Cf. Peter Dale Scott and Robert Parry, "A Long History of America's Dark Side," *Consortium*, October 7, 2010, www.consortiumnews.com/2010/100710a.html.

26. Cf. T.S Eliot: "I believe that at the present time the problem of the unification of the world, and the problem of the unification of the individual, are in the end one and the same problem, and the solution of one is the solution of the other." (T.S. Eliot, "Religion Without Humanism," in Norman Foerster, ed., *Humanism and America: Essays on the Outlook of Modern Civilization* [New York: Farrar and Rinehart, 1930], 112; misquoted in Peter Dale Scott, *Listening to the Candle*, 68; cf. Peter Dale Scott, "The Social Critic and His Discontents," in A. David Moody, ed., *The Cambridge Companion to T.S. Eliot* [Cambridge: Cambridge University Press, 1994], 63).

IV. "GAPS" OF CONSCIOUSNESS; OR, HOW WRITING *COMING TO JAKARTA* LED ME TO DEEP POLITICS

1. "Robert Hass: Online Interviews," with Sarah Pollock, Modern American Poetry, www.english.illinois.edu/maps/poets/g_l/haas/onlineinterviews.htm.

2. Friedrich Wilhelm Nietzsche, *Beyond Good and Evil* (Buffalo, NY: Prometheus Books, 1989), 103, §156.

3. Ellsberg has made the same comparison in speeches: see his "Introduction: Call to Mutiny," in E.P. Thompson and Dan Smith, eds., *Protest and Survive* (New York: Monthly Review Press, 1981), xvii. And others have endorsed his concern, for example Lyle V. Anderson, "Cybernetics, Culpability, and Risk: Automatic Launch and Accidental War," in P.T. Durbin, ed., *Philosophy of Technology: Practical, Historical and Other Dimensions* (Dordrecht: Kluwer Academic Publishers, 1989), 21.

4. Daniel Ellsberg, *The Doomsday Machine: Confessions of a Nuclear War Planner* (New York: Bloomsbury, 2017), 332 (emphasis in original).

5. James W. Douglass, *JFK and the Unspeakable: Why He Died and Why It Matters* (Maryknoll, NY: Orbis Books, 2008), xv.

6. McGeorge Bundy, Memorandum to President Johnson, October 22, 1965, *Foreign Relations of the United States, 1964–1968,* Volume XXVI, Indonesia; Malaysia-Singapore; Philippines, 334, history.state.gov/historicaldocuments/frus1964-68v26/d160. In addition, U.S. Ambassador to Indonesia Marshall Green in early December 1965 recommended financial assistance to Adam Malik "for the activities of the [civilian killer] Kap-Gestapu movement [DELETION] The Kap-Gestapu activities to date have been important factor in the army's program, and judging from results, I would say highly successful" (Telegram from the Embassy in Indonesia to the Department of State, December 2, 1965, *Foreign Relations of the United States, 1964–1968,* Volume XXVI, Indonesia; Malaysia-Singapore, 379, #179, history.state.gov/historicaldocuments/frus1964-68v26/d179).

7. A form of indirect violence is the extreme deprivation that is intensified by the increasing income disparity in America since about 1980. Books about poverty and despair in America often read almost as if they were about another country. I suggest, for example, Arlie Russell Hochschild, *Strangers in Their Own Land: Anger and Mourning on the American Right* (New York: New Press, 2016).

8. "Loving America," in *Tilting Point* (San Luis Obispo, CA: Word Palace Press, 2012), 20.

9. See "Peter Dale Scott on Enlightenment Values in the Age of Trump," WhoWhatWhy, November 20, 2017, www.whowhatwhy.org/2017/11/20/peter-dale-scott-enlightenment-values-age-trump/. America seems to be barely aware of how militarized it has become. In 2017, there was much talk of the Congressional inability to pass any legislation. Yet, "In a rare act of bipartisanship on Capitol Hill, the Senate [in September] passed a $700 billion defense policy bill . . . with a Pentagon budget that far exceeds what President Trump has asked for. Senators voted 89–9 to approve" (*New York Times*, September 18, 2017, www.nytimes.com/2017/09/18/us/politics/senate-pentagon-spending-bill.html). A similar House vote was 356 to 70, with 127 Democrats voting in favor.

10. It is no accident, I think, that both episodes concern women. It is even more relevant that in writing the second episode I was greatly helped, as elsewhere, by the guiding words of my mother. In the context of the whole trilogy, *Coming to Jakarta*, dedicated to my father, is a male, intellectual poem. But it tempers at the end toward reconciliation with the irrational world I have just criticized, which I now also see as a reconciliation of yang with yin within myself. I see similar reconciliations in the work of other poets, such as Wordsworth's two years at Racedown in 1795–97, when according to some commentators he was "on the verge of a complete breakdown which [his sister] Dorothy nursed him through" (Andrew Mitchell, "On the Road to Pantisocracy," *Fortnightly Review*, January 2011, www.fortnightlyreview.co.uk/2011/01/on-the-road-to-pantisocracy. For similar events in the life and work of Pound and Milosz, see Peter Dale Scott, *Ecstatic Pessimist* (forthcoming).

11. The Freudian notion of memory repression and recovery come under careful scrutiny during the recent vogue of so-called Memory-recovery therapy (MRT), which unfortunately led to cases where some people were convicted for alleged sexual abuses which never occurred. This scandal led to a backlash, to the extent that the publisher's promotion for a popular critique, *The Myth of Repressed Memory*, could

describe "the idea of 'recovered memory'" in general as "not actually a legitimate psychological phenomenon," but "closer to a dangerous fad or trendy witch hunt" (www.amazon.com/exec/obidos/ISBN=0312141238/roberttoddcarrolA). Although I have little or no sympathy for MRT, the experience I am about to describe in Palo Alto, corroborated by a witness, Alfred McCoy, left me absolutely convinced that some memories can be both repressed and recovered.

12. Psychologists tend to distinguish between the conscious "suppression" and the unconscious "repression" of memories. In this book, looking at the interaction between cultural and psychological forces effacing memory, the distinction can become very blurred. The memory of the Indonesian army's role in the 1965 massacre was vigorously "suppressed" by Suharto's psychological warriors, but to a greater or less degree "repressed" by most of the traumatized survivors. Writing today, I would say that my memory of the MG door was repressed rather than "suppressed," but we should not overlook the contribution of U.S. opinion managers to my act of repression.

13. There are other examples in *Coming to Jakarta* of this recovery of repressed memories. Unfortunately, in many cases the witnesses who might have corroborated them were not as sensitized as Al to the presence of a controlling irrationality in our daily affairs. Almost all had forgotten what they had witnessed (just as at first had Al and I), which was to be expected. But unlike Al, almost no one was able or willing to recover the memory when I urged them. So I was rendered cognizant of the widespread social conditioning of our thoughts, which were and are largely constrained to what could and can be easily shared. And *Jakarta*, from this perspective, had been a revolt from within against this social conditioning. *Le coeur a ses raisons*.

14. Peter Dale Scott, "The Sleep of Reason: Denial, Memory-Work and the Reconstruction of Social Order," in *Literary Responses to Mass Violence* (Waltham, MA: Brandeis University, 2004), www.brandeis.edu/ethics/pdfs/publications/Literary_Responses.pdf, 38–39; quoting from Alfred McCoy, *The Politics of Heroin: CIA Complicity in the Global Drug Trade, Afghanistan, Southeast Asia, Central America, Colombia* (Chicago: Chicago Review/ Lawrence Hill Books, 2003), xii (emphasis added); quoting in turn from *Coming to Jakarta*, V.ii, 147–148.

15. Peter Dale Scott, *American War Machine: Deep Politics, the CIA Global Drug Connection, and the Road to Afghanistan* (Lanham, MD: Rowman & Littlefield, 2010), 4–5.

16. A similar event, albeit far less dramatic, occurred in 1997, when I was writing a commissioned article on the U.S. war on drugs in Colombia. A friend had given me a small box of Xeroxed materials, mostly hard to obtain in North America but otherwise almost valueless, which I kept in my UC office. Returning there one day, I found the box emptied and inverted in the middle of the office floor, along with the pens and pencils I had also stored in it. Of course, it would have been much easier for the thieves to simply make off with the box. But that would not have conveyed the same forceful, one might have thought unforgettable, message. And yet once again I managed to forget the event, until recovering it almost two decades later in the course of editing this essay.

17. Scott, *American War Machine*, 3. In the 2011 version of this essay I explicitly declined to attribute this deep event to a "deep state." I wrote that "the term 'deep

state' was itself reflective of the social scientific structural bias—the urge to reduce all social phenomena to definable structures—that was my explanation for the resistance of intelligent critics like Noam Chomsky to studying deep events at all. That is why I have since preferred to refer to 'deep forces'—a term free of the structural connotations implicit in the word 'state.' I am coming now to envisage deep politics as revealing a realm beyond that of social structures and systems, much as quantum mechanics unsettled and moved beyond the Newtonian assumption of an ordered or structured universe." But still later I returned to the notion of a "deep state," while specifying that "Unlike the state, the deep state is not a structure but a system, as difficult to define, but also as real and powerful, as a weather system" (*The American Deep State*, 14).

18. Steven Levingston, Glenn Beck's paranoid thriller, "The Overton Window," *Washington Post*, June 15, 2010, www.washingtonpost.com/wp-dyn/content/article/2010/06/14/AR2010061405423.html. Obama's White House advisor Van Jones went outside this window when he signed a resolution (which I had helped draft) calling for an investigation of the 9/11 attacks. Though he soon retracted his support of this proposal, he was nonetheless forced to resign (Fred Barbash and Harry Siege, "Van Jones resigns amid controversy," *Politico*, September 6, 2009, www.politico.com/story/2009/09/van-jones-resigns-amid-controversy-026797).

19. Peter Dale Scott, "The Tao of 9/11," *Jacket* 34, October 2007. www.jacketmagazine.com/34/scott-p-d-5p.shtml; in Peter Dale Scott, *Mosaic Orpheus* (McGill-Queen's University Press, Spring 2009), 62.

20. "Indonesia Reacts to 'Act of Killing' Academy award Nomination," *Jakarta Globe*, January 23, 2014, jakartaglobe.beritasatu.com/news/indonesia-reacts-to-act-of-killing-academy-nomination. See chapter 6.

21. The same can be said of the Soviet Revolution, launched after the German High Command had arranged for Lenin to return to Russia in a sealed train. And there was a deeper dimension to the Boston Tea Party that preceded the American Revolution, in response to the new British Tea Act of 1773. It was not just a political protest. The Tea Act made legally imported tea cheaper, and was thus an economic threat to wealthy smugglers of Dutch tea, like John Hancock.

22. Peter Dale Scott, *The Road to 9/11*, 171. Cf. Ola Tunander, "Democratic State vs Deep State: approaching the Dual State of the West," paper presented at Government of the Shadows: Global Governance, Para-Politics and Organized Crime, University of Melbourne, August 10–12, 2006, www.prio.org/Publications/Publication/?x=3914; published in in Eric Wilson, ed., *Government of the Shadows: Parapolitics and Criminal Sovereignty* (London: Pluto Press, 2009), 56–72.

23. Peggy Noonan, *Wall Street Journal*, October 28, 2013: "What Woodward calls 'this secret world' I have come increasingly to think of as the deep state—again, the vast, unfathomable and not fully accountable innards of the permanent U.S. intelligence and national-security apparatus." (This paragraph was written before a very simplified notion of a "deep state" went viral in 2017, to explain the relative outsider Trump's difficulties with the establishment.)

24. Lofgren himself distinguishes his approach from those dealing with mysterious and/or repressed material: "Logic, facts, and experience do not sustain belief in overarching conspiracies and expertly organized cover-ups that keep those conspiracies

successfully hidden for decades" (Mike Lofgren, *The Deep State: The Fall of the Constitution and the Rise of a Shadow Government* [New York: Viking, 2016], 33). In this and other respects, I consider my concept of the deep state to be closer than Lofgren's to the original Turkish deep state (*gizli devlet*), a term used to describe sanctioned violence by drug-financed elements *against* public order. As others have pointed out, Lofgren's more mainstream analysis robs the notion of the deep state of this violent, conspiratorial dimension.

25. As late as October 2015 the Indonesian government (though now civilian) forced the cancellation of events in commemoration of the 1965 massacre: "Indonesia's largest writers' festival has been forced to cancel a series of events marking the 1965 massacre of alleged communists, after threats by authorities to revoke its operating permit. The announcement by organisers on Friday was unprecedented in the 12-year history of the Ubud Writers and Readers Festival and signalled heightened sensitivities in Indonesia around the 50th anniversary of the mass killings, in which about 500,000 people died . . .. Pressure had been applied by government, police and military officials, and local authorities were threatening to revoke the festival's permit, [the festival's founder and director] said" ("Indonesian writers' festival forced to cancel events linked to 1965 massacre," *The Guardian*, October 23, 1965, www.theguardian.com/books/2015/oct/23/indonesian-writers-festival-forced-to-cancel-events-linked-to-1965-massacre). Thanks to the increasing influence of Joshua Oppenheimer's two films on Indonesian public opinion, such acts of repression in Indonesia are now increasingly rare. See chapter 6.

26. Arthur G. Neal, *National Trauma and Collective Memory: Major Events in the American Century* (Armonk, NY: M.E. Sharpe, 1998), 4. Cf. Neil J. Smelser, "Psychological Trauma and Cultural Trauma," in Jeffrey C. Alexander, ed., *Cultural Trauma and Collective Identity* (Berkeley: University of California Press, 2004). 31ss.

27. Allard's murder was never explicitly dealt with in any of the many drafts of *Coming to Jakarta*. But it may explain why, when in II.iv I began to write about the Indonesian massacre, the first event I mention is the unrelated 1978 murder in Cambodia of Malcolm Caldwell, the Scot who first persuaded me to write about Indonesia. Caldwell's murder greatly distressed but did not terrify me, for I had never been actively involved like him in international politics. But Allard's murder in 1980 should perhaps have come to mind when a few months later I began to write about terror. After writing this chapter 1 now suspect that Malcolm may have served as a substitute for Allard, permitting me to deal more easily with something disturbing my subconscious.

28. Scott, *American War Machine*, 1–5.

29. I was then unaware of the quite lengthy file the FBI was already compiling on me.

30. McCoy, *The Politics of Heroin*, 461–463. At least two other witnesses to recovered deep memories in my poem, not so conditioned, could not remember them, even after I prompted them.

31. Cf. *Coming to Jakarta*, IV,iii: "There must be two of me/ I remember the surge of almost too vivid pleasure/ when the sheriffs lined up.," 106; *Minding the Darkness*, IV.vii, "There has to be two of me!/ one part welcoming our spread/ out into illogic

"... one part of me relieved/ this poem has worked back to' the one *Serat* or Way so many ancestors describe," 193. Cf. also the thought that came to Eckhart Tolle: "If I cannot live with myself, there must be two of me: the 'I' and the 'self' that 'I' cannot live with." "Maybe," I thought, "only one of them is real" (Eckhart Tolle, *The Power of Now: A Guide to Spiritual Enlightenment* [Novato, CA: New World Library, 2004], 4).

32. Peter Dale Scott, "How I Came to Jakarta," *Agni* 31/32 (1990), 297–304, www.peterdalescott.net/jak.html.

33. Peter Dale Scott, *Coming to Jakarta: A Poem about Terror* (New York: New Directions, 1989), 24–25. The complete section is on line at Poetry Foundation, www.poetryfoundation.org/poem/180097. My suspicions in the Caldwell murder have since expanded to include Indonesian secret services, who in the 1970s were much more influential in Cambodian politics, and massacres, than is generally recognized. See Peter Dale Scott, *The War Conspiracy* (New York: Skyhorse Publishing, 2013), 238; Peter Dale Scott, *American War Machine* (Lanham, MD: Rowman & Littlefield, 2010), 128.

34. See Peter Dale Scott, *The American Deep State: Wall Street, Big Oil, and the Attack on U.S. Democracy* (Lanham, MD: Rowman & Littlefield, 2014), 18–20.

35. Scott, *Coming to Jakarta*, IV.i, 102; quoting from Warren Commission, *Hearings*, 23, 166; Ed Reid, with Ovid Demaris, *The Green Felt Jungle* (New York: Pocket Books, 1964), 156–157; House Committee on Assassinations, Report, 151.

36. Peter Dale Scott, "Poets Who Grow Gardens in Their Heads," unpublished lecture, 2010. Cf. "Art as the Experience of Alterity: Theodor W. Adorno's Aesthetic Theory," *Poiesis* XII, 2010; Peter Dale Scott, *Ecstatic Pessimist* (forthcoming).

37. Theodor W. Adorno, "Commitment," *New Left Review* I, 87–88, September–December 1974; in Terry Eagleton and Drew Milne, *Marxist literary theory: a reader* (Oxford: Blackwell Publishers, 1996), 202. One can perhaps see in this an echo of Marx's thesis on Feuerbach: "Philosophers have hitherto only interpreted the world in various ways; the point is to change it."

38. Scott, *Coming to Jakarta*, 149–150.

39. Scott, *Minding the Darkness*, 242–243.

40. Cf. T.S Eliot: "I believe that at the present time the problem of the unification of the world, and the problem of the unification of the individual, are in the end one and the same problem, and the solution of one is the solution of the other." (T.S. Eliot, "Religion Without Humanism," in Norman Foerster, ed., *Humanism and America: Essays on the Outlook of Modern Civilization* [New York: Farrar and Rinehart, 1930], 112; misquoted in Peter Dale Scott, ed., *Listening to the Candle*, 68; cf. Peter Dale Scott, "The Social Critic and His Discontents," in A. David Moody, ed., *The Cambridge Companion to T.S. Eliot* [Cambridge: Cambridge University Press, 1994], 63).

V. THE CIA AND THE OVERTHROW OF SUKARNO, 1965–1967

1. The difficulties of this analysis, based chiefly on the so-called evidence presented at the Mahmilub trials, will be obvious to anyone who has tried to reconcile

the conflicting accounts of Gestapu in, for example, the official Suharto account by Nugroho Notosusanto and Ismail Saleh, and the somewhat less fanciful CIA study of 1968, both referred to later. I shall draw only on those parts of the Mahmilub evidence which limit or discredit their anti-PKI thesis. For interpretation of the Mahmilub data, cf. especially Coen Holtzappel, "The 30 September Movement," *Journal of Contemporary Asia*, IX, 2 (1979), 216–240. The case for general skepticism is argued by Rex Mortimer, *Indonesian Communism Under Sukarno* (Ithaca, New York: Cornell University Press, 1974), 421–423; and more forcefully, by Julie Southwood and Patrick Flanagan, *Indonesia: Law, Propaganda, and Terror* (London: Zed Press, 1983), 126–134.

2. At his long-delayed trial in 1978, Gestapu plotter Latief confirmed earlier revelations that he had visited his old commander Suharto on the eve of the Gestapu kidnappings. He claimed that he raised with Suharto the existence of an alleged right-wing "Council of Generals" plotting to seize power, and informed him "of a movement which was intended to thwart the plan of the generals' council for a coup d'etat" (Anon., "The Latief Case: Suharto's Involvement Revealed," *Journal of Contemporary Asia*, IX, 2 [1979], 248–250). For a more comprehensive view of Suharto's involvement in Gestapu, cf. especially W.F. Wertheim, "Whose Plot? New Light on the 1965 Events," *Journal of Contemporary Asia*, IX, 2 (1979), 197–215; Holtzappel, "The 30 September," in contrast, points more particularly to intelligence officers close to the banned Murba party of Chaerul Saleh and Adam Malik: cf. fn. 104.

3. The three phases are: (1) "Gestapu," the induced left-wing "coup"; (2) "KAP-Gestapu," or the anti-Gestapu "response," massacring the PKI; (3) the progressive erosion of Sukarno's remaining power. This paper will chiefly discuss Gestapu/KAP-Gestapu, the first two phases. To call the first phase by itself a "coup" is in my view an abuse of terminology: there is no real evidence that in this phase political power changed hands or that this was the intention.

4. U.S. Central Intelligence Agency, *Research Study: Indonesia—The Coup that Backfired*, 1968 (cited hereafter as CIA Study), 71n. [The paper is not to be found on the CIA Library website, but is cited there in a subsequent CIA study, "The Lessons of the September 30 Affair," www.cia.gov/library/center-for-the-study-of-intelligence/kent-csi/vol14no2/html/v14i2a02p_0003.htm].

5. Harold Crouch, *The Army and Politics in Indonesia* (Ithaca, New York: Cornell University Press, 1978), 79–81.

6. In addition, one of the two Gestapu victims in Central Java (Colonel Katamso) was the only non-PKI official of rank to attend the PKI's nineteenth anniversary celebration in Jogjakarta in May 1964: Mortimer, *Indonesian Communism*, 432. Ironically, the belated "discovery" of his corpse was used to trigger off the purge of his PKI contacts.

7. Four of the six pro-Yani representatives in January were killed along with Yani on October 1. Of the five anti-Yani representatives in January, we shall see that at least three were prominent in "putting down" Gestapu and completing the elimination of the Yani-Sukarno loyalists (the three were Suharto, Basuki Rachmat, and Sudirman of SESKOAD, the Indonesian Army Staff and Command School): Crouch, *The Army*, 81n.

8. While Nasution's daughter and aide were murdered, he was able to escape without serious injury, and support the ensuing purge.

9. *Indonesia*, 22 (October 1976), 165 (CIA Memorandum of 22 March 1961 from Richard M. Bissell, Attachment B). By 1965 this disillusionment was heightened by Nasution's deep opposition to the U.S. involvement in Vietnam.

10. Crouch, *The Army*, 40; Brian May, *The Indonesian Tragedy* (London: Routledge and Kegan Paul, 1978), 221–222

11. I shall assume for this condensed argument that Untung was the author, or at least approved, of the statements issued in his name. Scholars who see Untung as a dupe of Gestapu's controllers note that Untung was nowhere near the radio station broadcasting in his name, and that he appears to have had little or no influence over the task force which occupied it (under Captain Suradi of the intelligence service of Colonel Latief's Brigade): Holtzappel, 218, 231–232, 236–237. I have no reason to contradict those careful analysts of Gestapu—such as Wertheim, "Whose Plot?" 212, and Holtzappel, "The 30 September," 231—who conclude that Untung personally was sincere, and manipulated by other *dalangs* such as Sjam.

12. Broadcast of 7:15 a.m. October 1; *Indonesia* 1 (April 1966), 134; Ulf Sundhaussen, *The Road to Power: Indonesian Military Politics, 1945–1967* (Kuala Lumpur and Oxford: Oxford University Press, 1982), 196.

13. Ibid., 201.

14. Broadcasts of October 1 and 4, 1965; *Indonesia* 1 (April 1966), 158–159.

15. CIA Study, 2; O.G. Roeder, *The Smiling General: President Soeharto of Indonesia* (Jakarta: Gunung Agung, 1970), 12, quoting Suharto himself: "On my way to KOSTRAD HQ [Suharto's HQ] I passed soldiers in green berets who were placed under KOSTRAD command but who did not salute me."

16. Anderson and McVey concluded that Sukarno, Air Force Chief Omar Dhani, PKI Chairman Aidit (the three principal political targets of Suharto's anti-Gestapu "response") were rounded up by the Gestapu plotters in the middle of the night, and taken to Halim air force base, about one mile from the well at Lubang Buaja where the generals' corpses were discovered. In 1966 they surmised that this was "to seal the conspirators' control of the bases," and to persuade Sukarno "to go along with" the conspirators' plans (Benedict Anderson and Ruth McVey, *A Preliminary Analysis of the October 1, 1965, Coup in Indonesia* [Ithaca, New York: Cornell University Press, 1971], 19–21). An alternative hypothesis of course is that Gestapu, by bringing these men together against their will, created the semblance of a PKI-air force-Sukarno conspiracy which would later be exploited by Suharto. Sukarno's presence at Halim "was later to provide Sukarno's critics with some of their handiest ammunition" (John Hughes, *The End of Sukarno* [London: Angus and Robertson, 1978], 54).

17. CIA Study, 2; cf. 65: "At the height of the coup . . . the troops of the rebels [in Central Java] were estimated to have the strength of only one battalion; during the next two days, these forces gradually melted away."

18. Rudolf Mrázek, *The United States and the Indonesian Military, 1945–1966* (Prague: Czechoslovak Academy of Sciences, 1978), vol. II, 172. These battalions, comprising the bulk of the third Paratroop Brigade, also supplied the bulk of the troops used to put down Gestapu in Jakarta. The subordination of these two factions

in this supposed civil war to a single close command structure under Suharto is cited to explain how Suharto was able to restore order in the city without gunfire. Meanwhile out at the Halim air force base an alleged gun battle between the 454th (Green Beret) and RPKAD (Red Beret) paratroops went off "without the loss of a single man" (CIA Study, 60). In Central Java, also, power "changed hands silently and peacefully," with "an astonishing lack of violence" (CIA Study, 66).

19. Ibid., 60n; Arthur J. Dommen, "The Attempted Coup in Indonesia," *China Quarterly* (January–March 1966), 147. The first "get-acquainted" meeting of the Gestapu plotters is placed in the Indonesian chronology of events from "sometimes before August 17, 1965"; cf. Nugroho Notosusanto and Ismail Saleh, *The Coup Attempt of the "September 30 Movement" in Indonesia* (Jakarta: Pembimbing Masa, 1968), 13; in the CIA Study, this meeting is dated September 6 (112). Neither account allows more than a few weeks to plot a coup in the world's fifth most populous country.

20. Mortimer, *Indonesian Communism*, 429.

21. Of the six General Staff officers appointed along with Yani, three (Suprapto, D.I. Pandjaitan, and S. Parman) were murdered. Of the three survivors, two (Mursjid and Pranoto) were removed by Suharto in the next eight months. The last member of Yani's staff, Djamin Gintings, was used by Suharto during the establishment of the New Order, and ignored thereafter.

22. Howard Palfrey Jones, *Indonesia: The Possible Dream* (New York: Harcourt, Brace, Jovanovich, 1971), 391; cf. Arnold Brackman, *The Communist Collapse in Indonesia* (New York: Norton, 1969), 118.

23. Crouch, *The Army*, 150n.

24. Ibid., 140–153; for the disputed case of Bali, even Robert Shaplen, a journalist close to U.S. official sources, concedes that "The Army began it" (*Time Out of Hand* [New York: Harper and Row, 1969], 125). The slaughter in East Java "also really got started when the RPKAD arrived, not just Central Java and Bali" (letter from Benedict Anderson).

25. Sundhaussen, *The Road*, 171, 178–179, 210, 228; Donald Hindley, "Alirans and the Fall of the Older Order," *Indonesia*, 25 (April 1970), 40–41.

26. Sundhaussen, *The Road*, 219.

27. "In 1965 it [the BND, or intelligence service of the Federal Republic of Germany] assisted Indonesia's military secret service to suppress a left-wing *Putsch* in Djakarta, delivering sub-machine guns, radio equipment and money to the value of 300,000 marks" (Heinz Hoehne and Hermann Zolling, *The General Was a Spy* [New York: Bantam, 1972], xxxiii).

28. We should not be misled by the CIA's support of the 1958 rebellion into assuming that all U.S. Government plotting against Sukarno and the PKI must have been CIA-based (cf. fn. 122).

29. Daniel Lev, *The Transition to Guided Democracy: Indonesian Politics, 1957–1959* (Ithaca, New York: Cornell University press, 1966), 12. For John Foster Dulles' hostility to Indonesian unity in 1953, cf. Leonard Mosley, *Dulles* (New York: The Dial Press/James Wade, 1978), 437.

30. *Declassified Documents Quarterly Catalogue* (Woodbridge, Connecticut: Research Publications, 1982), 001191.

31. As the head of the PKI's secret Special Bureau, responsible only to Aidit, Sjam by his own testimony provided leadership to the "progressive officers" of Gestapu. The issue of PKI involvement in Gestapu thus rests on the question of whether Sjam was manipulating the Gestapu leadership on behalf of the PKI, or the PKI leadership on behalf of the army. There seems to be no disagreement that Sjam was (according to the CIA Study, 107) a longtime "double agent" and professed "informer for the Djakarta Military Command." Wertheim ("Whose Plot?" 203) notes that in the 1950s Sjam "was a cadre of the PSI," and "had also been in touch with Lt. Col. Suharto, today's President, who often came to stay in his house in Jogja." This might help explain why in the 1970s, after having been sentenced to death, Sjam and his co-conspirator Supeno were reportedly "allowed out [of prison] from time to time and wrote reports for the army on the political situation" (May, *The Indonesian*, 114). Additionally, the "Sjam" who actually testified and was convicted, after being "captured" on March 9, 1967, was the third individual to be identified by the army as the "Sjam" of whom Untung had spoken: *Declassified Documents Retrospective Collection* (Washington, DC: Carrollton Press, 1976), 613C; Hughes, *The End*, 25.

32. Wertheim, "Whose Plot?" 203; Mortimer, *Indonesian Communism* (Sjam), 431; Sundhaussen, *The Road* (Suwarto and Sarwo Edhie), 228.

33. Joseph B. Smith, *Portrait of a Cold Warrior* (New York: Putnam, 1976), 205; cf. Thomas Powers, *The Man Who Kept the Secrets* (New York: Knopf, 1979), 89.

34. U.S., Congress, Senate, Select Committee to Study Governmental Operations with Respect to Intelligence Activities. "Alleged Assassination Plots Involving Foreign Leaders," 94th Congress, 1st Session, 1975 (Senate Report No. 94-465), 4n; personal communications.

35. Declassified Documents Quarterly Catalogue, 1982, 002386; 1981, 367A.

36. Ibid., 1982, 002386 (JCS Memo for SecDef, September 22, 1958).

37. *Indonesia*, 22 (October 1976), 164 (CIA Memorandum of March 22, 1961, Attachment A, p. 6).

38. Scholars are divided over interpretations of Madiun as they are over Gestapu. Few Americans have endorsed the conclusion of Wertheim that "the so-called communist revolt of Madiun ... was probably more or less provoked by anti-communist elements"; yet Kahin has suggested that the events leading to Madiun "may have been symptomatic of a general and widespread government drive aimed at cutting down the military strength of the PKI" (W.F. Wertheim, *Indonesian Society in Transition* [The Hague: W. van Hoeve, 1956], 82; George McT. Kahin, *Nationalism and Revolution in Indonesia* [Ithaca, New York: Cornell University Press, 1970], 288). Cf. Southwood and Flanagan, *Indonesia: Law, Propaganda, and Terror,* 26-30.

39. Southwood and Flanagan, *Indonesia: Law, Propaganda, and Terror,* 68; cf. Nasution's statement to students on November 12, 1965, reprinted in *Indonesia*, 1 (April 1966), 183: "We are obliged and dutybound to wipe them [the PKI] from the soil of Indonesia."

40. Examples in Peter Dale Scott, "Exporting Military-Economic Development," in Malcolm Caldwell, ed., *Ten Years' Military Terror in Indonesia* (Nottingham, England: Spokesman Books, 1975), 227-261.

41. David Ransom, "Ford Country: Building an Elite for Indonesia," in Steve Weissman, ed., *The Trojan Horse* (San Francisco, California: Ramparts Press, 1974), 97; cf. 101. Pauker brought Suwarto to RAND in 1962.

42. John H. Johnson, ed., *The Role of the Military in Underdeveloped Countries* (Princeton, New Jersey: Princeton University Press, 1962), 222–224. The foreword to the book is by Klaus Knorr, who worked for the CIA while teaching at Princeton.

43. Shaplen, *Time*, 118; Hughes, *The End*, 119; Southwood and Flanagan, *Indonesia: Law, Propaganda, and Terror*, 75–76; Scott, "Exporting," 231. William Kintner, a CIA (OPC) senior staff officer from 1950–52, and later Nixon's ambassador to Thailand, also wrote in favor of "liquidating" the PKI while working at a CIA-subsidized think-tank, the Foreign Policy Research Institute, on the University of Pennsylvania campus (William Kintner and Joseph Kornfeder, *The New Frontier of War* [London: Frederick Muller, 1963], 233, 237–238): "If the PKI is able to maintain its legal existence and Soviet influence continues to grow, it is possible that Indonesia may be the first Southeast Asia country to be taken over by a popularly based, legally elected communist government. . . . In the meantime, with Western help, free Asian political leaders—together with the military—must not only hold on and manage, but reform and advance while liquidating the enemy's political and guerrilla armies."

44. Ransom, "Ford Country," 95–103; Southwood and Flanagan, *Indonesia: Law, Propaganda, and Terror*, 34–36; Scott, "Exporting," 227–235.

45. Sundhaussen, *The Road*, 141, 175.

46. Published U.S. accounts of the Civic Mission/"civic action" programs describe them as devoted to "civic projects—rehabilitating canals, draining swampland to create new rice paddies, building bridges and roads, and so on" (Roger Hilsman, *To Move a Nation* [Garden City, New York: Doubleday, 1967], 377). But a memo to President Johnson from Secretary of State Rusk, on July 17, 1964, makes it clear that at that time the chief importance of MILTAG was for its contact with anti-Communist elements in the Indonesian Army and its Territorial Organization: "Our aid to Indonesia . . . we are satisfied . . . is *not helping Indonesia militarily*. It is however, *permitting us to maintain some contact with key elements in Indonesia* which are *interested in and capable of resisting Communist takeover*. We think this is of vital importance to the entire Free World" (*Declassified Documents Quarterly Catalogue*, 1982, 001786 [DOS Memo for President of July 17, 1964; italics in original]).

47. Southwood and Flanagan, *Indonesia: Law, Propaganda, and Terror*, 35; Scott, "Exporting," 233.

48. Ransom, "Ford Country," 101–102, quoting Willis G. Ethel; cited in Scott, "Exporting," 235.

49. Sundhaussen, *The Road*, 141. There was also the army's "own securely controlled paramilitary organization of students—modelled on the U.S.R.O.T.C. and commanded by an army colonel [Djuhartono] fresh from the U.S. army intelligence course in Hawaii" (Mrázek, *The United States*, II, 139, citing interview of Nasution with George Kahin, July 8, 1963).

50. Pauker, though modest in assessing his own political influence, does claim that a RAND paper he wrote on counterinsurgency and social justice, ignored by the U.S. military for whom it was intended, was influential in the development of his friend Suwarto's Civic Mission doctrine.

51. Noam Chomsky and E.S. Herman, *The Washington Connection and Third World Fascism* (Boston, Massachusetts: South End Press, 1979), 206; David Mozingo, *Chinese Policy Toward Indonesia* (Ithaca, New York: Cornell University Press, 1976), 178.

52. Sundhaussen, *The Road*, 178–179. The PSI of course was neither monolithic nor a simple instrument of U.S. policy. But the real point is that, in this 1963 incident as in others, we see conspiratorial activity relevant to the military takeover, involving PSI and other individuals who were at the focus of U.S. training programs, and who would play an important role in 1965.

53. Sundhaussen, *The Road*, 228–233: in January 1966 the "PSI activists" in Bandung "knew exactly what they were aiming at, which was nothing less than the overthrow of Sukarno. Moreover, they had the protection of much of the Siliwangi officer corps" Once again, I use Sundhaussen's term "PSI-leaning" to denote a milieu, not to explain it. Sarwo Edhie was a long-time CIA contact, while Kemal Idris' role in 1965 may owe much to his former PETA commander the Japanese intelligence officer Yanagawa. Cf. Masashi Nishihara, *The Japanese and Sukarno's Indonesia* (Honolulu: University Press of Hawaii, 1976), 138, 212.

54. Sundhaussen, *The Road*, 99–101. Lubis was also a leader in the November 1957 assassination attempt against Sukarno, and the 1958 rebellion.

55. Ibid., 188; cf. 159n.

56. Suharto's "student" status does not of course mean that he was a mere pawn in the hands of those with whom he established contact at SESKOAD. For example, Suharto's independence from the PSI and those close to them became quite evident in January 1974, when he and Ali Murtopo cracked down on those responsible for army-tolerated student riots reminiscent of the one in May 1963. Cf. Crouch, *The Army*, 309–317.

57. Sundhaussen, *The Road*, 228, 241–243. In the same period SESKOAD was used for the political re-education of generals like Surjosumpeno, who, although anti-Communist, were guilty of loyalty to Sukarno (p. 238).

58. Crouch, *The Army*, 80; at this time Suharto was already unhappy with Sukarno's "rising pro-communist policy" (Roeder, *The Smiling*, 9).

59. Crouch, *The Army*, 81; cf. Mrázek, *The United States*, II, 149–151.

60. Sundhaussen, *The Road*, 241–243.

61. Through his intelligence group OPSUS (headed by Ali Murtopo) Suharto made contact with Malaysian leaders; in two accounts former PSI and PRRI/Permesta personnel in Malaysia played a role in setting up this sensitive political liaison: Crouch, *The Army*, 74; Nishihara, *The Japanese*, 149.

62. Sundhaussen, *The Road*, 188.

63. Mrázek, *The United States*, II, 152.

64. Cf. Edward Luttwak, *Coup D'Etat: A Practical Handbook* (London: Allen Lane/Penguin Press, 1968), 61: "though Communist-infiltrated army units were very powerful they were in the wrong place; while they sat in the Borneo jungles the anti-Communist paratroops and marines took over Jakarta, and the country." What is most interesting in this informed account by Luttwak (who has worked for years with the CIA) is that "the anti-Communist paratroops" included not only the RPKAD but those who staged the Gestapu uprising in Jakarta, before putting it down.

65. Nishihara, *The Japanese*, 142, 149.

66. Ibid., 202, cf. 207. The PRRI/Permesta veterans engaged in the OPSUS peace feelers, Daan Mogot and Willy Pesik, had with Jan Walandouw been part of a 1958 PRRI secret mission to Japan, a mission detailed in the inside account by former CIA officer Joseph B. Smith (*Portrait of a Cold Warrior* [New York: G.P. Putnam's Sons, 1976], 245), following which Walandouw flew on "to Taipeh, then Manila and New York."

67. Personal communication. If the account of Neville Maxwell (senior research officer at the Institute of Commonwealth Studies, Oxford University) can be believed, then the planning of the Gestapu/anti-Gestapu scenario may well have begun in 1964 (*Journal of Contemporary Asia*, IX, 2 [1979], 251–252; reprinted in Southwood and Flanagan, *Indonesia: Law, Propaganda, and Terror*, 13): "A few years ago I was researching in Pakistan into the diplomatic background of the 1965 Indo-Pakistan conflict, and in foreign ministry papers to which I had been given access came across a letter to the then foreign minister, Mr. Bhutto, from one of his ambassadors in Europe . . . reporting a conversation with a Dutch intelligence officer with NATO. According to my note of that letter, the officer had remarked to the Pakistani diplomat that 'Indonesia was going to fall into the Western lap like a rotten apple.' Western intelligence agencies, he said, would organize a 'premature communist coup . . . [which would be] foredoomed to fail, providing a legitimate and welcome opportunity to the army to crush the communists and make Soekarno a prisoner of the army's goodwill.' The ambassador's report was dated December 1964."

68. *Indonesia*, 22 (October 1976), 164 (CIA Memo of March 27, 1961, Appendix A, p. 8); cf. Powers, *The Man*, 89.

69. *Indonesia*, 22 (October 1976), 165 (CIA Memo of March 27, 1961).

70. The lame-duck Eisenhower NSC memo would have committed the United States to oppose not just the PKI in Indonesia, but "a policy increasingly friendly toward the Sino-Soviet bloc on the part of whatever regime is in power." "The size and importance of Indonesia," it concluded, "dictate [!] a vigorous U.S. effort to prevent these contingencies": *Declassified Documents Quarterly Catalogue*, 1982, 000592 (NSC 6023 of December 19, 1960). For other U.S. intrigues at this time to induce a more vigorous U.S. involvement in Southeast Asia, cf. *Declassified Documents Quarterly Catalogue*, 1983, 001285–86; Peter Dale Scott, *The War Conspiracy* (New York: Bobbs Merrill, 1972), 12–14, 17–20.

71. Jones, *Indonesia: The Possible Dream*, 299.

72. Mortimer, *Indonesian Communism*, 385–386.

73. U.S. Department of Defense, *Military Assistance Facts*, May 1, 1966. Before 1963 the existence as well as the amount of the MAP in Indonesia was withheld from the public; retroactively, figures were published. After 1962 the total deliveries of military aid declined dramatically, but were aimed more and more particularly at anti-PKI and anti-Sukarno plotters in the army; cf. fns. 46, 76 and 83.

74. *The New York Times*, August 5, 1965, 3; cf. Nishihara, *The Japanese*, 149; Mrázek, *The United States*, II, 121.

75. A Senate amendment in 1964 to cut off all aid to Indonesia unconditionally was quietly killed in conference committee, on the misleading ground that the Foreign Assistance Act "requires the President to report fully and concurrently to both Houses of the Congress on any assistance furnished to Indonesia" (U.S. Cong., Senate, Report

No. 88–1925, *Foreign Assistance Act of 1964*, 11). In fact the act's requirement that the president report "to Congress" applied to eighteen other countries, but in the case of Indonesia he was to report to two Senate Committees and the "speaker" of the House: Foreign Assistance Act, Section 620(j).

76. Jones, *Indonesia: The Possible Dream*, 324.

77. U.S., Congress, Senate, Committee on Foreign Relations, *Multinational Corporations and United States Foreign Policy, Hearings* (cited hereafter as Church Committee Hearings), 94th Congress, 2nd Session, 1978, 941; Mrázek, *The United States*, II, 22. Mrázek quotes Lt. Col. Juono of the corps as saying that "we are completely dependent on the assistance of the United States."

78. Notosusanto and Saleh, *The Coup*, 43, 46.

79. Nishihara, *The Japanese* (pp. 171, 194, 202), shows the role in the 1965–66 anti-Sukarno conspiracy of the small faction (including Ibnu Sutowo, Adam Malik, and the influential Japanese oilman Nishijima) who interposed themselves as negotiators between the 1958 PRRI Rebellion and the central government. Alamsjah, mentioned below, was another member of this group; he joined Suharto's staff in 1960. For Murba and CIA, cf. fn. 104.

80. *Fortune*, July 1973, 154, cf. *Wall Street Journal*, April 18, 1967; both in Scott, "Exporting," 239, 258.

81. *Declassified Documents Retrospective Collection*, 609A (Embassy Cable 1002 of October 14, 1965); 613A (Embassy Cable 1353 of November 7, 1965).

82. *The New York Times*, August 5, 1965, 3.

83. U.S. Department of Defense, *Military Assistance Facts*, May 1, 1966. The thirty-two military personnel in FY 1965 represent an increase over the projected figure in March 1964 of twenty-nine. Most of them were apparently Green Beret U.S. Special Forces, whose forward base on Okinawa was visited in August 1965 by Gestapu plotter Saherman. Cf. fn. 122.

84. George Benson, an associate of Guy Pauker who headed the Military Training Advisory Group (MILTAG) in Jakarta, was later hired by Ibnu Sutowo to act as a lobbyist for the army's oil company (renamed Pertamina) in Washington: *The New York Times*, December 6, 1981, 1.

85. *San Francisco Chronicle*, October 24, 1983, 22, describes one such USAF-Lockheed operation in Southeast Asia, "code-named 'Operation Buttercup' that operated out of Norton Air Force Base in California from 1965 to 1972." For the CIA's close involvement in Lockheed payoffs, cf. Anthony Sampson, *The Arms Bazaar* (New York: Viking, 1977), 137, 227–228, 238. [The role of commissions on Lockheed contracts is noted also by Geoffrey B. Robinson, *The Killing Season: A History of the Indonesian Massacres* (Princeton: Princeton University Press, 2018), 335n62.]

86. Church Committee Hearings, 943–951.

87. Ibid., 960.

88. Nishihara, *The Japanese*, 153.

89. Lockheed Aircraft International, memo of Fred C. Meuser to Erle M. Constable, 19 July 1968, in Church Committee Hearings, 962.

90. Ibid., 954; cf. 957. In 1968, when Alamsjah suffered a decline in power, Lockheed did away with the middleman and paid its agents' fees directly to a group of military officers (342, 977).

91. *Church Committee Hearings*, 941; cf. 955.

92. Southwood and Flanagan, *Indonesia: Law*, 59.
93. Crouch, *The Army*, 114.
94. *Declassified Documents Quarterly Catalogue*, 1982, 002507 (Cable of April 15, 1965, from U.S. Delegation to U.N.); cf. Forbes Wilson, *The Conquest of Copper Mountain* (New York: Atheneum, 1981), 153–155.
95. *World Oil*, August 15, 1965, 209.
96. *The New York Times*, June 19, 1966, IV, 4.
97. Ralph McGehee, "The C.I.A. and the White Paper on El Salvador," *The Nation*, April 11, 1981, 423. The deleted word would appear from its context to be "deception." Cf. Roger Morris and Richard Mauzy, "Following the Scenario," in Robert L. Borosage and John Marks, eds., *The CIA File* (New York: Grossman/Viking, 1976), 39: "Thus the fear of Communist subversion, which erupted to a frenzy of killing in 1965–1966, had been encouraged in the 'penetration' propaganda of the Agency in Indonesia. . . . 'All I know,' said one former intelligence officer of the Indonesia events, 'is that the Agency rolled in some of its top people and that things broke big and very favorable, as far as we were concerned.'" All references to deletions appear in the original text as printed in *The Nation*. These bracketed portions, shown in this article in bold-face type, reflect censorship by the CIA.
98. Victor Marchetti and John Marks, *The CIA and the Cult of Intelligence* (New York: Knopf, 1974), 245. For a list of twenty-five U.S. operatives transferred from Vietnam to Guatemala in the 1964–73 period, cf. Susanne Jonas and David Tobis, *Guatemala* (Berkeley, California, and New York: North American Congress on Latin America, 1974), 201.
99. Tad Szulc, *The Illusion of Peace* (New York: Viking, 1978), 724. The top CIA operative in charge of the 1970 anti-Allende operation, Sam Halpern, had previously served as chief executive officer on the CIA's anti-Sukarno operation of 1957–58: Seymour Hersh, *The Price of Power* (New York: Summit Books, 1983), 277; Powers, *The Man*, 91.
100. Donald Freed and Fred Simon Landis, *Death in Washington* (Westport, Connecticut: Lawrence Hill, 1980), 104–105.
101. *Time*, March 17, 1961.
102. Sundhaussen, *The Road*, 195.
103. Jones, *Indonesia: The Possible Dream*, 374; Justus M. van der Kroef, "Origins of the 1965 Coup in Indonesia: Probabilities and Alternatives," *Journal of Southeast Asian Studies*, III, 2 (September 1972), 282. Three generals were allegedly targeted in the first report (Suharto, Mursjid, and Sukendro); all survived Gestapu.
104. Chaerul Saleh's Murba Party, including the pro-U.S. Adam Malik, was also promoting the anti-Communist "Body to Support Sukarnoism" (BPS), which was banned by Sukarno on December 17, 1964. (Subandrio "is reported to have supplied Sukarno with information purporting to show U.S. Central Intelligence Agency influence behind the BPS" (Mortimer, *Indonesian Communism*, 377); it clearly did have support from the CIA- and army-backed labor organization SOKSI.) Shortly afterwards, Murba itself was banned, and promptly "became active as a disseminator of rumours and unrest" (Holtzappel, 238).
105. Sundhaussen, *The Road*, 183; Mortimer, *Indonesian Communism*, 376–377; *Singapore Straits Times*, December 24, 1964; quoted in Van der Kroef, "Origins," 283.

106. *Sabah Times*, September 14, 1965; quoted in Van der Kroef, "Origins," 296. Mozingo, *Chinese Policy* (p. 242) dismisses charges such as these with a contemptuous footnote.

107. Powers, *The Man*, 80; cf. Senate Report No. 94–755, *Foreign and Military Intelligence*, 192. CIA-sponsored channels also disseminated the Chinese arms story at this time inside the United States—for example, Brian Crozier, "Indonesia's Civil War," *New Leader*, November 1965, 4.

108. Mortimer, *Indonesian Communism*, 386. The Evans and Novak column coincided with the surfacing of the so-called Gilchrist letter, in which the British ambassador purportedly wrote about a U.S.-U.K. anti-Sukarno plot to be executed "together with local army friends." All accounts agree that the letter was a forgery. However it distracted attention from a more incriminating letter from Ambassador Gilchrist, which Sukarno had discussed with Lyndon Johnson's envoy Michael Forrestal in mid-February 1965, and whose authenticity Forrestal (who knew of the letter) did not deny (*Declassified Documents Retrospective Collection*, 594H [Embassy Cable 1583 of February 13, 1965]).

109. Cf. Denis Warner, *Reporter*, March 28, 1963, 62–63: "Yet with General A.H. Nasution, the defense minister, and General Jani, the army chief of staff, now out-Sukarnoing Sukarno in the dispute with Malaya over Malaysia . . . Mr. Brackman and all other serious students of Indonesia must be troubled by the growing irresponsibility of the army leadership."

110. *The New York Times*, August 12, 1965, 2.

111. Brackman, *The Communist*, 40.

112. McGehee, "The C.I.A.," 423.

113. Hughes, *The End*, 43–50; cf. Crouch, *The Army*, 140n: "No evidence supports these stories."

114. Hughes, *The End*, 150, also tells how Sarwo Edhie exploited the corpse of Colonel Katamso as a pretext for provoking a massacre of the PKI in Central Java; cf. Crouch, *The Army*, 154n; also fn. 6.

115. Anderson and McVey, *A Preliminary*, 133.

116. Benedict Anderson and Ruth McVey, "What Happened in Indonesia?" *New York Review of Books*, June 1, 1978, 41; personal communication from Anderson. A second newspaper, *Suluh Indonesia*, told its PNI readers that the PNI did not support Gestapu, and thus served to neutralize potential opposition to Suharto's seizure of power.

117. Thus defenders of the U.S. role in this period might point out that where "civic action" had been most deeply implanted, in West Java, the number of civilians murdered was relatively (!) small; and that the most indiscriminate slaughter occurred where civic action programs had been only recently introduced. This does not, in my view, diminish the U.S. share of responsibility for the slaughter.

118. *CIA Study*, 70; Sundhaussen, *The Road*, 185.

119. William Colby, *Honorable Men: My Life in the CIA* (New York: Simon and Schuster, 1978), 227. Crouch, *The Army* (p. 108), finds no suggestion in the Mahmilub evidence "that the PKI aimed at taking over the government," only that it hoped to protect itself from the Council of Generals.

120. McGehee, "The C.I.A.," 424.

121. Szulc, *The Illusion*, 16.

122. Southwood and Flanagan, *Indonesia: Law*, 38–39 (Cambodia). According to a former U.S. Navy intelligence specialist, the initial U.S. military plan to overthrow Sihanouk "included a request for authorization to insert a U.S.-trained assassination team disguised as Vietcong insurgents into Phnom Penh to kill Prince Sihanouk as a pretext for revolution" (Hersh, *The Price*, 179). As Hersh points out, Green Beret assassination teams that operated inside South Vietnam routinely dressed as Vietcong cadre while on missions. Thus the alleged U.S. plan of 1968, which was reportedly approved "shortly after Nixon's inauguration . . . 'at the highest level of government,'" called for an assassination of a moderate at the center by apparent leftists, as a pretext for a right-wing seizure of power. This raises an interesting question, albeit outlandish: did the earlier anti-Sukarno operation call for foreign elements to be infiltrated into the Gestapu forces murdering the generals? Holtzappel ("The 30 September," 222) has suspected "the use of outsiders who are given suitable disguises to do a dirty job." He points to trial witnesses from Untung's battalion and the murder team who "declared under oath not to have known . . . their battalion commander." Though these witnesses themselves would not have been foreigners, foreigners could have infiltrated more easily into their ranks than into a regular battalion.

EPILOGUE TO CHAPTER 5 (2015)

1. Peter Dale Scott, "How I Came to Jakarta," *Agni*, No. 31/32 (1990), 297.

2. OPSUS was a special intelligence unit under the command of Ali Murtopo, when he was the Intelligence Assistant at the army's Kostrad command under Suharto. OPSUS became the vehicle for the army's secret negotiations with the British and Malaysians, seeking, behind Sukarno's back, a peaceful resolution of the Konfrontasi crisis which Sukarno had provoked. Geoffrey Robinson also delicately asks whether "Kostrad's intelligence unit" may in addition have been involved in preparing Gestapu as "a deliberate provocation by the army" (The Killing Season: A History of the Indonesian Massacres [Princeton: Princeton University Press, 2018], 80; cf. 79).

3. Cf. footnotes 61 and 66 of chapter 5.

4. In similar CIA-backed plots against Allende in Chile (1970–73), a loyalist Army Chief of Staff was also murdered, making way for a right-wing General Pinochet who would subsequently carry out an army coup and massacre. But these were two plots separated in time, not a single piggybacked plot.

5. Paul Lashmar and James Oliver, "How We Destroyed Sukarno," *Independent* (London), December 1, 1998, www.independent.co.uk/arts-entertainment/how-we-destroyed-sukarno-1188448.html.Cf. Chris Kline, "Suharto: One of the greatest mass murderers of the 20th century," *Independent*, February 3, 2008, www.independent.co.uk/news/world/asia/suharto-one-of-the-greatest-mass-murderers-of-the-20th-century-777103.html: "In the midst of the mass executions, the British ambassador, Sir Andrew Gilchrist, sent a chilling telegram to London, saying: 'I have never concealed from you my belief that a little shooting in Indonesia would be an essential preliminary to effective change.'"

6. Stephen Dorril, *MI6: Inside the Covert World of Her Majesty's Secret Intelligence Service* (New York: Free Press, 2000), 718: "In co-operation with their colleagues from the Australian Secret Intelligence Service (ASIS), MI6's Special Political Action group launched up to six different disruptive actions, including . . . the recruitment of 'moderate' elements with the army."

7. John Roosa, review of Wanandi, *Shades of Grey*, Inside Indonesia, www.insideindonesia.org/review-from-the-dark-side.

VI. CATASTROPHE AND HOPE

1. The number of those killed during the partition of India is estimated to have been between several hundred thousand and two million (Ian Talbot and Gurharpal Singh (eds), *Region and Partition: Bengal, Punjab and the Partition of the Subcontinent* [Oxford and New York: Oxford University Press, 1999], 2). More than a million people are said to have been killed by the Khmer Rouge regime in Cambodia between 1975 and 1979.

2. Clifford Geerts, *The Interpretation of Cultures* (New York: Basic Books, 1973), 452. Cf. Peter Dale Scott, *Coming to Jakarta: A Poem About Terror* (New York: New Directions, 2000), 118–122.

3. Peter Dale Scott, *Minding the Darkness: A Poem for the Year 2000* (New York: New Directions, 2000), 212–214 online at muse.jhu.edu/login?auth=0&type=summary&url=/journals/manoa/v012/12.1scott.html; excerpting from Pramoedya Ananta Toer, "My Apologies, in the Name of Experience," 61 (April 1996), 1–14, Indonesia, cip.cornell.edu/DPubS?service=UI&version=1.0&verb=Display&handle=seap.indo/1106964456.

4. Bradley R. Simpson, *Economists with Guns: Authoritarian Development and U.S.-Indonesian Relations, 1960–1968* (Stanford, CA: Stanford University Press, 2008).

5. McGeorge Bundy, "Memorandum to President Johnson," *Foreign Relations of the United States, 1964–1968*, XXVI (October 22, 1965), *Indonesia*; Malaysia-Singapore; Philippines, 334, history.state.gov/historicaldocuments/frus1964-68v26/d160.

6. *New York Times*, June 19, 1966. *Time* in the same period (July 15, 1966) described the events in Indonesia as "the West's best news for years in Asia".

7. Jonah Weiner, "The Weird Genius of "The Act of Killing," *New Yorker Culture Desk*, July 16, 2013, www.newyorker.com/online/blogs/culture/2013/07/the-weird-genius-of-the-act-of-killing.html.

8. Peter Dale Scott, "Atrocity and its Discontents: U.S. Double-Mindedness About Massacre, from the Plains Wars to Indonesia"; in Adam Jones, ed. *Genocide, War Crimes and the West: Ending the Culture of Impunity* (London: Zed Press, 2004), 146–163.

9. Errol Morris, "The Murders of Gonzago," www.slate.com/articles/arts/history/2013/07/the_act_of_killing_essay_how_indonesia_s_mass_killings_could_have_slowed.html.

10. See Fred Landis, in Donald Freed and Fred Landis, *Death in Washington* (Westport, CT: Lawrence Hill, 1980), 103–118.

11. Jussi Hanhimäki, *The Flawed Architect: Henry Kissinger and American Foreign Policy* (Oxford: Oxford University Press, 2004), 401.

12. Simpson, *Economists with Guns*, 6.

13. Ibid., 8.

14. Ibid., 26. One of the results of this cultural "modernization," seen in Josh Oppenheimer's film "The Act of Killing," was that it conditioned the anti-PKI killer Anwar Congo to rejoice in the values of Hollywood, and specifically taught him also how to strangle his victims with a length of piano wire.

15. Simpson, *Economists with Guns*, 29.

16. See Peter Dale Scott, "Still Uninvestigated After 50 Years: Did the U.S. Help Incite the 1965 Indonesia Massacre?" *Asia-Pacific Journal: Japan Focus*, August 3, 2015, www.apjjf.org/2015/13/31/Peter-Dale-Scott/4351.html.

17. "Indonesia Reacts to 'Act of Killing' Academy award Nomination," *Jakarta Globe*, January 23, 2014, jakartaglobe.beritasatu.com/news/indonesia-reacts-to-act-of-killing-academy-nomination. In fact, according to one of Suharto's surviving medical examiners, who inspected the generals' bodies, there were no signs that they had been tortured before they were shot (Jon Emont, "The Propaganda Precursor to 'The Act of Killing,'" *New Yorker*, October 24, 2015, www.newyorker.com/news/news-desk/the-propaganda-precursor-to-the-act-of-killing.

18. Paige Johnson Tan, "Teaching and Remembering," *Inside Indonesia*, April–June 2008, www.insideindonesia.org/teaching-and-remembering.

19. Oppenheimer is American but lives in Denmark, and his film was a Danish-British-Norwegian co-production.

20. Mette Bjerregaard, "What Indonesians Really Think about The Act of Killing," *Guardian*, March 5, 2014, www.theguardian.com/film/2014/mar/05/act-of-killing-screening-in-indonesia.

21. Dean Irvine, "'The Look of Silence': The Film Making Indonesia Face Its Brutal History," *CNN*, November 14, 2014, www.cnn.com/2014/11/13/world/asia/indonesia-the-look-of-silence.

22. "Indonesia discusses massacres that killed 500,000," *BBC*, April 18, 2016, www.bbc.com/news/world-asia-36076069.

23. Margaret Scott, "Indonesia: The Saudis Are Coming," *New York Review of Books*, October 27, 2016, www.nybooks.com/articles/2016/10/27/indonesia-the-saudis-are-coming. Cf. M.C. Ricklefs, *Islamisation and Its Opponents in Java: A Political, Social, Cultural and Religious History, c. 1930 to the Present* (Singapore: National University of Singapore Press, 2012); Azyumardi Azra, *Indonesia, Islam, and Democracy: Dynamics in a Global Context* (Jakarta: Solstice Publications, 2006).

24. Anton McCabe, "Review: The Buru Quartet by Pramoedya Ananta Toer," *Socialist View*, Spring 2001, redlug.com/socview/svspring01I.htm.

25. *New York Times Magazine*, April 18, 1999, 112–114.

26. Irena Grudzinska Gross, *Czesław Miłosz and Joseph Brodsky: Fellowship of Poets* (New Haven: Yale University Press, 2009), 82.

27. Czeslaw Milosz, *New and Collected Poems, 1931–2001* (New York: Ecco, 2003), 103.

28. Milosz, *New and Collected Poems*, 245.

29. For more on the importance of Milosz to the Solidarity movement, see Peter Dale Scott, "Czeslaw Milosz and Solidarity; or, Poetry and the Liberation of a People," *Brick* 78 (Winter 2006), 67–74; Peter Dale Scott, *Ecstatic Pessimist: Czeslaw Milosz as a Poet of Catastrophe and Hope* (forthcoming). I regard *Ecstatic Pessimist* as a companion volume to *Poetry and Terror*.

30. As I said to Freeman in our 2012 discussion of IV.xii, my "good sense" in the poem, though in my opinion "worth saying," was just "not going to make any difference to anything."

31. Personal email of January 9, 2014. The "survey" he referred to is reproduced as chapter 5 of this book.

32. Irwan Firdaus, "Indonesia executes Bali bombers," *Jakarta Post*, November 9, 2008, www.thejakartapost.com/news/2008/11/09/indonesia-executes-bali-bombers.html.

33. Allan Nairn, "Trump's Indonesian Allies in Bed With ISIS-Backed FPI Militia Seeking to Oust Elected President," *The Intercept*, April 18, 2017, www.theintercept.com/2017/04/18/trumps-indonesian-allies-in-bed-with-isis-backed-militia-seeking-to-oust-elected-president.

34. Peter Dale Scott, *The American Deep State* (Langham, MD: Rowman & Littlefield, 2014), 9; citing "Brigade homeland tours start Oct. 1," *Army Times*, September 30, 2008, www.armytimes.com/news/2008/09/army_homeland_090708w. Many fear also the risk of their possible internment and confinement, since the Army Field Manual (FM 3.39; 2–40) now envisages "I/R [internment/resettlement] tasks performed in support of civil support operations [that] are similar to those during combat operations" (U.S. Army Field Manual, 3.39, chapter 2: Internment and Resettlement in Support of the Spectrum of Operations, 2–40). I have argued for a decade that Americans should demand the lifting of the State of Emergency enabling this that was proclaimed in September 2001 (itself now arguably illegal under the National Emergencies Act, 50 U.S.C. § 1601–1651; Scott. *American Deep State*, 40–41).

Index

Achilles, 160, 168
Adorno, Theodore, 182, 202
Aeneid (Virgil), 88, 158, 185, 202, 234
Aeschylus, 158, 177
Agamemnon (Aeschylus), 177
Agung, Sultan of Mataram, 63
Ahok (Basuki Tjahaja Purna), 236
Alamsjah, Ratoe Perwiranegara, 107, 148, 218
Allen, Richard, 108
Allende, Salvador, 151–52, 219–20, 224, 230
Anderson, Ben, 90, 222–23
Anti-war activity, xv, 18, 23–24, 56, 114–15, 127–28, 195, 285
Apollo, 171, 177
Aristotle, 180, 184
Arjuna, 90, 127, 159–60, 165, 176
Armstrong, Gregor, 13, 49–51, 61, 195
Armstrong, Hamilton Fish, 13, 49
Army Paracommando Regiment (RPKAD), 210, 213–14, 222
Army Strategic Reserve Command (KOSTRAD), 209, 214–15
Auerbach, Erich, 94
Augustine of Hippo, St., 167

Baker, Bobby, 108
Bali, 34, 90, 102–03, 123, 210, 236
Balinese culture, 93, 102–03

Ball, George, 123
banking industry:
  Bank of Indochina, 100–01;
  CIA and, 42–44, 54–55, 57, 61;
  Dawes Plan, 38;
  deep power and, 35–38, 44–45;
  Hibernian Bank, 142;
  International Credit Bank, 107–08;
  Lansky and, 107–08;
  Morgan Bank, 36;
  Nugan Hand Bank, 57, 61;
  Rockefeller and, 152;
  Rothschild system, 48–49, 54, 107–08;
  Schroder Bank, 42, 44
Beam, Jake, 97–98
Berkeley Mafia, 60–61, 65–66
Berle, Adolf, 36
Berlin, Isaiah, 74–75, 82–83
Bhagavad Gita, 92, 127, 128–29, 159–60, 165–66, 167–68, 176.
  See also Mahabharata
Bisson, Thomas Arthur, 175
book suppression, 109–10, 181, 202
Borson, Roo, 174
Bowart, Walter, 116
Brecht, Bertolt, 29
Buddhism:
  in Burma, 28;
  in Java, 146, 147;

277

original mind (*anatta*), 203
Bundy, McGeorge, 194, 229
Burke, Edmund, 184, 186
Burma, 28

Caldwell, Malcolm, 15, 18, 21, 23, 152, 201–02
Caltex, 215
Cambodia:
 Khmer Serai, 18, 202;
 mass killings in 1970, 17, 210, 227;
 Penn Nouth, 55;
 Sihanouk overthrow, 224;
 Vietnamese invasion of, 18
Carmichael, Stokely, 128
Carr, Steve, 169
Cassandra, 171, 177
CCAS (Committee of Concerned Asian Scholars), 42, 59
Central Organization of Indonesian Socialist Employees (SOKSI), 209
Chevalier, Haakon, 175
Chiang Kai-shek government, 27–28, 101
Chile:
 Allende overthrow, 218–19, 224, 230;
 CIA and, 16–17, 151–55, 155, 219–220, 224, 230;
 mass killings in, 151–52, 154, 219–20;
 Pinochet in, 152, 210–211
China:
 Chiang Kai-shek government, 27–28, 101;
 CIA and, 59;
 modernization and, 230–31;
 Suharto and, 135;
 Sukarno and, 135
Chomsky, Noam, 8, 24, 110, 148, 201, 205, 212
Chrétien de Troyes, 81, 94
CIA, 44, 49, 50, 59, 60, 97–98, 116, 122, 205–26;
 censorship by, 43–44, 200;
 in Chile, 151–55;
 drug trade and, 9, 22, 57, 61, 116, 169–70, 172, 196–98;
 Dulles brothers and, 42–44;
 in Guatemala, 42, 44, 54;
 Kennedy assassination and, 153;
 Lockheed and, 106–07, 108, 142, 205, 217–18;
 Muslim Brotherhood and, 190–91;
 Nixon and, 152–53;
 Schneider assassination and, 151–52;
 SOKSI trade unions and, 210;
 Sukarno's overthrown and, 16, 60, 106–07, 190, 205–26;
 UC Berkeley and, 60–61;
 World Assembly of Youth (WAY), 50, 106.
 See also Dulles, Allen
class, social, 31, 33, 95, 194
Colby, William, 148, 205, 223
Cold War, 83, 137, 139, 175, 229
Committee of Concerned Asian Scholars (CCAS), 42, 59
Cooke, John Starr, 116
Cooke, Sherman, 116
Council on Foreign Relations (CFR), 13, 49, 54–56, 61, 149, 162
Cowper, William, 193–94
Crouch, Harold, 208, 210
Cuba, 100–01, 109
cultural evolution, xv, 81, 147–48, 185
Curtius, Ernst Robert, 94

Dante, 20–21, 94, 161, 163, 168, 177, 179–80, 185, 203, 234
Dasaad, August Munir, 216–17
Davies, W.H., 81–82
deep events, xvi, 56, 198, 200
deep force, 115, 193, 197–98, 202
deep history, 192
deep politics, 5, 43–44, 111, 119, 170, 172–74, 194–96, 200;
 and engaged poetry, 194–96;
 and memory, 56

deep state, 38, 54–55, 106, 115–16, 173–74, 198–99
Dekker, Eduard Douwes, 233
Demaris, Ovid, 108
Dorril, Stephen, 226
doubleness, 180, 182, 184–85, 201
Douglass, James, 194
Doyle, Leonard, 60
dreams, 87, 89, 96, 142, 179–80
drug trade:
  in Bali, 34;
  CIA and, 22, 57, 61, 169–70, 196–97;
  deep state and, 198–99, 200;
  in Shanghai, 100–01
Dulles, Allen, 31, 32, 37–38, 42, 43–44, 49, 109
Dulles, Allen, Jr., 31–33
Dulles, John Foster, 16, 31, 32, 37–39, 42, 44, 49
Dulles, Lily, 31
Du Yuesheng, 100–01
Dylan, Bob, 186–87

Eastern Europe, 133–35, 137, 139
East Timor mass killings, 8, 17, 160–61, 173, 230
Edhie, Sarwo, 210, 211, 213–14, 222
Eliot, T. S., 163, 180, 182, 183
Ellsberg, Daniel, 23, 153, 163, 165–67, 194
Enlightenment, 34, 73, 228–29, 230, 231
Erlangga, 79, 80–81, 147
ethogeny, xv, 147–48, 185–86

Fairbank, John, 27–28, 41–42, 59
Fairbank, Wilma, 41–42
FBI (Federal Bureau of Investigation), 119, 145, 149–50, 153
Felt, Mark ("Deep Throat"), 153
Fifield, Russell, 55–56
Ford, Gerald, 17, 160
Ford Foundation, 24, 59–60, 61, 211, 212, 213
Forgan, J. Russell, 43–44
Foster, Michael, 79–80, 82–83

Gandhi, Mahatma, 127, 128–31, 149, 166, 167–68
Geertz, Clifford, 34, 136–37, 227
General Motors, 101–02
Geneva Accords of 1954, 114
Gestapu incident, 16, 190, 198, 205, 207, 208–12, 213–15, 216, 217–19, 219–24, 225–226
Ginsberg, Allen, 128
Goodman, Amy, 160–61
Gospel of Thomas, 167, 174, 187
Green, Marshall, 123, 191
Green Gang, 100–01
Guatemala, 41, 42, 44, 54–55, 220

Harris, Michael, 60
Hasan, Bob, 217
Hass, Robert, 88, 193
Heaney, Seamus, 182
Hegel, Georg Wilhelm Friedrich, 73–75, 79–83, 163
Heller, Erich, 81
Helms, Richard, 152
Henderson, William, 56–57, 149
Herman, E. S., 212
Hersri Setiawan, 172
Hinduism:
  in Bali, 90;
  caste system, 176–77;
  of Gandhi, 128–29;
  in Java, 146, 147;
  Krishna, 127, 165;
  Mahabharata, 90, 127, 135, 165, 176, 193, 225;
  meditation, 149;
  Untouchables and, 129
Hitchcock, Peggy, 116–17
Homans, George, 93–95, 161
Homer, 23, 177, 202. *See also Iliad* (Homer); *Odyssey* (Homer)
hope, 8–9, 20, 28, 51, 65, 86, 111, 137, 139–40, 167, 181, 182, 183–87, 194, 231–33, 235
Hughes, John, 222
Human Be-In, 115–17
Hunt, Howard, 153

Hussein, Saddam, 142
Hutcheon, Linda, 180

Idris, Kemal, 214
Ignatieff, George, 97
Iliad (Homer), 88, 107, 108, 147, 166, 168
India:
    Gandhi, 128–31;
    Hinduism, 128–29;
    independence movement, 128–31;
    influence on Indonesia, 149, 165;
    mass killings in, 130–31, 227;
    Muslims in, 130–31;
    neutralism and, 16;
    partition of, 130–31;
    Royal Indian Air Force, 127
Indonesian Army, 16, 53, 122, 136, 142, 148, 161, 189–91, 190, 195, 198, 207–17, 218, 220–21, 226, 229, 231, 236. *See also* SESKOAD (SEkolah Staf KOmando Angkatan Darat/Army Staff and Command School)
Indonesian Army General Staff, 207–09, 221–22, 223, 225
Indonesian Communist Party (PKI), 16, 122, 189, 208–10, 212–13, 215–17, 220–23, 229, 231–32
Indonesian mass killings of 1965:
    American involvement in, 16, 60, 106–07, 190, 205–26;
    Geertz essay on, 136–37;
    Pramoedya on, 227–28;
    Suharto and, 173;
    summary of, 15–17
Indonesian Muslims, 189–91, 210–12, 232–33, 236
inspiration, 85, 110, 163, 179, 181, 185, 234
Iran, 41, 44, 142, 152
Iraq, 62, 63, 142, 174, 191
ISIL/ISIS, 189, 236

Java:
    Agung, Sultan of Mataram, 63;
    Central Java, 208, 209–10, 216–18;
    Dutch occupation of, 63, 102, 228;
    East Java, 208, 210, 221;
    mass killings in, 140–41;
    Multatuli in, 233;
    Pramoedya in, 227, 228, 229, 231, 233–34;
    Suharto and, 214;
    West Java, 208, 213
Javanese culture, 63, 89–90, 90, 93, 165, 227–28, 231
Johnson, Lyndon B., 50, 108–09, 186, 191, 194, 215, 229

Kadane, Kathy, 191
Kennedy, John F., 9, 36
Kennedy administration, 213, 215
Kennedy assassination, 8, 22, 108–09, 110, 146, 153, 173, 181, 198
Khashoggi, Adnan, 142
Khmer Serai, 18, 202
Kierkegaard, Søren, 81
King, Martin Luther, Jr., 128, 186
Kintner, William, 190
Kissinger, Henry, 17, 152, 160
KOSTRAD (Army Strategic Reserve Command), 209, 215
Krishna, 127, 159, 165, 174
Kundera, Milam, 236

Langbaum, Robert, 180
Lansdale, Edward, 154
Lansky, Meyer, 100–01, 107, 108
Laos, 220
Lattimore, Owen, 27–28, 175
Leary, Timothy, 115–17
Lenin, Vladimir, 36, 134–35
Levinson, Ed, 108, 109
Libya, 142, 233
Liem Sioe Liong, 142
Lippmann, Walter, 50–51, 195
Lockheed, Inc., 106–07, 108, 142, 148, 205, 217–18
Lodge, Henry Cabot, 95, 97
Lofgren, Mike, 199
Lowenstein, Allard, 23, 199

Index

Madiun Affair of 1948, 212, 221–22
madness, 8, 33, 68, 75, 149, 168, 171–72, 193;
  right relationship to the irrational, 160, 163;
  social and cultural, 33, 73, 137, 142, 171–72, 174, 193–94, 229
Mahabharata, 90, 127, 135, 159–60, 165, 176, 193, 227
Mailer, Norman, 128
Malaysia, 161, 214, 216, 220–21, 225–26
Malraux, André, 100–01
Maltman, Kim, 174
Mandelstam, Nadezhda, 61
Martens, Robert, 191
martial law, 211, 216, 236
Marx, Karl, 74, 163
Marxism, 18, 146, 231
mass ritual suicide (*puputan*), 102–03
McCarthy, Joseph, 28, 171, 175, 177
McCarthyism, 28, 171, 175, 177
McClure, Michael, 115
McCoy, Alfred, 169–70, 172, 196–97, 199–200
McGehee, Ralph, 205, 219–20, 222–24
McVey, Ruth, 209, 222–23
McWillie, Lewis, 109
Memmi, Albert, 180
memory:
  conscious gaps in, 62, 193–94;
  deep politics and, 56, 170, 172–74, 194–96;
  memory repression and recovery, 62, 91, 170, 172–73, 183, 195–96, 196–200;
  memory work, 193–94
Merton, Thomas, 194
MI6 (British intelligence), 221, 226
Milosz, Czeslaw, 24, 137, 179, 182, 185, 202, 234–35
Morris, Errol, 229
Mortimer, Rex, 221
Mossad (Israeli intelligence), 107–08
Mozingo, David, 213
Mrázek, Rudolf, 135, 135–36
Multatuli (Eduard Douwes Dekker), 233

Murtopo, Ali, 226
Muslims:
  in Bali, 90;
  in India, 130–31;
  in Indonesia, 189–91, 210–12, 232, 236

Nairn, Allan, 161, 236
Nasution, Abdul Harris, 208, 212–14, 215, 217, 221
Neal, Arthur G., 199
Nehru, Jawaharlal, 130, 131
neutralism, 16, 135
The New York Times, 17, 43, 108, 114, 121–22, 160, 191, 200, 217, 221, 229
Nietzsche, Franz, 193
9/11, 173, 197, 198, 234
1960s, 32, 111, 113, 115, 140, 181, 187, 230;
  nostalgia for, 111, 181
Nishihara, Masashi, 215
Nixon, Richard M., 111, 142, 152, 153, 224
Nixon administration, 108, 153, 224
nonviolence, xvi, 128, 130, 149, 165–66, 168, 187, 195
NORAD agreement, 96–97
Nugan Hand Bank, 57, 61

Odysseus/Ulysses, 20–21, 86, 147, 168
Odyssey (Homer), 147, 166, 168, 185
oil companies:
  Alamsjah and, 148;
  CIA and, 41, 42, 219;
  deep state and, 198–99;
  OPEC, 142;
  Suharto coup and, 148, 219;
  Sukarno and, 16, 42, 146, 148, 215;
  Vietnam and, 56–57, 149
Operation Phoenix, 154, 220
Operation Sunrise, 43
Oppenheimer, Josh, 16, 232, 235
Oppenheimer, Robert, 159–60, 165–66, 174, 175–76

OPSUS (Special Operations Service), 225–26
Oswald, Lee Harvey, 109, 146, 153
Overton window, 173, 183, 191, 198

Pagels, Elaine, 167
Pakistan, 129–31
Parkin, Raleigh, 12, 99–102
Pauker, Guy, 53, 56–58, 61, 190, 212, 213–14, 215
Paz, Octavio, 182
Penn Nouth, 55
People's Park incident, 117–18
Philippines, 154, 229
Phillips, David, 152, 153–54
phone tapping, 28, 76–77, 169–70, 172, 183, 196–98, 199–200
Pinochet, Augusto, 152, 210–11
PKI (Indonesian Communist Party), 16, 122, 189, 208–10, 212–13, 215–17, 220–23, 229, 231–32
poetry:
 engaged poetry, 194–96, 200, 202–03;
 as "higher politics," 185;
 memory recovery and, 200;
 poetic healing, xvi, 9, 37, 170, 172, 181–82, 183, 186–87, 195–96;
 process poems, xvi, 91, 183–87
political science, 56, 170, 201
Pound, Ezra:
 banking industry and, 38, 44–45, 48, 54–55;
 detention of, 19–20, 21, 37;
 on poems, 185;
 poetic healing and, 20, 182;
 politics of, 18–19
Pramoedya Ananta Toer, 227, 228, 229, 231, 232, 233–34
PRRI/Permesta, 212, 215, 225–26
psychology, 173;
 crisis at Watertown, 6–12, 21, 66, 110–11, 147, 158, 179;
 homeostasis, psychological, 183;
 and poetic healing, xvi, 9, 37, 170, 172, 179, 181–82, 183, 186–87, 195–96;

psychic rebellion and healing, 201–03;
PTSS (Post-Traumatic Stress Syndrome), 181–82, 191;
trauma, 179–87, 199.
See also doubleness; dreams; second nature
PTSS (Post-Traumatic Stress Syndrome), 181–82, 191
puputan (mass ritual suicide), 102–03
Purna, Basuki Tjahaja (Ahok), 236

al-Qaeda, 198, 236

Rachmat, Basuki, 209
RAND Corporation, 211, 212
Ransom, David, 60
Reagan, Ronald, 8, 89, 111, 118, 162, 179
Rebozo, Bebe, 142
Rector, James, 118
Reddaway, Norman, 226
Reid, Ed, 108
Reston, James, 219, 229
Rockefeller, David, 152
Rockwell-Standard, 190, 218
Roosevelt administration, 27, 38, 43, 44–45
Rosenbaum, Tibor, 107–08
Rotblat, Joseph, 176
Rothschilds, 48–49, 54, 107–08
RPKAD (Army Paracommando Regiment), 210, 222
Ruby, Jack, 5, 106, 109
Rumi, Jalal ad-Din Muhammad, 234
Rusk, Dean, 55, 191

Saleh, Chaerul, 216–17, 220–21
Sarkar, Himansu, 149
Sartre, Jean-Paul, 71–74, 187
Saudi Arabia, 141, 142, 233, 236
Schamus, James, 180
Schneider, René, 151–52
Schurmann, Franz, 42, 48, 114
second nature, 184–86

Seculum (trilogy) (Scott), 20, 73, 94, 196, 203;
  Listening to the Candle, 20, 24, 66, 69, 83, 85, 88, 145, 163, 167, 203;
  Minding the Darkness, 20, 64, 83, 145, 158, 203, 227, 232
September 30th Movement (G30S/PKI), 207, 231–32
SESKOAD (*SEkolah Staf KOmando Angkatan Darat*/Indonesian Army Staff and Command School), 57, 58, 60, 212–14, 218
Shaplen, Robert, 124
Sihanouk, Norodom, 224
Silvers, Bob, 24, 146
Simone, Nina, 186, 200
Simpson, Bradley, 190, 229
Smart, Christopher, 193–94
Smith, Richard Harris, 43
SOKSI trade unions, 209
Solidarity movement, 137, 235, 236–37
Soong, T. V., 27–28
South Africa, 49, 101–02
Soviet bloc, 16, 95, 133–35, 137, 139, 215
SPD (Sozialdemokratische Partei Deutschlands), 50–51
Stanley, Owsley, 116
subconscious:
  and creativity, 7, 10, 154–55, 179–80.
  See also doubleness; yin and yang
Suharto:
  Alamsjah and, 107, 148, 216–17;
  CIA and, 16–17, 207–211;
  Gestapu incident, 198, 213–15, 218, 221, 222–23;
  Lockheed and, 142, 148, 217–18;
  mass killings and, 229, 230, 231–32;
  Murtopo and, 226;
  OPSUS plot and, 225–26;
  protests against, 172;
  regime of, 161, 173;
  Soviets and, 135;
  U.S. assistance to, 190, 216

Sukarno:
  Berkeley Mafia and, 60–61;
  CIA and, 16, 107, 207, 211, 215, 219–24, 225–26;
  election of, 153;
  Gestapu incident, 198, 207–10, 232;
  ideology of, 146, 233;
  Indonesian Army General Staff and, 135, 208–09, 225–26;
  Lockheed and, 107, 142;
  Malaysia and, 225–26;
  MI6 and, 226;
  neutralism of, 16, 135;
  oil industry and, 16, 42, 148, 216;
  overthrow of, 16, 56, 61, 161, 189, 207–24, 225, 232;
  U.S. government against, 122, 123, 214–17, 228
Sullivan and Cromwell, 42, 44, 54–55
Sundhaussen, Holm, 210, 213–14, 220
Sun Life Insurance Company, 99–101
Sutowo, Ibnu, 216–17, 219
Suwarto, 214
Szulc, Tad, 220

Terrell, Jack, 169
terror memories, xiii–xiv;
  political, xv, 9, 15, 16–17, 140, 152–54, 169, 172, 183, 189, 193, 197, 198, 199, 210;
  psychological, 7, 11–12, 20, 62, 88–89, 168, 181–82, 230
Tinkham, George, 44–45
Tonkin Gulf incidents, 24, 229, 230
trauma, 179–87;
  and creativity, 179;
  cultural trauma, 199;
  poetic healing, 170, 172, 179, 181–82, 183, 186–87, 195–96
Truman, Harry S., 176
Tunander, Ola, 198

United Fruit, 41, 42, 44, 54–55
United Nations, 28, 37, 38, 125
United States of America, 174–75, 179, 181, 186, 187–92, 193–95, 198

University of California, Berkeley, 47, 54, 58, 60–61, 65, 119, 154, 175, 212
Untung, 208–09, 221
U.S. State Department, 16, 27–28, 123, 166, 213, 222

Van Buren, Martin, 54
Vesco, Robert, 107–08
Vetin, Boris, 190
Vidal, Gore, 109, 146–47
Vietnam:
    Cambodian invasion by, 18;
    Four Points program, 114;
    oil industry and, 56–57, 149;
    Operation Phoenix, 154, 218
Virgil, 158, 168, 177, 202, 234

Walandouw, Jan, 215, 217
Wall Street, 108
War and Peace Studies Project, 49–50
Warren Commission, 109
Watertown crisis, 6–12, 21, 66, 110–11, 147, 158, 179

WAY (World Assembly of Youth), 50, 106
Weiner, Tim, 190
Whitehead, Alfred North, 74
Widjojo, Agus, 232
Widodo, Joko (Jokowi), 236
Williams, William Carlos, 105, 182
Wintersteen, Marian, 32
Wordsworth, William, 72–73, 140–41, 142–43, 168, 182, 185, 194, 202, 234
World Assembly of Youth (WAY), 50, 106

Yani, Ahmad, 208–209, 214, 216, 217, 221, 225–26
yin and yang, 20–21, 29, 64, 73, 94, 134, 145, 148, 154, 163, 180–82, 184, 196, 203
Yvain, 79, 80–81, 137, 147

Zechariah, 158–59
Zelnik, Reginald, 114

About the Authors

Peter Dale Scott's latest book of poems, *Walking on Darkness*, appeared in 2016 from Sheep Meadow Press. His other chief poetry books are the three volumes of his trilogy *Seculum*: *Coming to Jakarta: A Poem About Terror* (1988, 1989), *Listening to the Candle: A Poem on Impulse* (1992), and *Minding the Darkness: A Poem for the Year 2000*. In addition he has published three other collections of shorter poems: *Crossing Borders* (1994). *Mosaic Orpheus* (2009) and *Tilting Point* (2012). An anti-war speaker during the Vietnam and Gulf Wars, he was a co-founder of the Peace and Conflict Studies Program at UC Berkeley. In 2002 he was awarded the Lannan Poetry Award.

His most recent political books are *The Road to 9/11: Wealth, Empire, and the Future of America* (2007), *The War Conspiracy: JFK, 9/11 and the Deep Politics of War* (2008), *American War Machine: Deep Politics, the CIA Global Drug Connection, and the Road to Afghanistan* (2010), *The American Deep State: Big Money, Big Oil, and the Attack on U.S. Democracy* (2014, 2017), and *Dallas '63: The First Deep State Revolt Against the White House* (2015, 2018).

His books have been translated into six languages, and his articles and poems have been translated into twenty. The former U.S. poet laureate Robert Hass has written (*Agni*, 31/32, p. 335) that "*Coming to Jakarta* is the most important political poem to appear in the English language in a very long time."

His website is www.PeterDaleScott.net. His Facebook page is www.facebook.com/PeterDaleScott.

About the Authors

Freeman Ng is a former Google software engineer and the author of *Joan*, a YA novelization of the life of Joan of Arc, *Who Am I?* a personalizable, multicultural picture book, and *Haiku Diem 1*, a haiku collection illustrated by neural net generated digital art.

More of Freeman's digital art can be found at www.DeepWall.art.

His website is www.AuthorFreeman.com.

www.ingramcontent.com/pod-product-compliance
Lightning Source LLC
Chambersburg PA
CBHW022010300426
44117CB00005B/111